S0-BOK-540

COLLECTING
American Paintings

IDENTIFICATION & VALUES

A. EVERETTE JAMES JR. SCM, MD

COLLECTOR BOOKS

A Division of Schroeder Publishing Co., Inc.

Front cover: A.C. Heaton, Edith Flisher, Edwin W. Blashfield, and Ernest L. Major.

Back cover: Marguerite S. Pearson, William Frerichs, and Eugene H. Thomason.

Title page: Charles Wright, Henry Ossawa Tanner, and Louis Ritman.

Cover design by Beth Summers
Book design by Terri Hunter

COLLECTOR BOOKS
P.O. Box 3009
Paducah, Kentucky 42002-3009
www.collectorbooks.com

Copyright © 2006 A. Everette James Jr. SCM, MD

All rights reserved. No part of this book may be reproduced, stored
in any retrieval system, or transmitted in any form, or by any means
including but not limited to electronic, mechanical, photocopy, recording,
or otherwise, without the written consent of the author and publisher.

The current values in this book should be used only as a guide. They
are not intended to set prices, which vary from one section of the
country to another. Auction prices as well as dealer prices vary
greatly and are affected by condition as well as demand. Neither the
author nor the publisher assume responsibility for any losses that
might be incurred as a result of consulting this guide.

 Searching For A Publisher?

We are always looking for people knowledgeable within their fields. If
you feel that there is a real need for a book on your collectible subject and
have a large comprehensive collection, contact Collector Books.

Contents

About the Author

Everette James, a native of rural Martin County, North Carolina, was educated at the University of North Carolina in Chapel Hill, Duke Medical School, Harvard, and the Johns Hopkins School of Public Health. Dr. James taught at Harvard, Johns Hopkins, University College London, and Vanderbilt. He has published more than 24 books and 525 articles and established St. James Place, a restored historic Primitive Baptist church exhibiting over 400 examples of North Carolina pottery. He and his wife, Dr. Nancy Farmer, have donated their

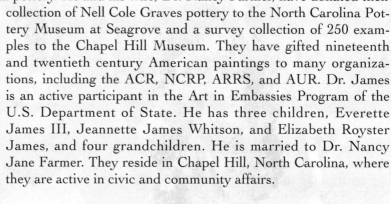

collection of Nell Cole Graves pottery to the North Carolina Pottery Museum at Seagrove and a survey collection of 250 examples to the Chapel Hill Museum. They have gifted nineteenth and twentieth century American paintings to many organizations, including the ACR, NCRP, ARRS, and AUR. Dr. James is an active participant in the Art in Embassies Program of the U.S. Department of State. He has three children, Everette James III, Jeannette James Whitson, and Elizabeth Royster James, and four grandchildren. He is married to Dr. Nancy Jane Farmer. They reside in Chapel Hill, North Carolina, where they are active in civic and community affairs.

Introduction

The origin of this text began several decades ago in a number of interesting experiences I had when beginning to collect American paintings. The chapters are written with a degree of independence; hence there is some duplication. Hopefully it can be examined as a reference text or read as a novel. This text is written for the initiate, and for the collector who has assembled a number of paintings through random acquisitions that provide no thematic identity and little satisfaction with either the process or the achievement.

Collecting American paintings should allow you to derive great pleasure from the accumulations as well as the distribution of your paintings. For me it has been a monumental journey of learning, mainly from my own travails and tribulations, but also from the advice and encouragement of others. Both mistakes and triumphs have been part of my education. Self instruction and sound advice have at times been determinant in my conduct as a collector.

Given the appropriate circumstance, I have greatly benefitted from the helpful advice of art historians, fellow collectors, and dealers. The extraction of data has been as varied as the information provided. Hopefully, I will be able to convey the proper expectations in each relationship so that you, as a collector first, reach a plateau of information to instill confidence, allow enjoyment in participating, and have long-term pleasure from your acquisitions.

For me my initial activities as a collector required patience and discipline. Residency time at Harvard Medical School was a period of intense study, allowing little time for Newbury Street but enough that I made contact and gained knowledge from my first mentor, Robert Vose. When I returned to Harvard, the Business School, in the late 1970s, I was prepared to take my knowledge to another level. I spent a number of hours in Vose Gallery and even more at the Boston Museum of Art (BMFA) and the Boston Public Library researching the BMFA and especially the women artists. Other dealers in the area like Ara Danekian, Roger Howlett, Al Walker, Bill Young, John Driscoll, Rob and Annette Elowich, the Godwins, and Pat Pierce, and many others offered me paintings from the BMFA. That gave me great incentive to return to Boston to talk at the Massachusetts General Hospital, the Boston Children's, the Brigham, and the Lahey Clinic. I also traveled up into the far reaches of New England seeking "bargains" of the landscape paintings, scenes from the North Shore and Cape Ann. I met George Young and Ron Bourgeault and attended their auctions. Over the years,

I gained confidence in my knowledge and bought many paintings at Bourne Auction on the Cape and from Jim Baaker in Boston as well as Skinner's in Bolton. Diane Fesko was invaluable in her advice. I also met a number of pickers in that area who have supplied works at Brimfield in the past few years.

When my medical career changed venue so did my art interests. We were moved from residency at the Massachusetts General Hospital (MGH) to a fellowship and postgraduate study at Johns Hopkins; my art interests changed but I still fostered my New England contacts. Bereft of funds, I "collected" in my mind. The year as an Honorary fellow of the Royal Society of Medicine in London allowed me little opportunity to acquire paintings but I visited art museums of the British Isles and had time to reflect about how I wanted to participate in art circles. I returned in the spring of 1975 to Baltimore. The proximity of the Baltimore Museum of Art, the National Galleries, and the Phillips Gallery in Washington gave me renewed exposure to American paintings. Many of the staff and directors of these institutions were patient and helpful to me and I acquired a few paintings at Sloan's and Weschler's auctions and from galleries in Washington.

When I took the chair at Vanderbilt University in the mid-1970s, I did not find immediately the interest in American art in Nashville. However, there were a half dozen eager collectors and we were about in the same phase in acquiring American paintings. Since I was changing a department in the medical school from less than 30 staff to over 200, I had little free time and confined my "art endeavors" to trips to Washington and to New York. However, I was active at Cheekwood Art Center and Gardens. Kevin Grogan was director and he has been very helpful as an advisor and friend. We have "transitioned" through his career at Cheekwood, Fisk, and now as director of the Morris Museum of Southern Art in Augusta, Georgia.

I was chair of the Acquisition Committee at Cheekwood, and took the responsibility seriously and encouraged other donors to contribute. Walter Knestrick was a very generous local collector as was John Hill. Local artist groups gave me courage to have an exhibit of my collection of American impressionism and later as my second, of Women Artists (1840 – 1940). My exhibit "America the Beautiful" traveled to several museums including the Dixon Gallery and Gardens in Memphis.

I loaned three paintings to the exhibit on Connecticut Impressionism held jointly at Cos Cobb (Green-which), Storrs, and Old Lyme. I had thoroughly enjoyed traveling about this beautiful state seeing the areas the impressionists painted. I acquired major paintings by some of the lesser known but very accomplished artists and they have been cherished acquisitions.

The early 1980s were spent acquiring and sharing our growing collection. The personal contacts during this period were very rewarding. At this time I was publishing medical texts on ultrasound, digital radiology, nuclear cardiology, and MRI and began publishing manuscripts about American arts in several venues.

From just an acquirer from dealers in a cash mode to avoid any of the pitfalls, I now found myself with some opportunities that were more complex. Some were grand experiences like trading paintings with Dr. Robert Coggins or joining in acquiring the estate of artists such as Maurice Gerberg, Eliot and Walter Clark, and Alberta Shulz to name a few. However, some of these activities resulted in delays and misunderstandings of timing and have been quickly forgotten.

As one's knowledge of the field improves so does one's confidence. One of my passions has been tonalism and the human visual response to this genre as well as the more popular impressionism. I was a curator, and exhibited, and published a monograph on tonalism which was an "intellectual" success but failed to inspire the public. From this I learned that tonalism may be an "acquired taste."

One of my fondest memories in art was the "discovery" or rediscovery of Eugene Healon Thomason (EHT), writing a text with my son and with Lib Thomason as contributors, and through Knoke Galleries having a retrospective of his work. Several major "EHTs" were sold to museums. More recently, there has been a restructure of interest through the excellent marketing effect of the Charleston Renaissance Gallery. I have continued to publish material about the "Ashcan Artist of Appalachia" and feel that this has been a contribution.

Collecting American paintings has made me more aware of the commercial "importance" of works and artists, but writing has forced and driven my research and analysis as well. However, exhibiting can be even more of a learning experience. It is not just about arriving just before the opening and having everyone present applaud the loans from your collection. Even with this caveat, I encourage you to share your treasures and that negative results or commentary comes with the territory. Just have realistic expectations and enjoy the fellowship. Leave the blue ribbons to the horse-set and the trophy cups to the golfing types.

Sharing of your collection is one of the most fulfilling activities whether it is a loan, transparency, or out-

right gift. It is certainly rewarding to have a lovely color illustration of your favorite landscape to be used by the likes of a Bill Gerdts in a textbook. I have taken advantage of this opportunity many times but have sometimes had the credit as "private collection." However circumspect you might be, readers often find out the ownership. Despite the label "private collection" I have had many telephone offers for "Ladies in Woods" by Marion Howard, and it and numerous other works in our collection have been subsequently published with specific ownership identified. It does not take a great deal of research or analysis to realize, in general, that publication of a work enhances its value.

One of your legitimate activities as a collector is to encourage other collectors, especially the beginners. I truly hope this text will prove effective in this regard. My ideas in *Collecting American Paintings* are not offered as templates. However, I feel the basic concepts are reasonable and should help most collectors of this broad sweep of the literary brush.

Two nonanticipated opportunities have had a profound effect upon my experience and added to whatever expertise I am accorded in the art field. Because of my training as a physician/scientist we have had a great deal of experience utilizing imaging procedures to evaluate age, composition, and condition of paintings. Despite numerous presentations and articles, my most lasting activity was to produce an extensive monograph funded by the Eastman Kodak Company. Thousands of these were sent to conservators, museums, dealers, and collectors. The feedback has been a decade of positive responses and continues today as computerized techniques are being applied. Conservators/restorers have found it particularly useful. It can be a crucial adjunct to raking light, microscopic, and UV analysis as well as scan CT mode for additional layer by layer information.

The most singular event of my career in American paintings came through a friend and medical colleague, the late Lee Minton. We were asked to evaluate a little used, almost unknown collection of paintings residing in the bowels of the Parthenon in Centennial Park, Nashville, Tennessee, the symbol of the city. We were shown the storeroom where an art find of monumental proportions awaited us: the Indiana Jones equivalent in painting as it were. Before us in primitive racks were Chase, Homer, West, Redfield, Inness, Gifford, A. P. Ryder, Blakelock, and other greats of American art. They were, along with outstanding examples of lesser known but very accomplished artists, all framed in valuable period frames, some monumental. Through the good graces of Wendell Garrett at *Antiques Magazine*, we published our cover article for the American painting issue in 1980. This gave us, however undeserved, respect in the field, presentation opportunities, and resulted in a renovated space in the Parthenon for permanent display. My ophthalmologist colleague went on to be a London antiques dealer and now has the Pawley's Island cultural festival named in his memory. I take pride in our contribution and the fact the Cowan Collection is recognized as a very important one of American paintings.

I have found that in collecting a theme of art leading to some type of public sharing, you come to consider the paintings your offspring and you become emotionally attached. The remedies I have used to ease the pain are to insist that the body of the works stay intact, the recipient will have them on public display,

A. Everette James, Nancy J. Farmer, and "Sugar"

and I write a catalog or monograph. This process takes time and energy but can result in a meaningful contribution and a documented method of sharing. This will be an undercurrent theme in this text. Sometimes my family is thoughtful enough to fashion a small catalogue raisonne which eases the pain of separation and that helps, but the easiest method to combat retrograde nostalgia and remorse is to embark on another project. After the Indiana (Hoosiers) Collection activity, I began my Southern Collection 1840 – 1950 plans for acquisitions and exhibition as well as a catalog and a series of publications throughout the literature.

I attempted to acquire as much data as I did examples. These interests have led to continued experience with museums specializing in "Southern art," collections of Southern and African-American quilts, publications on the portrayal of African-Americans in Southern art (1850 – 1950), and ongoing activity with the John Hope Franklin Center at Duke and the Universtiy of North Carolina at Chapel Hill Center for Study of the American South. The exhibitions and monographs provide ongoing interests and balance the need not to be physically (and fiscally) encumbered by the sheer numbers and need for space.

My wife Nancy and I find the most pleasurable activities are the gifts in kind, which will have more than a chapter devoted to this subject subsequently. Our gifts to Pfieffer University and Granville County were just as rewarding as to Vanderbilt Medical School, the Cosmos Club, or the gift to Duke University for entirely different reasons. We have come to learn that proper sharing in an appropriate context is the most rewarding experience we have as collectors. This can range from the U.S. Department of State to a companion gift for the Cowan Collection, donation for an auction at the North Carolina Museum of History, the Round Hill auction in Jamaica to the decoration of the Massachusetts General Hospital or the offices of the American Roentgen Ray Society. Sharing has multilayered and often ongoing pleasures and brings one's American painting collecting to a reward level.

Over the decades so many people have contributed to this text that the list would be infinite and I would invariably miss someone vitally important. I would like to summarize but provide generic "thank you's" to the dealers for good advice, fellow collectors for understanding and comfort, scholars and historians for sharing, and family for continued support, especially my partner in every endeavor, Dr. Nancy Jane Farmer. I would like to thank the following people for the use of their artwork to illustrate this text: Howard Godel, Dave Knoke, Jim Williams, Roger H. Ogden, Rob Hicklin, Bill Vose, Shirley Lally, and others as indicated. These illustrations from private lenders were crucial for the text. Also important was the editing of Nancy Farmer, Ed and Claire Alexander, and David Knoke.

This text is written for the early collector but we trust our other colleagues will not find it overly simplistic. The opinions contained herein are mine (warts and all) and do not necessarily reflect any other person's ideas.

This has been a wonderful experience for me to analyze my own behavior, consider my own strategies and activities, trip lightly down memory lane, and to share data and advice with the reader. I hope reading this text will prove as enjoyable and rewarding as writing it for Collector Books has been for me.

Art Speak

Every profession and activity has its own nomenclature which may be baffling and at times off-putting for the initiate. Mastery of some of the essential terms will enhance both the acquisition process and later appreciation by the collector. I have selected a number of terms that occur with regularity in the analysis of art and ones that should be at least familiar to the competent collector. Some are general descriptors while others are specific to the art.

A great part of the pleasure of collecting art is to share it. This can be enhanced for collectors by their ability to describe the paintings they have acquired. The facility of characterization and description will greatly embellish this sharing process.

These are terms I have commonly encountered in my many pleasurable art activities and I trust that the reader will benefit from this exercise. They are presented alphabetically only to facilitate their retrieval if you wish to find them expeditiously at some future time.

Abstract art — The elements of form may not be recognizable. Kandinsky is credited with creating the first work in 1910 but many other painters used abstraction generically including Turner.

Expressionism or abstract expressionism — Art characterized by spontaneous and individual artistic expression presented in a nonobjective manner.

Academy — The place of rigorous study and highly structured teaching based on classical standards.

Aesthetics — The philosophy of art. A Greek word meaning to perceive. Study of the human perception of beauty.

After — Copied from the original of another artists.

American Scene Painting — Movement in which artists have chosen distinct areas of American life or landscape and rendered them in a literal style.

Armory Show — The International Exhibition of Modern Art in 1913 at New York City's 69th Regiment Armory Building. First large scale exposure for American and European avant-garde.

Art Brut — Jean Debuffet's term for visionary, naive, primitive art.

Arts and Crafts Movement — Begun by William Morris about 1850 and focused upon artistic level of industrial designs.

Ashcan School — A form of realism that evolved from "the Eight" who favored urban life as subject matter. Usually with thick application of pigment of the lower register.

Atelier — Workshop.

Attribution — Indication of a measure of uncertainty regarding authenticity.

Authentic — Art that has established origin.

Avant-Garde — Art ahead of its time.

Barbizon – A group of naturalist painters working outside the village of Barbizon in France 1830s – 1890s. Often landscapes of the countryside in brown, russet tones.

Bitumen — Mineral pitch when used as pigment. Can cause severe crackleur and darkens with exposure to sunlight.

Canon — Usually a historical term; meaning universally accepted character of an art form.

Catalogue Raisonne — A complete description of an artist's work.

Circle of — This term denotes the influence of a particular artists.

Classicism — Art based upon classical models and qualities.

Color — Is usually characterized by hue (tint), intensity (strength), and value (lightness or darkness).

Complementary Color — A color having maximum contrast with another color.

Crackle (cracquelure) — The network of hairline cracks in pigments and varnish on antique paintings. ("Crazing" is a term also used.)

Deaccession — To purge one's holdings.

The Eight — Members of the Ashcan School founding group Henri, Sloan, Prendergast, Glackens, Lawson, Shinn, Davies, and Luks.

Fine Art — Those categories of artwork historically judged as the most aesthetically significant (also called "High Art").

Folk Art — Art of common society; "art of the people."

Foxing — The discoloration of paper due to dampness; manifest as brown spots.

Genre — A type of art.

Gouache — A painting medium made of opaque pigments in a water base.

Ground — A coating of the support suitable for receiving pigment.

Hudson River School — American realist landscape

painters 1820 – 1880. Cole, Moran, Church, Durante, Gifford, Bierstadt, and others. Popularized by John Wilmerding, art historian.

Icon — A universally symbolic image. From the Greek to mean image or portrait.

Impasto — Thick or heavy application of paint.

Limners — Untutored artists who executed naive and literal portraits.

Linear — A work of art in which contour rather than masses of colors is the primary means of compositional definition.

Linear perspective — A process of delineating three dimensional objects in a picture plane. This is done by considering them in terms of reading planes.

Luminism — An American art movement in the mid-nineteenth century that was characterized by control of tonal gradations and absence of brush marks.

Manner of — Stylistic similarity to another artists but not a copy ("style of" also).

Medium — The physical material of which the painting is made.

Metier — The subject by which the painter is known.

Mixed media — the use of several different materials in the same painting.

Modern art — Art which developed with increasing preoccupation with form. Began in mid-nineteenth century with Courbet.

Monochromatic — Painting in predominantly one color (grisalle, grayed tones). Tonalist works are often monochromatic.

Mural — Large painting applied directly to a wall surface or completed separately and affixed later.

Narrative art — The representation of story elements by images depicted.

Nocturne — A night scene.

Nonobjective art — Art that makes use of color, form, and texture, with no recognizable subject matter.

Oeuvre — An artist's entire production. French for work.

Old Master — A distinguished painter before 1700.

Optical mixing — The joining of juxtaposed colors by the visual and cognitive apparatus of humans.

Overpainting — A layer of paint applied on top of another.

Painterly — Painting representing forms by color and tonal relationships (opposite of linear). Often used to describe the vibrancy of a work.

Palette — Surface upon which painter sets out pigments. As well, the spectrum of colors used by an artist. For example, the bright, light palette of Impressionism.

Pastel — A painting executed by sticks formed by colored powders mixed with gum.

Patina — Mellowing with age.

Perspective — Representing three dimensional objects on a two dimensional surface. They then appear as they do in nature.

Picture plane — The frontal boundary of a painting; pictorial elements are arranged in depth.

Pigment — Colored matter that is mixed with a vehicle to make paint. It may be permanent or nonpermanent (fugitive).

Plein air — A movement of the late nineteenth century seeking naturalism through handling of atmospheric conditions. Outside in air. Espoused by the Impressionists.

Primary colors — Those that cannot be produced by a combination of any colors (red, yellow, and blue) mixed together.

Priming — A layer applied over a sized canvas before painting on the surface (usually zinc or lead in linseed oil).

Print — An impression or proof taken from a block or plate.

Provenance — The history of ownership of a painting.

Realism — Fidelity to natural appearances without attention to minute details. The regionalists often adopted this technique.

Regionalism — An authentic American style of painting concentrating on realistic depictions especially of the rural Midwest and South in the 1930s.

Reline — To mount a painting with its original canvas on another support.

Representational — Art that strives to depict objects as they appear visually.

Restoration — The attempt to return a work of art to its original condition. (Conservation is often used but its intent is restore to some aesthetic goal.)

Romanticism — An art style of the first half of the nineteenth century in which the artist's and observer's imaginations were paramount.

Salon — The French term for an annual exhibition.

Saturation — The degree of brilliance of a hue or tint of a pigment.

Secondary colors — Colors formed by a mixture of primary colors (orange, green, and violet).

Shade — The degree of darkness of a hue.

Sketch — A painting or drawing made as a draft for a later composition.

Social realism — Manner of depiction of the ills of a society by an artist.

Staffage — Figures in landscape painting that are included to establish scale and perspective.

Still life — Paintings of inanimate objects.

Stretcher — The wooden frame upon which the canvas support is laid out. Keys or wedges can be used to tighten the canvas.

Style — The appearance characteristic of that artist or school of painters.

Support — After priming it is the untreated surface upon which the pigment is applied.

Syntheism — Emphasis of reduced forms to essentials and colors applied flat with nonshaded fields bounded by distinct contour lines (related to postimpressionism).

Tempering — To mix colors in painting.

Tertiary colors — Produced by mixing two secondary colors.

The Ten — Ten American artist who separated from the National Academy of Design (NAD) and exhibited first in 1898.

Triptych — A painted work of three panels arranged side by side.

Trompe L'oeil — A painting so precise it gives the illusion of being the object depicted.

Underpainting — The first layer of a painting in monochrome that lays out the composition.

Vanishing point — The point in a painting on the horizon at which parallel lines seem to disappear.

Vehicle — Material that carries pigments in suspension.

Watercolor — A pigment pulverized with a water soluble binder and dissolved in a water vehicle.

Yellowing — The discoloration of an oil painting due largely to the varnish cover and excessive use of oil as a vehicle.

This is certainly not an exhaustive list of art terms and I would refer you to texts cited in the bibliography. However, knowledge of these terms will enhance your pleasure as a collector.

Silver Poplars, *Allen Tucker (1866 – 1939), 28" x 34", oil on canvas, signed and dated 1921 L.R. Provenance: exhibited in the Allen Tucker Memorial Exhibition, Nov. 10 – Dec. 6, 1980, at the Arts Students League of New York, #7. Courtesy of Knoke Galleries of Atlanta.*

Collecting

Collecting paintings has many motivations and objectives. John Sloan, a leader of the "Eight," said "People buy pictures to demonstrate that they have money. Acquiring pictures leads to a kind of social success." I take issue with this, because I feel this description characterizes "acquirers" and not collectors.

Collectors manifest many different personal characteristics as do artists, but there are several common traits that are possessed by "true" collectors. Although they collect what they like, this self-realization only exists after much personal experience in the form of viewing, reading, and discussion with artists, museum curators, knowledgeable dealers, and fellow collectors. Auctions and museum openings generally provide them a classroom for a quick survey study of art and a social gathering to facilitate this necessary interaction with curators, art historians, and fellow collectors or aspiring collectors. Openings are pleasurable, but you can also make them informative. Be bold and ask, declare, deliberate, denounce, disagree, and demand data about the art you intend to collect.

You will soon begin to recognize your preference for a specific genre, subject matter, or painting technique. You will then become more focused in your selection of auctions, dealers, and exhibitions. To become a competent collector you should dedicate a certain amount of time to the objects you intend to acquire. This is where you should initiate the process, not when you write the first check. Study the paintings as well as your behavior before the acquisition. This serves as a manner of consummating the creativity.

You are not compelled to "understand" a visual image as your modus operandi in the usual sense. You should appreciate it at more than a superficial level; however, this process may require time for analysis, and processing of your biases and forgotten experiences recorded somewhere in your subconscious. Devote some time to become knowledgeable about your selection or you could acquire a painting without "collecting" it. Many acquirers of art, either representational or abstract, feel that once they identify the subject or recognize what they believe to be the artist's

Sunset Off Ten Pound Island, *Gloucester, Fitzhugh Lane, 12" x 20".*
Courtesy of Vose Galleries of Boston.

any overall introspection to characterize you as a genuine collector. Most collectors start out as random acquirers and, after they have gathered a few paintings, begin to wonder a bit about where this process is going and if they are receiving full emotional benefit from the activity. You might then turn to someone you deem more experienced and ask their opinion and advice about which direction to pursue and how to proceed. They will often be pleased you sought them out. I will use nineteenth and twentieth century American paintings as a paradigm.

Many novice collectors like to state "I collect what I like" and with that pronounce-

A Snow Squall, *Thomas Cole, 31¼" x 41¼". Courtesy of Vose Galleries of Boston.*

intent, then they truly understand the painting. Understanding a visual image is a complex process. You will only come to understand your collection over time. With the purchase you have only initiated the process which is neither a one lane or one-way street. If you decide to give up ownership of an earlier choice, do not regard it as failure. There are always other avenues open to you.

You will often find yourself in a state of transition regarding acquisitions and de-accessions reflecting what you prefer at any particular time. This can continuously be refined, resulting in objects being de-accessed, donated, traded, and acquired. Desire, acquire, analyze, refine, de-access, acquire again; for many collectors it is a rewarding and never-ending process. At certain intervals you should distance yourself from the immediacy of the process, become truly introspective, and give yourself time to think about your collection. For awhile after you have initiated the acquisition process, discipline yourself not to collect but to learn.

You may initially spend a great deal of time analyzing the individual elements of your collection without

ment have placed themselves in what they believe is a no-lose position. After all, if you have it, by definition you like it, and this response also makes "it" sacrosanct from the judgement of others. Safe, but not scintillating, this posture also obviates the pleasure (and risk) of the opinion of other judgments. It also requires no scholarship, since the acquisition process is presumably based upon one's intuitive behavior. This position ("I collect what I like"), if viewed exclusively, means that historians, critics, and curators can be logically excluded from the process and the acquirer will never get to know much about their collection or themselves as a collector; a poor imitation in my opinion.

You should enjoy the growth process that comes with enlarging your collecting experience and gaining the insight of those knowledgeable in the field. If you start the process correctly, refinement of your tastes will enhance the acquisition and ownership pleasures. Learning about new artists, styles, or movements will often make the acquisition of an example the logical endpoint of an intellectual journey, rather than a reflex response. Remember the "If it itches, scratch it" philosophy. A scratch in the wrong place could lead to bleeding your emotions and finances dry, but more important this type of acquisition experience will not endure.

I find that many collectors, after some years of activity, are not satisfied with their acquisitions because they did not attempt to understand their paintings or their motives as these objects were being acquired. Their "whole" ended up being less than "the sum of the parts." An eclectic collection can be both rewarding and pleasing, but the chances are less than with a collection which evidences rational thought, resolve, and acquisition discipline from the beginning. A "statement" collection predictably gives the collector more pleasure and is more understandable than an accumulation of random acquisitions.

Before collecting my first painting, I visited many of the major cities of the world and spent a great deal of time in their museums. From this initiating process I came to realize what I wanted to collect and knew I was more attracted to traditional representational works than the modern and nonrepresentational images. Landscapes were easy to understand and appreciate, and I especially enjoyed the visual effects and the light colors of impressionism. For over a decade, I followed this commitment, but later after some independent study, have included in my collection a number of examples of related artistic movements such as the Barbizon aesthetic and tonalism. I also became interested in examples of these aesthetics painted in certain art colonies that used modified versions of these techniques such as the ones at Old Lyme, Con-

Hunting Scene, *William de la Montagne Cary (1840 – 1922), 12" x 16", oil on canvas.*
Courtesy of Knoke Galleries of Atlanta.

necticut; Rockport, Massachusetts; New Hope, Pennsylvania; and in Brown County, Indiana.

As important as deciding on the style and subject matter you wish to collect is, first determining the level, amount of time, and financial commitment you would feel comfortable with. This is a significant decision. What do you want to achieve?

Two physician colleagues of mine were very well-known and highly regarded collectors. One owned several thousand paintings, and the other once told me that he wanted "only a dozen or so great paintings." These goals dictate a markedly different collecting style and a different resource allocation for each example you acquire. If you enjoy collecting a large number of paintings, you are much less likely to feel comfortable with or can afford a large expenditure for any single great example by a well-known and highly desirable artist. This is a much different posture than a collector who acquires one or two paintings a year. My adage is "pay more, buy less," but that also depends upon the anticipated final result — the intent you have in acquiring the collection.

There are all manner of motivations for collecting art, and you should examine yours and realize that any change of intent will definitely affect your collecting strategy. At some time, you should redefine your goals to give your collection a more clearly identifiable theme. Your paintings will no longer be a random acquisition of images but the individual elements of a definable whole.

Over the years, as I gained confidence in the validity of my choices and began to share my collection with the public, I soon recognized that even my initial collecting was influenced by the intended future loans and exhibitions of my paintings. The half dozen, almost life-sized female figure paintings (70" x 40") I acquired because they were great values, were decidedly more appropriate for Grand Central's La Femme exhibit or the Art in Embassies program of the U. S. Department of State than they are for almost any home, including my own. I was an early participant in each of these undertakings and enjoyed being part of a public function each providing a service.

Public display of your paintings will also make you very "frame conscious." You will make every effort to restore the original frames if they substantially add to the visual impression of the work. If the frame detracts or does not particularly embellish the painting, however, opt for a period reproduction or a refurbished period frame. The final appearance of the composite entity should even be calculated initially into your collection strategy.

You should begin with the intent to enjoy not only the result of your acquisitions, but the process itself. Some introspection will lead you to an enhanced understanding of your early motivations and provide you with reasonable criteria to reinitiate the process and later judge the success of your efforts. You are ready to begin the process again by choosing the next painting to acquire.

Many collectors believe that selecting a painting is a formidable exercise and may even feel intimidated by the prospect. If you truly believe this, you initially may have someone else determine the suitability of a particular work for you. In this instance, the person you select as your agent should have intimate knowledge of your needs, desires, and resources. Alternatively, you can "buy what I like," and through an often lengthy process of trial and error, you may learn what the expression really means to you. "What I like" may change often and quite rapidly at first. I would not recommend this approach.

The most satisfying method of acquisition is for you to develop personal skills in evaluating paintings and, with the assistance of a reputable dealer, art consultant, or auction house representative, eventually make your own choices. After all, the final criterion in evaluating a painting is its specific desirability to you and that is largely a personal judgment. Do not feel you have to be "right" or "wrong." Individual collectors have their own visual perception, sense of values, and personal interests that combine to make them uniquely qualified to, in general, render this evaluation for themselves. It is *your* collection, so do not be faint of heart. The time to begin should always be "now."

Investing

With the many alternatives for one's discretionary assets, the question of paintings as a sound financial acquisition seems to arise repeatedly. This communication will share my thoughts about nineteenth to early twentieth century American works.

Certainly, the scions of traditional American wealth had paintings as part of their valuable possessions and as part of their largesse they built museums, donated collections, and supported many artistic endeavors. However, the Mellons, Carneigies, Paleys, Guggenheims, and others acquired their wealth in other endeavors.

Even legendary collectors of great wealth like Charles Lang Freer, William T. Evans, Walter Annenberg, Richard Manoohgian, Daniel Terra, Joseph Hirshorn, and George A. Hearn were of sufficient wealth that their painting acquisitions are the results of wealth acquired by astute business judgment in other areas.

One can cite a small handful of painting collectors who profited from this activity in a truly spectacular way. The late Wendell Cherry, founder of the hospital management chain Humana, acquired and sold a Picasso (*Yo Picasso*) for over 40 million dollars in profit in less than a decade.

The late John McDonough, a physician from Youngstown, Ohio (the home of the Butler Art Institute), sold his impressionist collection at auction for a large multiple of his acquisition price. However, the artists in his collection were the leaders of American impressionism (Hassam, Robinson, Chase…) and Dr. McDonough's acquisition prices would be above the resources of the average collectors and certainly the amount Mr. Cherry paid for the Picasso was. An old adage in the financial world "it takes money to make money" is at least a partial truth in art as well.

Given the circumstance that you have a finite limitation of funds, what might some measures be to enhance the possibility that you can enjoy the pursuit, take pleasure in the ownership of the paintings, and deaccess, for whatever reason, them for a profit. The trite expression might be to "have one's pate and eat it as well."

The Banjo Lesson, *Henry Ossawa Tanner,
oil on canvas, 49" x 35½", 1893. Courtesy of
Hampton University Museum, Hampton, Virginia.*

First, assess accurately what your resources are and what they will reasonably acquire. If you have $70,000 and want a William Merritt Chase, decide which of his students you admire the most. Perhaps you should consider Charles Webster Hawthorne or one of the female students. I once found an interesting self portrait of Hawthorne that he had used as a demonstration piece in one of his classes. After finding a period frame for it, I donated it to the Cheekwood Museum/school with a very favorable fair market appraisal.

To embellish the idea that the painting by students of the most accomplished and famous will increase in value, I will cite a few other examples. The Boston Museum of Fine Arts (BMFA) School had a succession of leaders from Frank Weston Benson and Edmund Tarbell to Joseph R. DeCamp, William McGregor Paxton, and others. The training was rigorous and lengthy and the draftsmanship and painterly qualities of the students reflected this intensity and breadth. Many of the most talented pupils were women.

For various reasons, they did not receive the acclaim they deserved and until only a few years ago were significantly underpriced. Some of their work was on par with that of their mentors (Gretchen Rogers, Lillian Wescott Hale, Margaret Fitzhugh Brown, Lee Lufkin Kaula, Marguerite Stuber Pearson), and others are sufficiently gifted and accomplished that their works should continue to increase in value. If, however, you can afford to invest $150,000 – 200,000 in a major Benson or Tarbell, they will likewise appreciate but not as much on a percentage basis.

The market for major artists exists as a phenomenon of the general knowledge about them and their works. Most collectors know the leading teachers and major figures of the Art Students' League, the Pennsyl-

vania Academy of Fine Arts, or the colony at Old Lyme or Rockport; but there were very competent artists there that are not as well known. In fact, they might not have sold a large number of paintings during their careers and their legacy represents a large number of paintings closely held by their descendants.

Closer view.

Outside Charleston (Plantation Life), *Gilbert Gaul, 10" x 18", oil on canvas. Southern genre paintings will greatly increase in value.*

In the 1970s and 1980s, a number of dealers acquired these estates and marketed the paintings by preparing a text/monograph about the life and career of the artist to accompany a traveling exhibit. This process provided a format where collectors could learn about the artist, judge the scope of their work, and feel they were participants in a dynamic process of discovering or rediscovering a deserving artist.

Since dealers might have to raise the capital to acquire these estates, you might have an opportunity to purchase paintings at favorable prices and sell them after the publication and during the exhibition cycle. Certain artists such as Walter and Eliot Clark, Robert Emmett Owen, and Eugene Healon Thomason 1 had several "estate exhibitions and sales." This creates a market through exposure and awareness of the public. The resale value of these artists' works has increased as the information about them became more widely disseminated.

The above scenario provides you another opportunity to acquire a painting and later, if you so desire, realize a profit but an acquisition opportunity as well. You may, indeed, encounter a dealer with a painting executed by one of these artists. The dealer may not know about the monograph and retrospective exhibition; therefore, very little is found about the artist except a small entry in a reference text and modest auction sales records. The price will likely be quite conservative and favorable for resale.

In theory, the price of paintings at auction is "wholesale" and this is generally correct if certain circumstances exist and the collector behaves in a disciplined manner: presale study of the condition of the work and previous auction prices, and comparison of its technical qualities with other works by the artist.

Man Hunting, *William M. Paxton,*
Impressionist outdoor landscape. Private collection.

Garden Scene, *Eliot Clark, 24" x 20". Private collection.*

Following this preparation and a discussion with the staff of the auction house, decide what you are prepared to pay for a painting and be resolute during the excitement of the sale itself. If you follow this strategy, you should acquire paintings at a very favorable price; deaccession will usually result in a profit.

Themes and locales if thought of creatively can result in a prudent acquisition for later resale. Paintings of regional interest purchased outside of a particular environment but offered for sale in the area of avid collectors, will sometimes result in a spectacular profit. I once acquired a very large Charleston harbor scene for a modest price and sold it through a Charleston dealer

for a large multiple of the acquisition cost. The painting was so large that I had always had difficulty exhibiting it and I had several examples of the artist's work which made deaccession painless.

If a collection of paintings has a clearly identifiable statement, the whole may be worth considerably more than the sum of the individual works. To gather these paintings, however, will require some effort and independent scholarship.

For example, in the late nineteenth and early twentieth centuries, Indiana had an extraordinary number of good artists creating paintings in a modified impressionist manner. Among the dozen accomplished artists, only Theodore Clement Steele had received significant national exposure. His contemporaries William Forsythe, J. Otis Adams, J. Elwood Bundy, Adolph Shulz, Otto Stark, Edward Williams, V. J. Cariani, William Eyden, and others were very fine artists whose works were largely in private hands in Indiana.

These paintings could be acquired for modest sums, but the collector should physically be prepared to make the journey, purchase the works using their own judgment, and document the collection themselves.

Over several years, we accumulated over 60 examples of Hoosier impressionism and traveled the exhibit to several states including a number of venues in Indiana as well. This included Terre Haute, Huntington, Richmond, Evansville, and Indianapolis. A catalog was published and the collection was acquired intact by the oldest insurance company in the state. The profit in this instance was not so much the commercial value but the satisfac-tion of bringing a representative survey collection of the Indiana impressionists to the public. The monetary profit was negligible.

Most of us consider profit in commercial, monetary terms and overlook the fact that "profit" can result in increased value of our paintings used in other ways, such as trades and donations. Some of the most favorable exchanges I have ever made were trades of paintings to either dealers or fellow collectors.

Interestingly, three of my most memorable experiences involved expatriate artists about whom very little was known, by me as well as my colleague with whom I was to execute the trade.

I had purchased at auction several years before in New York a large, almost monochromatic, painting by Eugene Vail that was not favorably received by the ladies at home and had been parked in a stairwell at a local club.

Following the Grand Central exhibit "Post Impressionism," I was very attracted to a painting of

Shinnecock Hills (New York), *Charles Wright, 12" x 16", oil on canvas. Student William Meritt Chase. This same scene by Chase is in the permanent collection of the Cleveland Museum.*

The Blue Kimono, *Marguerite Pearson of Rockport, Massachusetts,*
21½" x 23¾", oil on canvas. Student of Tarbell and Benson. Following her death her paintings
greatly increased in value. Pierce Gallery, James Collection.

Woodstock, New York, by one of the founders of the colony there but the asking price was more than I felt comfortable with (by several orders of magnitude). The dealer suggested that he might be interested in a trade from my collection. When he visited me, I showed him the paintings we had on loan or exhibition, first hoping that he would find a suitable painting for his inventory before viewing the "family favorites" at home.

To my amazement and pleasure, he selected the work in the stairwell by the expatriate artist. The difference in my acquisition price for my painting and the asking price for his was over 20 times. Later he told me he sold my painting for more than he had priced the Woodstock piece, thus, we both were pleased. Grand Central made a tidy profit, and I acquired a painting at a very favorable exchange for me. The general message from this litany is that dealers have a particular clientele with specific needs. For this reason, they can pay you a "retail" or "super retail" price for a painting and still realize a substantial profit. For the same reason, you may observe a dealer buy a painting at auction for much more than you would be willing to pay and above your general idea of its retail value.

I once asked a well-known dealer about a questionable purchase another dealer had made at auction. He responded by saying "he has already got it sold." If you can project the potential of a painting you own to the intentions of a particular dealer, you can be financially rewarded.

Today there are clearly defined regional markets and paintings that depict an identifiable area or place. These are sold at a premium. Two examples of cities with a strong regional collecting public are New Orleans and Charleston. A painting by one of the early Louisiana artists of that area or the rendering of a Charleston scene will sell for a premium.

If you need to have your turnover to occur in an expeditious fashion, consign the painting to the appropriate regional auction.

You can substantially increase the value of a painting by improving its aesthetic appeal without changing its artistic merit or authenticity. Many paintings have a dull appearance after 50 or more years that is often due to yellowing of the varnish which was probably applied by the artist shortly after executing the work. Removing the dull, yellowed varnish and application of a fresh coat is an inexpensive and safe procedure and can dramatically change the market value of a painting. Relining an unstable canvas not only preserves the work but enhances its value as well.

Restoring a period frame or replacing an undistinguished contemporary one can significantly alter the aesthetics of the composite and make the painting much more desirable (see section on Condition). A painting that has a "pristine" appearance will have greater commercial appeal that will be translated into financial terms in the marketplace. Irrespective of the value of the painting, we are all influenced by aesthetics. The frame contributes greatly to the desirable image.

Lady in White, *Ernest L. Major, 26" x 22", oil on board. Major was a noted Boston artist at the turn of the nineteenth century and taught at BMFA. James collection.*

Not ordinarily considered in the context of financial advantages is the use of donations resulting in tax credits which indeed represent a form of "profit." Donating paintings is an excellent method to achieve tax relief on income. In the past, when taxes were very high on passive income, the incentive to defray taxes with charitable donations was greater than they presently are. However, the donation of paintings can be a worthwhile endeavor from a monetary sense and has positive societal implications as well. This is especially true if the donated work or works have increased substantially in value since their acquisition. These will be "written off" at the fair market value appraisal and the owner will have the gratitude of the receiving institution. (See Donating, page 294.)

While there are undoubtedly other considerations regarding the issue of whether collecting paintings can be profitable, these reflect my experience and appear most valid to me. A number of these considerations and strategies require time and individual effort on your part.

However, they will also make you a more astute collector and significantly increase your pleasure in the process.

Understanding and documenting your collection will make it more valuable, not only to you but to others as well. Will a painting someday be considerably more valuable simply because it has your identifying collection label on the stretcher? That may represent a form of "profit" that supercedes any monetary measure.

Are paintings a good investment? Yes and no. In a strict commercial sense, it depends upon your alternatives. Judicious choices of good quality paintings will probably do better than bonds, mutual funds, or very conservative financial instruments.

Good choices will appreciate more than 90% of your commodity future contracts unless you are hedging against your large hog operation; but stay out of the lagoons. If your funny-looking kid with the politically incorrect hair color and the slide rule is going to let you have 100K worth of his IPO, Fantastica dot Com, the Willard Metcalf landscape should no longer wait even if it is a mere $750,000.

For those of us who enjoy all of the aspects of collecting paintings, from the studied accumulation of data, to the primal urge of auction bidding, to the adrenaline rush of an exciting acquisition from a dealer, to the satisfaction of a donation or the consummation of a highly profitable sale, paintings are a good investment but somewhat illiquid. In the meantime you will improve the aesthetics of your personal environment.

Mary Reading, *Edmund C. Tabell*,
50½" x 40½".

Tools of the Trade

You should delight in utilizing your own knowledge and tastes to acquire art objects, hopefully at below their actual value. This practice has the spirit of adventure and the excitement of uncertainty, and, if successful, affirmation of your expertise and good judgment.

Finding "bargains" may involve a search in obscure and sometimes isolated places with only a remote chance of uncovering a treasure. Part of the uncertainty and related excitement will be due to the fact that you will not have the benefit of a knowledgeable seller, the opinion of a conservator regarding the condition of the work or even an adequate provenance or a validated signature.

You may find yourself in an antique mall next to the socks and undershirts or in a "junque" shop winding through vintage washing machines, farm implements, and vacuum cleaners.

The tag on the painting may reveal such worthless information as "oil picture," "early work," or "listed artist." To embellish this data may be "from an estate" or "found in..." The proprietor or booth operator may also inform you that "this picture has some age on it."

Given these circumstances, you are definitely left to your own devices. If knowledge is power, then you are rendered powerless by the information provided by the seller. Your opportunity, however, is to acquire a treasure or to accumulate sufficient personal knowledge to ensure that you should make a prudent choice. Accepting this circumstance you, as a wise collector, should plan to gather the necessary information to make an educated decision in purchasing the particular painting you have uncovered.

To acquire the necessary data, even the most astute collector should never enter an antique mall, junk shop, or even an estate sale without the proper devices of the trade. Your gear should include a portable black light, a magnifying glass, a tape mea-

Picnic, *Martha Walter, 24" x 30", oil on board, signed lower right,*
Provenance: Estate of Martha Walters, David David Gallery, Philadelphia, Pennsylvania.
Courtesy of Knoke Galleries of Atlanta.

sure, a multipurpose knife, and a reference text featuring those artists you collect. Several favorites include *Who Was Who*, Davenports, Benezit, Youngs, and Mallett.

The condition of a painting is a major determinant of its value. Part of your assessment is to evaluate whether a painting has been restored, the amount of repair that has been done, or whether a significant restoration will be necessary. Black light inspection will allow you to make a general analysis of the location and extent of "inpainting."

The determination of authenticity, which has been given a separate discussion, depends upon a number of factors including style, composition, subject matter, provenance, and the presence of a valid signature.

Oftentimes, a signature can be seen with black light inspection when it is not delineated by visual examination with ambient light. Also, if a signature has been altered or reinforced, black light inspection will allow a more accurate evaluation of what has been done. Never spend significant money for a painting until you have inspected it by black light.

The general condition of a canvas can also be evaluated by a careful inspection of the edges. Removal of a painting from its frame will enable you to examine the edge to determine friability of the support and, if the work is an oil canvas, often determine whether a reline will be necessary. This has implications of risk as to the final condition and financial exposure for you to have the restoration process done.

Paintings are fitted into frames by all manner of devices; therefore, for removal of the painting without undue trauma, a multipurpose knife with is several functions is a necessity. Nail clippers and files, ballpoint pens, tie clasps, etc. have met with very mixed results in my experience. Once out of the frame or away from the glass covering, your inspection process becomes infinitely more precise.

The magnifying glass has multiple uses. Without a raking light inspection, it is often difficult to determine the severity of crackle or crackleur that is an expected process of aging of an oil composition. If the edges of the crackle are widely separated and the pigment layer has turned or curled at the boundary, extensive conservation methods may be required to stabilize the surface to prevent flaking and paint loss.

A magnifying glass will allow a more accurate visual inspection of the edges and the depth of the crackleur. Signatures, inscriptions, dates, and titles can also be discovered or uncovered to greater advantage using a magnifying glass.

Value is obviously a subjective determination, with many components and parameters affecting this judgment. In general, the most important is the identification of the artist and the painter's standing in the art world. Despite the fact that you have specialized as a collector, it would be naive to believe that you know the names of more than a select few artists. I believe that 95% of collectors of American impressionism could not identify all members of "The Ten."

Having intimate knowledge of their training, exhibition records, and honors and awards of a large body of artists would exceed the storage capacity of any human brain. A reference text will greatly improve your opportunity to identify an undiscovered "treasure." However, the reference text should be used only if you have already become interested in the painting on aesthetic grounds.

It is usually unwise to pursue the documentation of a work unless you are emotionally or visually attracted to it or you may end up as an "autograph collector" with poor nonrepresentative examples of well-listed artists.

You should collect first for your pleasure, and these artists are listed in the reference because they painted collectible works. However, not all of an artist's productivity has merit so do not relegate yourself to being an autograph acquirer; decide if the painting appeals to you aesthetically. The painting you acquire must reflect the characteristics that placed this artist in the books.

If the frame is undistinguished then you may wish to acquire a period frame or one of standard size like 16x20, 20x24, 24x30, 30x36. . . that is why you need a small tape measure.

The pursuit of paintings brings to mind a number of analogies regarding the tools you will need. One would not anticipate a round of golf without a putter, sport fishing without a rod, or hunting without the presence of a weapon.

You will want to know the characteristics of your quarry and where they are likely to be found. These are the instruments of those particular quests, and so are the black light, the multipurpose knife, the magnifying glass, the tape measure, and the artist's reference book.

If you want to engage in the described analysis in relative secrecy, store your gear in a camera bag and find a secluded corner in the "sandbox" or "loo." Actually the seller may be so impressed with your studied approach that they may let you decide upon the price, an unlikely but wonderful prospect.

Selection

Collectors initially believe that selecting a painting is a formidable exercise and may even feel intimidated by the prospect. Early on in their collecting they may have someone else determine the suitability of a particular work for them.

In this instance, the person you select as your agent should have intimate knowledge of your needs, desires, and resources. Alternatively, you can "buy what you like," a philosophy already discussed. Through an often lengthy process of trial and error, you may learn what the expression really means to you, and "what I like" changes often and quite rapidly at first.

Probably the most satisfying method of acquisition is for you to develop some personal skills in evaluating paintings and, with the assis-

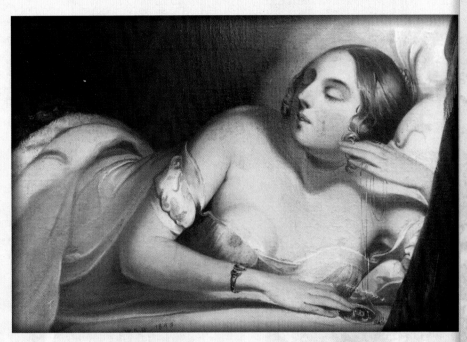

Rowena, *William Barclay, 26" x 32", oil on canvas. Private collection.*

tance of a reputable dealer, art consultant, or auction house representative, eventually make your own choices.

Aspiring collectors often wish to know where to begin and ask me about the initiation. The generic answer is go to wherever the greatest spectrum of art is exhibited for you to see and learn about. You should visit as many museums as possible, view the offerings at the large auction houses, and attend discussions and lectures on paint-

New England Landscape, *Chauncey Ryder, 12" x 16", oil on board, National Academy, signed lower left. Courtesy of Knoke Galleries of Atlanta.*

ings and techniques that have some chance of being interesting and informative to you. You should review as many auction catalogs, art books, exhibition monographs, and atlases as makes sense for your lifestyle, and how knowledgeable you want to be.

After a general survey of art history, auction catalogs are very helpful to reinforce the visual images and for you to determine the specifics of those you want to collect and become aware of fair market value. Soon, the style of art, painting technique, and subject matter that you prefer will be identified. Once this has been established, the next step is for you to structure your reading of art texts specializing in this genre and begin visiting dealers who offer this particular art for sale. You should attend auctions where these paintings are being offered and observe the process and record the prices achieved. I will enlarge upon this strategy later.

This is akin to charting stock prices before investing in them. This activity will provide you a sense of the most important artists painting with a particular technique, their general price range, and what characterizes the representative and most collectible works for these individual painters.

The Picnic, *Paul Bartlett, 24" x 20", oil on canvas. Bartlett trained at the Art Students League and was influenced by John Sloan. His paintings are rare; he was known primarily as a sculptor. His wife was an accomplished artist as well.*

Newfoundland Fishwharf, *William Partridge Burpee (1870 – 1952), 25" x 30", oil on canvas, signed lower right. Exhibited at The William A. Farnsworth Library & Art Museum, Rockland, Maine, July 16 – Sept. 5, 1976. Courtesy of Knoke Galleries of Atlanta.*

From reading about painting techniques and viewing examples on public exhibition, you should and will gain knowledge of how to evaluate the composition of a painting and whether the technical elements are appropriately utilized to create a competent and pleasing work that will endure. You should also develop some judgment with regard to evaluating the condition of a painting and whether any conservation or restoration will be required. More will be offered later regarding the importance of painting condition. However, the condition of the pigment and outer layers exterior to the support are of great importance in evaluating the status of a painting. If

Village Scene With Church, *Ben Shute (1905 – 1986)*, 21¾" x 30¼", *watercolor, signed upper left, July 29, 1948. Courtesy of Knoke Galleries of Atlanta.*

Cottages in Spain, *Anthony Thieme (1888 – 1954)*, 30" x 36", *oil on canvas, circa 1930, signed lower right. Courtesy of Knoke Galleries of Atlanta.*

the condition is poor, restoration can be costly and so extensive that very little of the original work of the artist remains after this process. Visual inspection can provide an overview of the condition of a work, but a personal black light viewing for inpainting, signature reinforcement or addition, and overpaint should be a standard part of your routine.

Dealers and auction houses will usually provide a condition report upon request. However, you should utilize both your personal assessment and the report of the seller before judging the suitability of a painting.

Several unaided assessments can only be made after you have had personal experience in evaluating many paintings. You will deal with your comparing the individual painting you are considering with the spectrum of works by that artist. Is this the best, the worst of their spectrum, or something in between? Think about judging from 1 to 10.

The provenance (pedigree) and exhibition record of the painting should be requested before you consider purchasing it. The pedigree can add substantially to the importance and desirability of any particular work. Provenance will be discussed again in this text.

Madonna & Child, *Elliott Daingerfield (1859 – 1932), 40" x 32", oil on canvas, signed lower left, 1914. Courtesy of Knoke Galleries of Atlanta.*

Fall Landscape, *Robert Vonnoh, 25" x 30", NA, oil on canvas, signed lower right. Courtesy of Knoke Galleries of Atlanta.*

Painters generally submit their best works to important exhibitions and juried shows. To be included, the paintings must meet certain criteria. Therefore, paintings selected by the artist and included in exhibitions will generally have greater appeal and value. You should always seek the pedigree (provenance) in determining whether to make an acquisition. Some judgment should be exercised in evaluating the provenance; "from the estate of the artist" may not mean that it was retained as a personal treasure by the artist. The painter may have been dissatisfied with the work and thus not have offered it for sale. Provenance will be discussed many times in this text.

The name of a famous gallery on a stretcher label enhances the value but may also mean that they deaccessed it by "dumping" at auction. Thus, use your eye and don't succumb to just label collecting. These dealers may also have placed the work on consignment with another dealer and the work failed to sell in the secondary market. A well-known museum could have purged the work from their holdings as an example they did not want to exhibit and they might gain both space and money by selling it. Thus, knowledge of provenance is usually, but not always, enhancing, as it can even lessen the value of a painting.

Ownership by an astute collector, if established, can add value to any work. If the painting has been exhibited, judged, and then received an award, these phenomena will also enhance its value. You, as a collector, in uncovering this type of data, have an opportunity to experience one of the singular joys of the acquisition process. Many dealers will do the prerequisite research, but while the information is important to you, it is more rewarding for you to acquire the data yourself.

An important criterion in evaluating a painting is its specific desirability to you as the collector, and that is largely a personal judgment. Individual collectors can have their own visual perception, sense of values, and personal interests that combine to make them uniquely qualified with the prerequisite date to render this evaluation. After all, it is your collection.

Choosing a painting is a very enjoyable process — no matter how inexact; mistakes are reversible, your tastes may change, and the intellectual experience is often exhilarating. My advice is to be an active part of the process because you best know your needs and the extent of your resources.

Seated Woman by a Pond,
Edmund C. Tarbell, 24" x 28".
Courtesy of Vose
Galleries of Boston.

Sunrise, Barnegal Beach, New Jersey,
1875, Francis A. Silva (1835 – 1886), 13½"
x 23¾", oil on canvas, signed and dated.
Courtesy of Godel & Co.
Fine Art, New York, New York.

Mother and Child by the Hearth, 1867,
Lilly Martin Spencer (1822 – 1902), 34½" x
27½", oil on canvas, signed and dated.
Courtesy of Godel & Co. Fine Art,
New York, New York.

Authenticity

A major, if not the chief, determinant of value of any painting is the author of the work. A corollary to this statement is its authenticity; that the painting should be by the hand of the artist that it is purported to be.

Establishing authenticity is a combination of scientific analysis, reasoning, gathering of appropriate data, and employing an informed opinion. Each of these has merit and should contribute to an accurate assessment if utilized in the proper manner and appropriate sequencing of the analysis employed.

Establishing authenticity is not only significant for the proper assessment of the value and importance of a painting but can be one of the greatest satisfactions of the collecting experience.

The first observation in assessing authenticity is usually the painter's signature. Do painters sign all their works? No they do not. Do they sign them in the same manner? Also a resounding no. However, there are signature reference books that are often helpful in that they demonstrate valuations over the course of a painter's career.

Julian Alden Weir, a major figure in American art circles at the end of the nineteenth century and a member of "the Ten," later signed his paintings "J.

Closeup of signature, Alice R. H. Smith.

Isle of Palms, *Alice Ravenal Huger Smith, signed. Private collection. Exhibited at Vanderbilt University Club, Cosmos Club, Chapel Hill Museum, Meredith College, Wesleyan College, Knoxville Art Museum, Huntsville Art Museum.*

Alden Weir" wishing to emphasize his Alden family connection. Henry Curtis Ahl, the Newburyport artist, signed his works "Ahl Jr." paying homage to his father, Henry Hammond Ahl, a well-respected artist known for his Barbizon paintings and church murals throughout New England. As the son's work became more widely recognized, he later signed his paintings "H. C. Ahl."

Signatures obviously should be contemporaneous with the execution of the painting. This can be most accurately determined by ultraviolet (UV) or black light examination. If the signature has been added at a later date, the most likely conclusion is that the work is a forgery. However, this may not always be the case. It is not unheard of that signatures may be applied to genuine unsigned works of a deceased artists by the surviving spouse, by a relative, or by a dealer embellishing the "authenticity." Thus, a forged signature may not always designate a fake painting.

Style and subject matter are two other parameters employed in ascribing authenticity to a work. Most artists' methodology in constructing a painting will become a "signature" whereby an expert can authenticate an individual painting or at least attribute the work to the hand of a particular artist. This requires a great exposure to the nuances of that artist's technique over time and a critical analysis by the person authenticating the work.

Closeup of signature, Marie Faure, 1904.

Sometimes authorship of a text

Closeup of signature, Robert L. Reid, collaboration signature, denotes commission.

Tobacco Farm, *Scudder,* 20" x 24", oil on board, purchased in antique mall. Inscription on reverse indicated by commission of a wealthy North Carolina planter family. Records revealed Cape Cod artist painting in South, 1940s. Gift to Tobacco Farm Life Museum.

on that particular artist or compiling a catalogue raisonne of their known works can make an individual the expert. This is at best an inexact science and their evaluation is an expert *opinion* although it is often naively accepted in the art world as *fact*.

In the circumstance of certain artists, the financial or commercial implication are sufficient that the temptation for perfidy and misrepresentation, being commensurate, represent a formidable incentive. An example is Ralph A. Blakelock, who along with Albert Pinkham Ryder, were America's greatest visionary artists. Blakelock lived an emotionally troubled life and like many creative people suffered from depression. He produced, with his multiple glazing techniques of painting composition, many moody, evocative, general landscapes and scenes of Indian encampments.

In the first decade of the twentieth century, Blakelock, while interred in a mental institution, had several works sell publicly for record prices for an American artist. Soon a number of works allegedly painted by Blakelock appeared for sale from all quarters. These were signed, often the signature appeared to float upon the surface of the varnish; and over the ensuing years, it became apparent there existed many more fake Blakelocks than genuine paintings by the artist.

A major difficulty in their detection is that these paintings were composed contemporaneous with Blakelock's active period; thus, they could not be differentiated upon the materials used. This circumstance led to a facility in Lincoln, Nebraska, headed by Professor Norman Geske to evaluate the authenticity of works by Blakelock. Over the years, the grading system from genuine, to attribution, to fake has become sufficiently accepted that the value of genuine Blakelocks has continued to rise and recently over $400,000 was realized for one at auction. Collectors possessing genuine Blakelocks or paintings attributed to him were pleased.

A very difficult group to sometimes authenticate are works composed in art colonies or schools. A number of artists belonged to a certain school such as the regional groups in such convivial locations as Old Lyme or Rockport where the famous and lesser known artists composed works in immediate proximity and of the same subject. This, over time, obscured the boundaries of attribution based upon style and subject matter for these artists.

Various schools, such as the Boston Museum of Fine Arts School, Woodstock, the Pennsylvania Academy of Fine Arts, and Chase's School at Shinnecock on Long Island, had students that could often

Waiting for the Return, *24" x 20", oil on canvas, circa 1945, painted at Ringling School, Little Switzerland, North Carolina. Could only be attributed to one of three instructors on a stylistic basis.*

produce works not unlike those of their mentors. This does not infer that the body of paintings produced by these artists rivaled the abilities of their mentors but the individual works could.

We once acquired a large modified portrait attributed to Evangeline Walker, a BMFA graduate and private student of Phillip Leslie Hale. A photograph of Walker proved that she was the subject of the work and further research revealed that the painting was executed by Hale and apparently not signed. BMFA students, especially the Tarbellites, created works similar in technical qualities and almost identical in style to their more famous teachers.

Sometimes artists in teaching demonstrations might execute a painting during a class. These were often not signed and might not represent fully completed works in the opinion of the artist. John Grabach, a well-known New Jersey artist from the Art Students' League had a school in Newark. We once acquired a well executed work unsigned on artist board. It was inscribed on the obverse "Grabach, for class" and dated. The style was characteristic of Grabach's work and the date appropriate. In our minds, this is a work by John Grabach, but we have archived it as an attribution in that it is not signed conventionally and the authenticating evidence is circumstantial.

Uncovering a signature by removal of varnish or pigment is an exciting moment in a collector's experience. Even finding an indistinct or obscured signature by a loop or magnifying glass, or clarifying one by microscopic examination or study using indirect or sometimes UV light is a rewarding process.

We once acquired a work by Henry Moser on the basis of artistic merit alone to find upon removal of the varnish his signature. Our early "Bellows" was actually attributed to Robert Henri as the subject was a young girl. George Wesley Bellows studied and was influenced by Henri, the leader of "the Eight." Early in his career, Bellows painted these modified portraits before he turned to his better known subject matter of land and seascapes and especially prize fights (one sold for 27 million dollars recently). Our painting was on the original stretcher and in the original period frame.

Female (Life Study), *John Grabach, 24" x 20," oil on board, signed on back and inscribed with initials and sitter's name. Records at New Jersey confirm artist and date. Replacement frame is period. Grabach was a teacher of the Newark and Hull Schools of Art and a member of the National Academy. Private collection.*

Authentication by an inscription on the back of the painting or on its stretcher or even frame is less preferable than a signature on the visual surface of the painting, but its veracity depends on the context. The exact place or circumstances of composition might well be identified, leading to a very well substantiated attribution. We once acquired a landscape that was unsigned but of excellent technical quality. Removal of the backing revealed the artist's signature and the designation of a farm later identified as one belonging to a relative of the artist, Aaron Gorson. I would feel as secure about the authenticity of this work by Aaron H. Gorson as a characteristic industrial scene fully signed, but our archives have this as an attribution bowing only to convention and not to the usual canons of evidence.

One should apply logic and common sense to deciding about the genuineness of a painting. Questions of authenticity can often be answered by examining the surrounding circumstances. As a first premise, the fake or forgery should benefit the perpetrator, whether misrepresenting a Rembrandt or an obscure member of the Hudson River School. The incentive is almost always financial gain.

A Young Girl, *George Wesley Bellows, 28" x 23", oil on canvas, signed in right left corner, "Geo… W Bell…." Original stretcher and frame.*

We had the frame restored and the painting cleaned and relined. A partial signature "Geo… W Bell…" could be clearly discerned in the lower right corner. Obviously, one would be delighted to have an attribution, even a Henri, become a signed Bellows, but also, we had even felt somewhat justified about the previous attribution on a stylistic basis emphasizing the point that style and subject matter are a part of the evidence. Attribution is not an exact science.

Farm Outside Pittsburgh, *Aaron H. Gorson (1872 – 1933), 20" x 24", oil on canvas, signed on reverse. This was purchased at a flea market as an excellent, unsigned work. Removal of liner revealed signature and description. Confirmed by Gorson family. Gorson studied at Acadamie Julian in Paris and with Whistler.*

Closeup of signature,
Childe Hassam. Note on
signature, "s" slightly
obscured by watermark.

Havana Cuba, *Childe Hassam, 1895, 16" x 12",*
watercolor.

If you are considering whether or not a painting is of a particular hand, determine whether it would have been profitable to have faked a painting at the proposed time. The paintings of very few artists were sufficiently valuable during their careers to serve as a proper incentive to fake the authorship. While George Wesley Bellows or Vincent Van Gogh works sell for millions today, they were not particularly valuable and were not faked during their lifetime, but Ralph Blakelock was because of the value of his paintings during his career. Bellows and Van Gogh would not have had fakes created contemporaneously out of "whole cloth" but the work of a lesser known contemporary might today be purposely misattributed to represent one of these artists.

If one considers the intent of the faker, which is deceit, then it would appear illogical to expect that the subject matter of the faked painting be atypical in subject of the work or medium employed in composition. Using the characteristic works by an artist as a reference, it would be anticipated that the perpetrator would choose subject matter and style of execution for which the artist is known.

Collectors prefer paintings that represent the best images of the artist's talent and typical works that faithfully demonstrate the qualities of that artist. Atypical paintings are more likely to represent works composed during training or a personal experiment by that painter, but not fakes. Fakes will be attempts at the characteristic style and medium for that particular artist.

We once acquired a Childe Hassam that was a tropical scene considered either a fake or an attribution, but research uncovered that it was painted in Havana, Cuba, in 1895 and had been matted in New York City in 1897 and later sold in St. Louis at a time when Hassam was not sufficiently valuable to have made a fake of his work likely.

We had an Alfred H. Hutty challenged on the basis of the medium. Hutty was noted for his watercolors of Charleston and the painting was mixed media, mostly pastel. Research of the provenance showed that the painting had been executed in Charleston of an identifiable site outside the city and purchased in Woodstock, New York, where Hutty had another home, by a collector from Brooklyn and later offered by an antique shop in New Bedford, Massachusetts. This was stylistically characteristic of a Hutty and any form of conventional or even unconventional logic strongly suggests that was, indeed, an authentic painting by the artist.

Returning for a moment to evaluation of style which is the use of pattern recognition by an expert to offer an opinion regarding authenticity. It is not science, but a highly respected methodology with historical precedence. Its analogy in the field of law would be expert opinion or expert testimony and in medicine the conclusion of a skilled diagnostician. The facts are the nature and age of the compositional materials, the manner of their application, and the image achieved. The opinion is based upon the gestalt of an individual with certain knowledge and experience to render their conclusions of determinative value.

This is not flame photometry of pigment analysis or computerized recognition of stroke pattern as one might apply to fingerprints. It is not column chromatography of DNA but is a valuable impression to be used as a part of the body of evidence that can be employed to render a judgment regarding the authenticity of a painting.

South Carolina Landscape, *Alfred Hutty (Charleston, South Carolina), 14" x 22", pastel, unusual medium and initialed signature. Authenticity proven by provenance estate records purchased in Woodstock, New York, where Hutty had his studio.*

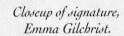

Closeup of signature, Emma Gilchrist.

At the Beach, *Emma Gilchrist, 24" x 20", oil on canvas.*

Authenticity is one of the most challenging areas in art. Rembrandts, highly revered by centuries by important museums, have been either declared "not by the hand of" or as outright forgeries. Certain forgers are so highly regarded that the experts have publicly given them high marks and it is well known that a number of perfidies attributed to the most valuable of the post-impressionists have sold for millions.

More recently a Cranache, owned by a well recognized public museum, was shown to have been stolen by the Nazi pillage in which numerous valuable works were taken both from public institutions and collectors. In the process of returning the work, the authenticity of "the Cranache" was reevaluated and the work was considered to be either an attribution or the school of.

Painting authentication is an ongoing and dynamic process. It is subject to the best evidence rule and to revision and can be capricious, arbitrary, and even illogical. Like in many cases of endeavor, the art world is inhabited by the informed, the uninformed, and the misinformed, often defending their position and opinion with equal fervor.

"Study for Landscape," *Thomas Moran, 11 ¼" x 8", oil on canvas. This small incomplete oil was a study for an almost identical larger work.*

Winter Landscape, *attributed to Walter Launt Palmer (1854 – 1932), 16" x 20", oil on canvas, exhibited NAD for 60 years. Authenticated by Van Horne estate records. Style is consistent with Palmer's most common subject.*

Collectors should seek the advice of those accepted in the field as experts, avoid the internecine conflicts that are fairly common, and engage in their own independent research and inquiry about those works they plan to acquire or hope to purchase and accept the results of their genuine best efforts.

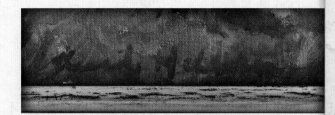

Closeup of signature, Knute Heldner.

Sailing, *T. Bailey, 30" x 25", oil on canvas, "T. Baily" was a collaboration of four or five artists painting in Swampscott, Massachusetts.*

Reverse of rare painting by Catherine Wiley, impressionist, note elaborate professional stretcher.

Obverse of W.A. Cooper portrait,
preliminary sketch.

President Trent, *W.A. Cooper,*
24" x 20", oil on canvas.

Landscape, *Attributed to Dennis Miller Bunker, 16 ¼" x 21 ¾",*
oil on canvas, signed DMB.

Value

Before any acquisition, the dealer or collector should have some specific sense of the value of the work. The most definable determination is its commercial value. In the instance of the collector, the assessed value may or may not be equivalent to the asking price.

When you are attracted to a painting for its visual appeal or aesthetics, then your establishment of its commercial value becomes the next step.

There are a number of reference books on values. For the biographic information, I use the three-volume *Who Was Who in American Art* by Peter Hastings Falk. Other general references are more related to prices and auction and private sales. *Davenports, American Art Index, Mallets, Bartlett and James* are but a few. Remember these figures do not always tell you the importance of the work, sometimes not even the dimensions.

Other sources of values are the prices quoted by dealers on pieces they have illustrated in such outstanding publications as *Antiques, Art in America,* or *Maine Antiques Digest.* Remember you are being quoted retail prices so you must decide if you want to pay wholesale, retail, or even "super retail."

Examine the painting; evaluate the painter. First look at the condition of the support (canvas, artist board, masonite, paper, wood panel, and many other materials). Canvas will, in general, be the most amenable to therapy and also black light and raking light analysis. Missing pigment will have to be painted in; but more important, is the status of the adjacent canvas to the visual defect.

This is only an introductory consideration to have you realize that after the determination of ownership (author) of the work, then condition becomes the next consideration. I once bought a work by one of the legendary American artists that was perceived to have significant problems with condition. I thought these changes were the result of restoration and purchased the work for $1,500, removed the restoration and kept the painting in my private collection for over 25 years, finally donating it to a public inventory for over 30 times what I paid for it.

The stretcher can reveal a great deal about a painting. If original, it can tell you the age or the origin of the work. The artist will often inscribe data on the stretcher; this may be for themselves, an agent, an acquirer, or for a public exhibit. We bought a lovely nocturne several months ago, thought to be by the accomplished but not well-known artist, Alexander Tupper. The technically wonderful nocturne showed very academic training. A signature became more apparent with a change in varnish. Tupper trained with two of the greatest artists of their era, John Henry Twatchman, the great impressionist, and Frank Duveneck, leader of the "Duveneck Boys." However, most intruiging was the exhibition label on the stretcher stating the exhibit was on the North Shore, the piece was entitled "Glouchester Harbor" and the artist's address.

This established several data points simultaneously and gave "personality" to the piece. It allowed us to know that it was painted contemporaneously with the height of Twatchman's career and that is why it appears Twatchman-like. A moody, mystical Twatchman of comparable quality would cost $250,000 – 400,000. While the Tupper would be worth only a fraction of that, it has many of the artistic merits and is much more affordable. This type of data places your painting in context.

When using the price lists you only have the subject and dimensions but not the visual appeal. So if you buy a Potthast believing it is a bargain at $45,000 rather than the $100,000 plus fetched by the good examples of his work, compare yours with the Potthasts in museums, texts, or those offered in leading antique magazines. How does yours measure up?

You do not want a poor or nonrepresentative example by any artist. Would you want a Lamborghini without an engine or a cracked 1920s Oriental vase by the Jugtown potter Ben Owen, Sr.?

An important point is that you must have one incontrovertible criteria — satisfaction of your aesthetic senses. You will never enjoy a painting that does not depict the representative work of that artist. A bad Childe Hassam is a bad painting. Decide upon your visual attraction first, then go to the reference books, look at the stretcher, determine condition, and then get your advisor's opinion, in that order.

Collect the Best

A Cup of Tea, *Lee Lufkin Kaula,*
St. Johnsburg, Vermont, 30" x 25".
Private collection.

Collecting paintings is a dynamic process and while the acquisition activity is usually emphasized, it is a process by which growth can only be accommodated by thoughtful deaccession. Collecting is a learning process and increase in knowledge and refinement of tastes is reflected in the choices and changes made during both aspects of the activity.

An area of some disagreement among dealers, curators, and collectors involves the relationship of the quality of the work to the fame of the artist in the selection process. Simply posed, would it be better to own a sketch by Edmund Tarbell or William Merritt Chase or a major work by Lillian Wescott Hale or Charles Webster Hawthorne? This answer is not always simple because the human motivation to collect paintings is quite varied. However, if the collector is a true connoisseur collecting mainly for his own pleasure, then the answer is obvious.

A collection should reflect the discrimination of the acquirer mirroring both his scholarship and experience. The scholarship should be ongoing but the original effort most appropriately should be a broad body of art encompassing sev-

Haystack, *William Partridge*
Burpee (1870 – 1952), 18" x 24",
oil on canvas, signed lower right.
Courtesy of Knoke Galleries of
Atlanta.

eral genres. After a time certain periods and painting techniques will be favored, then a collector can be more specific in his individual study and observation. Both confidence and conviction will grow.

When you decide upon a specific period and genre, then you can come to understand what is representative. You can also determine the limits of an acquisition cost. Possibly several examples in nineteenth century American art might prove illustrative about these concepts. For example, if one decided to collect the Hudson River School, leaders among this group would include Frederich Church, Thomas Moran, Sanford Robinson Gifford, and others. A major example of their work would have an acquistion cost of millions of dollars, a representative painting several hundred thousand, and even a minor example over $100,000. The second and third tier Hudson River School artists approach the high tens of thousands for major examples and $20,000 – 40,000 for representative ones.

Large, competent, unsigned paintings by the Hudson River School can be acquired for less than $10,000. These have aesthetic

The Fiske Madonna, *Elliott Daingerfield (1859 – 1932), 36" x 30", oil on canvas, signed lower left, dated 1895. Courtesy of Knoke Galleries of Atlanta.*

Barn in Snow, *Brantley Smith, 25" x 30", oil on canvas. James collection.*

appeal and represent some of the qualities that make the Hudson River School desirable. Understand, however, you are eschewing name recognition and some fellow collectors will not be impressed with your choices. An alternative is to simply say you cannot afford to own the best of the Hudson River School, so you will allocate your finite resources to another genre.

The most popular style of painting is impressionism characterized by a light, bright pallette, color to simulate form, pleasant subject matter, and an inherent vibrancy to render these works almost universally appealing. If a painting demonstrates these characteristics, it represents an honest example of impressionism irrespective of the artist's standing. If the composition, draftsmanship, and other technical criteria are outstanding, one can have confidence that the painting will provide pleasure over time.

If you plan to have a collection and not just a few paintings, then you should anticipate multiple acquisitions, each with a unit cost and implications for the total. Also a collection and an assemblage are not the same. A random gathering of paintings will usually appear to be just

Meditation, *Lilla Cabot Perry,* 45¾" x 35¼", oil on canvas. Courtesy of Knoke Galleries of Atlanta.

The Pig Woman — A Southern Idol, *Knute Heldner (1877 – 1952),* 42" x 40½", oil on canvas, signed lower right, dated "32," excellent condition, relined. Courtesy of Charleston Renaissance Gallery.

what it is — a series of acquisitions without an identifiable theme or obvious plan of acquisition.

Certainly a series of random acquisitions of major paintings would be impressive, but less so than a collection demonstrating outstanding examples of a particular genre. The "collect what I like" school is very often a response to the acquirer's resistance to scholarship or simple lack of knowledge. Sometimes it reflects a "collection" acquired by a dealer for a collector. The very best friend a collector can have is an informed, reputable dealer to act as an advisor. Four of five dealers have been invaluable to me in my career as a collector. I consider them an important part of my learning process especially in judging the quality of a painting. By the time I bought my first major painting, I had visited dozens of museums, read a number of texts, attended many exhibitions, participated in auctions, and made several inappropriate acquisitions. The best advice I received from those dealers I formed long-term relationships with was for me to understand what I acquired and to master the methodology to judge a major or representative example of an artist's work.

Violette, *August Lundberg, 24" x 20", oil on canvas. Private collection.*

The Morning Lesson, *Carl Nordell (1885 – 1957), 58" x 45", oil on canvas, signed lower center, dated 1917, original PAFA label on reverse. Courtesy of Knoke Galleries of Atlanta.*

If your dealer has a number of examples of a particular artist's work, you can get some idea of the spectrum of the examples. If this is not the circumstance, look for the artist in museums, texts, or in the inventory of other dealers. When you have identified a major work you are attracted to and can afford it, acquire the work. If it is not a major painting by the artist or you cannot afford a major work by that artist — pass. If the artist had students or followers, you may be able to afford a painting of equal artistic merit by a student or follower over an example by the famous painter. Do not buy an atypical painting by an artist or one that does not represent a characterisitc effort no matter how famous the artist or inexpensive the work.

If you can put together an identifiable collection of major examples by good artists, then the whole will have visual appeal, represent an artistic statement, and will be important and an ongoing pleasure for you. Collect major examples whether the artist is famous or simply accomplished.

The Christening, *William DeHartburn Washington (1833 – 1870), 30½" x 25", oil on canvas, signed lower right, dated 1868. Courtesy of Knoke Galleries of Atlanta.*

Gilbert Gaul's Farm, Sumner City, Tennessee, *Gilbert Gaul (1855 – 1919), 26" x 34", oil on canvas, signed lower left, dated 1879. Courtesy of Knoke Galleries of Atlanta.*

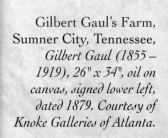

Spring Day, *Ellen Day Hale (1855 – 1940),
34" x 34", oil on canvas, dated 1879, marked
lower right. Courtesy of Vose Galleries of Boston.*

Laurel, *William Chadwick (1879 – 1962), 30" x 30",
oil on canvas, signed lower left. Courtesy of Knoke
Galleries of Atlanta.*

A Thoughtful Moment, *Isabel Vernon Cook, circa
1910, 40" x 30", oil on canvas, signed lower right.
Courtesy of Knoke Galleries of Atlanta.*

New York in Snow, *Cornelius Hawkins,
20" x 16", oil on canvas.*

Sources

Your Relationship with Your Art Dealer

The fundamental relationship for a collector is that with his dealer or dealers. Collectors are often intimidated by the prospect of this relationship but knowledge and experience can remove these fears.

The collector should consider what specific aesthetic he is attracted to as a first step. In examining and rejecting other aesthetics, the collector will gain the perspective to judge the various painting techniques that might also be considered. This will allow you to have an even-handed discussion with almost any dealer and may allow you to appreciate related painting techniques such as tonalism and the Barbizon aesthetic or the Visionarys.

Prepared with your own preference you should avail yourselves to many examples so you can become aware of the technical characteristics, typical images, and spectrum of that genre. This will give you confidence that you can at least tell a representative from a poor example of the technique giving you confidence in your exchange with the dealer especially regarding any particular painting. Never buy an atypical example of an artist unless the painting appeals to you by another criteria.

This does not mean you should assume a subservient role or that you need to equal the dealer's body of knowledge about the artist, the genre, or that particular work. What the dealer is obligated to do is to justify the purchase of a particular painting by you. This should begin with the recitation of facts by your dealer about the subjects indicated, the artist, the genre, the condition, and then the dealer's opinion of importance.

Certain assertions are meaningless. Do not be impressed by the other collectors that have purchased an artist's work by artist from the dealer, the value your fellow collectors will ascribe to your acquisition, or the price another dealer is offering similar examples for. These are not terribly relevant and certainly should not in any way be determinative in your acquisition.

If your dealer is the least bit put off by your inquiry about factual information, examine the relationship and consider that you might need another dealer. This is information you should know and it is a dealer's responsibility to provide it for you. Once past this initial exchange, a discussion of aesthetics, importance, and the acquisition costs will logically follow.

If your dealer seems over impressed with the aesthetics of the considered purchase without context, remember your opinion is also valid. If I disagree with this subject assessment, I usually try to say as little as possible. Nothing is to be gained by being contentious and the next offering of a painting from this dealer may be something you find very desirable.

If you are attracted to a painting but believe the price to be excessive, you may ask for a justification or just inquire "is that your best price?" You can make an oblique reference to your financial plans for acquisition by stating that the quoted figure represents "a bit more than I had planned to spend." Dealers understand this and will almost never embarrass you by asking "how much did you plan to spend?" After all, you are talking about a single entity and not your general commitment for art. If you indicate to any seller how important a purchase is to you, then they will usually respond by indicating their understanding — factual responses and justification will be a logical result of this revelation.

Tell the dealer what you want. If you do not collect nonrepresentative works, European art, or artist's pastels or whatever, tell the dealer so they will know what to present to you and not waste their time or yours or cloud the issue of a valid acquisition. I tell a new dealer that I collect nineteenth and early twentieth century American art. This is specific, should convey that I probably have some knowledge of the subject, and indicates the futility in attempting to entice me to collect something else the dealer has in their inventory. It saves us both time and the embarrassment of my having to politely refuse a series of inappropriate offerings.

The dealer clearly knows what his mandate is and what my expectations are. The challenges are defined and in dealing with a subject as emotion laden as the selling and acquisition of paintings, clear guidelines are very helpful.

In every aspect of this enterprise, the greater the competence and sophistication of the collector, the more pleasurable the process will be. As important, the dealer will derive the greatest satisfaction from a circumstance in which they have clear guidelines of the desires of the collector and are able to meet them.

Getting Your Dealer's Attention

One of the great impediments for the aspiring collector is the perceived formidable challenge of earning the good graces of that mythical figure possessing all the toys — the art dealer. The prospect of this encounter has been known to render catatonic even lions of industry and just ordinary billionaires. Folks who will buy a Bertram in 12.8 minutes using their uranium card or ladies who will charge the Star of Siam against their line of credit can be intimidated upon entry to the establishment of a famous art dealer. This state of affairs unfortunately is based upon cultivated and cultured misconceptions and even misrepresentations.

These homilies I offer should take care of your worst baseless fears and I assure that you will leave your dealer in awe. Any similarity to reality is both contrived and circumstantial. The characterizations, while revealing, are almost entirely fanciful. You should feel free to embellish but not significantly deviate from any of the ploys and basic principles imparted herein.

First, always have someone with a decidedly British accent "tele" ahead and inform the dealer of your arrival without indicating who you are or even rightly might be. He should note discreetly that you will represent at least two genders. If convenient, travel in pairs increasing some four- to five-fold your impact — make the dealer feel he has been ganged up on or at best simply overmatched. You should understand that part of this is about intimidation, like Air Jordan on the break when he reveals his considerable tongue or the late Sam Ervin telling you he was just a country lawyer.

Landscape, *Robert Nisbet, 24" x 20",*
oil on canvas, purchased from regional
dealer in Old Lyme.

Crabbing in Blue Creek, *Rufus*
Zogbaum, 8" x 10" mixed media on
brown paper, Zogbaum's works on paper,
like Maurice Prendergast's, are considered
more valuable than his oils.

Spanish Villa, *Maurice Gerberg, estate purchase.*

Having someone of the opposite gender has solid historical precedence. After all, where do you think Clark would have ended up if it had not been for Miss "Sakejowea." Probably in Nome or part of the Nes Perse version of Mulligan stew. You think Emelda could have picked out all those shoes without Ferdinand's advice? Why, even Adam didn't grab the first apple he saw, did he? Then there is Slick Willie… but you get the gist and strategy even if it doesn't end up perfect.

You then tool around for 45 minutes after your announced ETA so the dealer will have his game face on and a chance to put all the "dogs" (in frames) back in the storage racks. Always carry a briefcase which the opposition might imagine contains a "wire," at least a black light or even an electron microscope disguised as a PB and J sandwich.

Some collectors like to carry *Who Was Who*, Davenports, Benezet, and the *Memories of Duveen* but you can pretend to retain all that in your head. Carry a cell phone that is so little and skinny it looks like a poker chip. After you have given this dealer your best "aw shucks" homeboy rendition or "Miss Pittypat" greeting which will confuse the living hell out of him, her, or whatever, using your immobilizing stare like a long-

The Old Soldier, *Mayna Avent, 20" x 16" watercolor, purchased in frame shop.*

Roses, *Callie Braswell,*
16" x 20", found in
antique mall.

tongued lizard fixing a bug, whip out the cell phone and say "s'cuse me."

Then within earshot pretend to be talking to Zurich about the relation of rupees to hog undersides and what your IPO is going to open at on the Hong Kong Exchange. Then over-contritely look like your Chesapeake Retriever did when you caught him head-first in the third garbage can and say, without meaning it for one instant, "sorry."

Now it is time to announce that you have come to look at some paintings as if this were a revelation and you might be there to outfit your next safari instead. Do not say the Director of the Metropolitan sent you and then refer to him by his first name because the dealer will swear they are going to be having tea and curds in the foyer at four. Also, it's gauche to try the "do you know" by saying your very best friend in art, some legendary collector with his own museum, had suggested you drop by. The dealer will then have to swear he "arranged" for your friend to acquire much of his collection — the good part at least.

Just bob and weave like Muhammad Ali and see if this dealer can lay a glove on you. The first query will usually be as to what you are looking for but will be couched in terms like "aesthetic," "genre"; the artistic equivalent to "speaking in tongues." Forget about trying to remember so you can interpret his lines, just get

yours down like "well, we do admire impressionism but in a modified form suggesting some Barbican elements." The dealer's eyes will glaze over and you can know you took that hurdle like Edwin Moses or Princess Anne.

Next will be the bottom line query, but it might very well be disguised in a little foreplay like where the painting might be planned to hang in your Palm Beach or Blue Hill home, chalet at Zermot, doublewide on Big Pine Key (Kay), or "lean to" on Pine Ridge and the approximate size of the work. These subterfuges, however long they take, will finally get down to "it," how much are you anticipating spending for this next important acquisition.

The very best answer is "I really had not thought about that" which could mean price is no object, it does not really matter that I failed to take that into account because this is not for real — and the dealer does not know which, but wants desperately to believe the former. The ball is now in the dealer's court and it is his move. He does not even know what your game or game plan is.

You can keep it this way if you reveal as little as possible by gesture, body habits, or verbal utterance from this point forward. Let him describe the paintings shown you in intimate detail. It is his sell and he has to make his case compelling — do not help. If you feel you should be interactive, ask about provenance or condition — never about price. If the dealer's entreaties beg for a response, comment upon the "composition, the painterly qualities, draftsmanship, perspective…" but go very soft on the approving adjectives.

You can be reasonably assured that the best works in the dealer's judgment are out on the wall, but most established dealerships will have many more paintings in the racks of their immediate storage. You should discreetly suggest a "look see" by asking if there might be anything else in the inventory of interest. The dealer may refuse but will not be offended but impressed at your savvy.

You will probably see one or several paintings that, given the proper circumstance, you might wish to purchase. Without referring to the price directly, express your interest by requesting the dealer to write the title, name of the artist, dimensions, and price on one of his business cards. This will depersonalize the matter of buy and sell for the moment. It will also change the venue of the eventual sale to where you have at least an

equal footing. After all, if the deed is done on his turf in the first chukka, ownership of the bat and the ball may not be relevant.

Besides getting a better read on your own desires, your finances, and who this artist really is by a bit of independent research, you can bargain with the dealer later and develop a separate game plan for that. Do you believe Wyatt and Doc just walked up to the O.K. Corral? Or that Newton was just snoozing under any ole tree? You think that computer geek shrunk that microchip 'cause it fell in his laundry?

Your departure is almost as important as your entrance. Whip out your mite-sized cell phone and pretend to speak to your investment banker on one line while giving instructions to your imaginary chauffeur to fetch you; not at this dealer's establishment but at his competitor of equal fame who is nearby; in an hour. This ploy may very well soften the future asking price for the paintings you have written down on the dealer's card.

Act as if your identification and that of your companion should not require a revelation or is immaterial, leaving the dealer to guess — and hope — who you just might be. Solemnly, stroke the dealer's hand and thank him genuinely for his time, concern, patience, and hospitality. That oughta do it until he calls you the next day telling you the National Museum of Art had expressed interest in "your" piece but he had told them it was on hold.

You compliment him for his loyalty and consideration and tell him your foundation has that work at the top of their list for acquisition for the traveling exhibition of your holdings to be shown at Palm Beach and Santa Fe during the season. You, however, feel it might well be suitable for a gift to the Diplomatic Reception rooms of the U.S. Department of State. In any event, you found the visit both enjoyable and enlightening.

Winter at New Hope, *Edward Willis Redfield (1869 – 1965), 22" x 16", oil on canvas. Founder of New Hope Colony. Although sparkling impressionistic works by Redfield have sold for over $100,000, early examples such as this can be acquired for $20,000 – 25,000. James collection.*

Acquiring at Auction

When retail prices for paintings seem to be beyond your financial reach, an alternative may be to acquire paintings at auction. This avenue, however, should not be taken by the uninformed, the unwary, or the faint of heart. To be successful, you must apply the appropriate study, spend the requisite time in evaluating the paintings, and exercise self-discipline on the auction floor.

Knowledge is the best insurance you can have. Excellent data sources to prepare for auction are catalogs and post-sale price lists. Study these over a period of months to several years, which is much like charting stocks, before you attempt to enter the active bidding process to personally acquire at auction.

A method I recommend is to order a catalog prior to the sale and after serious analysis determine what you would pay for those paintings that you would like to acquire. Write that figure down.

From the post-auction price list, compare your prediction or theoretical offering price with what the paintings realized at the sale. If your prediction was not in close agreement with what the painting brought, try to determine the reason for this disparity by learning more about the artist, or ask knowledgeable dealers and fellow collectors their opinion for the realized price. Make certain you know the range of that artist's works. A great Chase or Heade will cost 5 – 10 times the acquisition price of an ordinary one but the differential in value may be greater than that.

This process may seem simplistic but would you play a round of golf not knowing where the out of bounds markers are? In tennis you have the linespersons and anglers have "no fishing" signs but art collectors have none of these helpful safeguards.

When you are sufficiently informed and experienced to begin your career as an auction bidder, there are several disciplined activities that you should follow. After receiving the auction catalog, go through it several times to determine which paintings interest you most. Evaluate how specific the information is about the authenticity and condition.

Plan to visit during the auction exhibition and arrange to go through the paintings you are interested in with one of the staff. You must discuss the technical and aesthetic merits of the paintings and, more importantly, the condition reports. Condition is of great importance in determining the value and desirability of a painting. After you have gone past visual appeal you should have a systematic and rigorous method to assess condition.

Before acquiring, you will want to determine what support the painting is applied to. Rigid supports, such as paper or canvas mounted on board, masonite, or aluminum, present inherent difficulties in future restoration or conservation. Therefore, those paintings mounted in such a manner should be in very good condition if you plan to buy them at auction or any other mode of acquisition for that matter.

Aluminum, for example, is often covered by canvas, even covered in the rear, and the novice would neither see it nor recognize the feel of it. Paintings mounted on masonite are very difficult (and expensive) to restore. Removing these paintings from certain mounts is very traumatic and must be done with great care and often attendant expense.

You should examine carefully the back of the painting. In addition to being able to evaluate the condition, you may discover labels that can reveal much about the provenance of the work. Artists often inscribe interesting data about the painting there, such as the time and place it was executed or the title they personally gave to the painting.

The leading auction firms are usually forthright and circumspect in their evaluation of paintings, especially with collectors they know to be very demanding. Ask for the proverbial black light examination, especially if the appearance of the painting does not match the condition report given to you by the auction staff.

If a painting is in poor condition and will require significant restoration (including inpainting) avoid it unless you feel confident about the expense it will involve as well as the outcome of the restoration.

The types of paintings many collectors search for are the pristine ones that have not had any "work" but reflect the fact that they have passed through life in an environment which allowed the support and pigment layer to age generally.

"Trade paintings" (those that have been passed around among galleries or have been in many previous auctions) should be avoided because there is often a very good reason they have repeatedly changed hands among knowledgeable owners.

Ask for the provenance of the painting. The auction house may not tell you specifically the consignor but will often indicate if it is or is not a private party. Any exhibition record, award, or catalog or monograph publication will enhance the value of a painting. These need to be documented.

After previewing the auction, make a list of the paintings you like and decide, on an individual basis, how much you would commit for each; afterwards prioritize your selections. Then add the total and plan to keep a mental running account during the sale. Planning to spend $15,000 and spending $45,000 is not prudent collecting.

You have several options of bidding in acquiring paintings by auction. The most passive route but the one with the greatest risk is the absentee bid form because you have the potential and possibility of acquiring all of your selections. A safeguard is to be overly conservative in your bid on each painting, so your only chance of being successful is if one painting were to sell at an unrealistically low price. If this happens, you should be concerned that you missed something in your evaluation and appraisal. Thus, select the paintings that you really covet and bid only on those; this takes discipline but success in almost any other endeavor does as well.

Alternatively, you can have someone act as your agent during the sale for a fee. With proper instructions to your representative, you can avoid unwanted multiple acquisitions.

Another technique of acquisition at auction is the telephone bid. This has to be well organized and orchestrated, and is a service that is not available from all auction houses or for all the sales of any. If available, this is not as complicated as most collectors believe. The staff person will phone you at a pre-established time.

Keep in mind that during the bidding process you may have a sense of isolation, because you have no prima facae or personal information as to what is really happening with the other phone bidders or on the floor of the auction house. Telephone bidding requires discipline and even some cognitive imagery to maintain your frame of reference to properly guide your instantaneous judgment.

The most preferable method of acquisition, and the one which offers the greatest control and least risk to you, is to attend the auction in person. The only inherent rise is the disorientation which occurs if you get caught up in the competition in the process.

To always exercise discipline is difficult in this exciting arena. Over the years, I have used a technique to maintain my frame of reference during the bidding. I write down the highest bid I will execute in the catalog before the sale and simply do not exceed that amount. Other tactics can be effective, but the usual ones of secretive bidding or sitting or standing in the back of the room to determine who is participating often do not make any significant dif-

ference in what you will expend to acquiring paintings at auctions.

Discipline comes from within — put aside the concept of winning and losing; this is not a billiards game or test of your honor. When the bidding is escalating rapidly, it is important not to enter until the offers for acquisition curve levels off.

Try to indicate your bid so that you will have the last offer just prior to a major price increment ($9,750 just before $10,000, for example). While these levels are only symbolic barriers, they affect the behavior of most individuals. When you are present at the auction, you can usually be in control of these factors, but only within the limits of your self discipline.

You should have a current idea of your expenditure at the auction from moment to moment so as to proceed in a fashion toward the limit you have given yourself. This will allow you to bid accordingly and in context for the next painting offered. This I call the "running exposure" determination.

There are bidding techniques that can be used as strategy. Sometimes you can attempt to intimidate a competing bidder by jumping the bidding increments. For example, if bids have been at $500 increments, raise the next bid by a factor of $1,000, if you can do so, and still remain within your pre-sale limit. This may convince the competition that you are so resolute, they should cease and desist.

The last paddle standing is the "winner," and the competition may think that only one more bid by them will take you out of the bidding. Appear to have the resolve to acquire the painting irrespective of the price (I emphasize *appear*).

As I have noted, it is important to know where the inventory offered at auction comes from. Should this information be taken into consideration? The paintings you should most actively seek are those from private holdings which are reaching the open market for the first time. Dealers will also bid very aggressively for these "fresh" paintings.

Deaccessions from museums can be a source of good and desirable paintings and usually have a definitive provenance. Museums may deaccess a painting because they have other examples by that same artist or if that particular work does not fit their current statement or image they wish to convey. Often, museums will set a modest reserve because they genuinely want to deaccess the work and do not want it to be a "buy in." Remember they have to go through an arduous screening process with the governance of their institution to be allowed to offer the work publicly.

Red Sails, *Edgar Payne (1882 – 1947), 22" x 26", oil on canvas, signed lower right, auction estimate was retail. Typical execution of common subject by artist. Purchased at auction.*

You should also know your bidding competition and as much about the origin of the painting as you can. Speculators will buy paintings on the presumption that they will fetch higher prices as private resales or at future auctions. They cannot afford to pay retail sums but you can.

As I have previously discussed, galleries sometimes dump paintings at auction which they are having difficulty selling and cannot trade with another gallery. These are generally referred to as "trade" paintings. In my experience, they are often poor or nonrepresentative examples by famous artists. They often appear dark and dull. Unless you are an "autograph collector," you should avoid these examples because they will not wear well as part of your permanent collection and upon resale, they will typically not increase in value. Also, make certain to avoid the practice of acquiring "bargains"; however, if you do succumb, do not be too self-judgmental. You will be numbered among most of America's great collectors who almost universally engaged in this bit of folly early in their careers. After

all, everyone is searching for a bargain, but an undesirable painting acquired cheaply is never one.

The issue of bargains merits further commentary. Because of the temptation to own impressive titles, inexperienced collectors will acquire unattractive examples because they are perceived as bargains. As an investment, they are not "cheap" in artistic terms, and they only serve to emphasize their naivete and inexperience to any sophisticated audience, such as fellow but competent collector, gallery owner, colleague, art historian, or museum curator whose approval one might like to have.

Unless you have unlimited funds — in some ways, an unfortunate circumstance — you must recognize that there may be certain artists whose representative examples are beyond your resources. Rather than buy a work with little aesthetic appeal and without the painterly qualities that made that particular artist famous and desirable, simply do not succumb to the temptation to own something by that painter. A desirable alternative is a good drawing or a work in a noncharacteristic medium for that artist (pen-and-ink, pastel, watercolor, or mixed media, depending upon the artist). This work can be affordable, can be appealing, and will demonstrate the technical qualities of that artists. Most dealers will advise you to collect "big names" but their bias is in favor of these artists as well as the monetary incentive of the sale.

After purchasing several poor but genuine examples of the work of Edmund Tarbell, as an alternative, I acquired a wonderful pastel of the artist's sister-in-law, Lydia. Several years ago when the painting was loaned to the United States Embassy in Paris, it became very clear to me how attached I was to the work because it is aesthetically lovely, demonstrates the best qualities of the artist, and was his sister-in-law.

Conversely, after several years of unsuccessfully convincing myself that another painting by a major American artist, a landscape, was not an acceptable example for my collection, I deaccessed this nonrepresentative Julian Alden Weir which had been purchased at auction early in my career because I thought it was a "bargain." It was consigned by me to auction and, protecting my anonymity, proved the P.T. Barnum theory by unexpectedly producing a sizeable profit in the transaction. Later, through a conservator friend, I was able to acquire a good example of Weir's artistry.

I wanted a Weir because he is an excellent artist and an important figure in American impressionism, but I first bought a minor and undesirable example for the wrong reasons. This was an error even though I gained financially. Good examples of J. Alden Weir are expensive and I could not afford to acquire one at retail. Thus, I should not have acquired a J. Alden Weir at all unless I acquired one privately and I was fortunate enough to do just that at a later time.

Many of "The Ten" and "The Eight" command prices at auction equal to or greater than those works by these artists acquired privately or in any other manner. If the examples of these artists are excellent or the paintings are by some of the "rare" members of these groups, dealers are willing to pay even more than the average collector. This reflects the fact that the dealer wants to have an example in his inventory. A dealer may also be acting at auction as an agent for a serious and well-funded collector (and they are not all Japanese industrialists).

I would recommend as in searching auction catalogs to find great examples by the students of the leaders of "The Ten" or "The Eight" or from the schools they represent, such as the Art Students League or the Boston Museum of Fine Arts School. This idea will be expanded in my discussion of the regional artists and the concept of seeking the students.

Major examples by lesser-known artists, I believe, are the best values the average collector should aspire to. At auction you will often be able to compete more successfully for a major Gretchen Rogers or Ellen Day Hale than a minor example of the work of Frank Weston Benson or Joseph R. DeCamp; all of these artists were from the Boston Museum School of Fine Arts. Most of the bidders will have never heard of Charles Wright but would "run the table" for an unfinished (and unappealing) William Merritt Chase, his teacher. I selected Wright because I purchased one that was similar in subject and composition to a Shinnecock example by Chase (which is in the Cleveland Museum). My painting was selected for exhibition of Chase's students by the late Ron Pisano, the William Merritt Chase scholar. My still life by the late student Edith Flisher reflects the best qualities of a Chase — her mentor.

When you view a pre-sale exhibition and see an appealing painting by an unknown artist, a few minutes research in one of the dictionaries or reference texts might reveal that the artist trained in Paris with Theodore Robinson or painted in Old Lyme with Childe Hassam. You may also find that the artist had several one-person shows or a retrospective exhibition with a brochure. A few hours in a reference library will sometimes be rewarded by a catalog with illustrations of the entire spectrum of the artist's work.

A number of times I have had the good fortune from research to find that the auction piece had been represented in an exhibition brochure, allowing documentation of public exposure and comparison of the painting with other examples by that artists. You can then judge if you are acquiring an outstanding example, a representative, or a minor example of the artist's work. You may not choose to spend your time in this manner, so remember your time is yours to occupy as are your other resources.

Everyone has a personal conviction about what constitutes an appropriate allocation of resources for their art collection. It is also personal what you believe a reasonable expenditure for an individual painting.

In this consideration, you should calculate the additional expense for conservation, restoration, or reframing, if this is going to be necessary. These costs vary but are real, and a pre-sale determination of these costs may be a prudent investment of your time.

I once bought two painterly and wonderful female figure studies (70" x 40") by Raymond Rogers Perry Neilse but had not estimated the cost of restoration or reframing. To meet these estimated costs, I sold one painting to a dealer the night of the auction. Several years later I decided to reacquire that painting and after some independent research found it in the Ralph Lauren mansion (shop) on Madison Avenue. Since I thought it might make an interesting addition to my other Neilsen, I talked with the store manager who was very understanding and said that the painting was "not for sale" but revealed to me their purchase price, which was more than 20 times my acquisition cost. Was I to be joyful or frustrated? You must go see it sometime at the entrance of the mansion on Madison Avenue.

Once I acquired at auction a very large early Sanford Robinson Gifford that had been deaccessed by a famous museum of American art. The painting was well documented and had been exhibited, but it demonstrated such detractions as significant crackleur, "yellowed" varnish, and a damaged frame. They felt that their other examples by Gifford were more exhibitable. Radiographic studies and consultation with a conservator that I respected confirmed that the work was structurally sound and would require little or possibly no inpainting after it was relined. The removal of the varnish made it bright and sparkling again. Thus, once restored, the painting could very well represent the genius of some of the great members of the Hudson River School. I purchased the work at the auction, and, after restoration and suitable framing in a wonderful reproduction frame, I ended up with a major example of this desirable school for less than one-tenth its current appraisal value. The painting has been on exhibition and holds up well alongside the other members of the Hudson River School. In this instance, auction probably afforded me an opportunity to acquire a painting that I could not have acquired as inexpensively by any other method but required some initiative to properly assess its condition. I took a risk but I would like to think it was an educated one.

This discourse has meant to create the idea that purchase at auction is unduly risky or complex. I have endeavored to emphasize the importance of appropriate preparation and due diligence before acquiring art at auction. Do not expect to "get lucky" or to stumble into a great painting acquisition. Many of your competitors will also have approached this process in a scholarly, disciplined manner, significantly diminishing the element of chance for them. Knowledge is the substance upon which prudent acquisitions at auction are based. Discipline and organization are the techniques that provide the foundation for the successful collector.

I believe that the effect of foreign investors on the prices of American paintings has been over-emphasized. Admittedly, the Japanese, for example, seem to have had unlimited funds and an insatiable desire for the most major examples of impressionism and post-impressionism. They bought overpriced paintings. With the marked down turn of their economy, many have been resold at a loss.

However, for the majority of collectible American paintings, there appears to be little competition from foreign investors. The unbridled enthusiasm for the most important American paintings by the Japanese and Europeans did momentarily have implications for auction prices because the frame of reference for other works of similar style and subject matter became momentarily distorted.

The financial climate has changed in the 1990s. October 1987 and certain tax changes made many investors wary, nervous, and much more conservative. While you might consider investments other than stocks and conventional money instruments, keep in mind art is generally not liquid and requires special knowledge to deaccess effectively. Bond yields have been described as boring, and tax laws have made real estate ventures much less popular than before. Commodities are too risky for most investors, and the IRS has chosen to tax gains in this instrument as they occur rather than after they are realized.

Given this environment, it is quite understandable that among the buyers of paintings are participants that can only be characterized as investors and speculators and not collectors. Some of these acquirers have little knowledge about the paintings they are buying or art in general. This commitment by them is regarded solely as an investment. What has this to do with auction acquisitions — everything, because it sets the environment and parameters.

A number of young people have made a great deal of money in the past several years. They see an art collection as a symbol of wealth and are active and very aggressive in their acquisitions. These new collectors do not have the benefit of history of prices for a particular artists and initially have little knowledge or experience in evaluating the condition or aesthetic value of a painting. Thus, they are more inclined to overpay for a painting by a known artist or unwittingly for a painting that is in poor condition than the "pros" who are resting on the sidelines. Having never had a painting restored, these inexperienced collectors cannot be expected to accurately calculate, or, in truth, anticipate the cost of the restoration in addition to the purchase price. They usually remain uninformed because their motives are not to learn about art but to use it for symbolic purposes to demonstrate their newly acquired affluence instead. Just identify these lemmings but do not follow them. You may not be able to compete because their premise and purchasing power are different.

Another phenomenon that I think is significant in increasing the auction prices is telephone and electronic bidding. Many collectors have now become very comfortable with this method of acquisition of paintings. They often bid over the telephone without personally inspecting the paintings, an unwise practice in my opinion. You should never acquire a painting unless you have held it in your hands and visually inspected it.

Photographs in sales brochures and auction catalogs are so clear and sharp, as well as having brilliant color contrast, that they may have more eye appeal than the actual painting itself. I have been at auctions and watched phone bidders drive the price of a dull, lifeless painting beyond anything reasonable. I also noted that the appearance of the painting in the auction catalog was much more attractive than viewing it in person. I am very certain the "successful" bidder was very disappointed when they actually held their purchase.

I emphasize that you should never bid on a painting until you have personally examined it. Even appointed factors and designated bidders used by some collectors should be carefully selected and specifically instructed before they act in your behalf. My advice — make your own acquisitions. Having someone bid for you at auction only makes sense if they can position themselves on the "right" side of the bid and you cannot.

To repeat a previous concept, if your maximum intended investment for a painting is $50,000 and the bidding is in $5,000 increments, you will want to be holding the $40,000 and not the $45,000. Also, do not forget that at $55,000 you have spent $60,000 (10% for fees and premium) prior to shipping and insurance. You really do not need someone to do the math for you, but do it before the auction; it is your roadmap. Buyer's premium, tax, and shipping are realities.

Although I have no scientific data, I believe that dealers are increasingly executing bids on behalf of their collectors. Thus, you can no longer feel comfortable with the fact that a painting is selling to the dealer at auction for a "wholesale" price. Do not assume that the dealer is acquiring the painting for inventory, and, therefore, must purchase the painting for a price so that the work can later be sold in their gallery for a profit. Instead the dealer may be acquiring the work for a col-

lector, investors, or speculators who have instructed them to purchase the painting almost irrespective of the bidding price. In the 1990s there appears to be less speculation in the art world than in the 1980s, but it is still significant and affects auction prices.

So-called "blockbuster" paintings with great visual appeal, well established provenance, and uncomplicated subject matter will usually sell for premium prices at auction (they win the beauty contest). For example, painterly landscapes containing human figures composed in light, bright pigments will generally fetch high prices and attract many interested bidders at auctions. Dealers also believe that they can pass on to their buyers any increased costs at auction associated with the acquisition of this type of painting. As a private collector, you might adopt the same attitude, but most of us would like to think we were receiving at least "present value" for our financial commitment at the time of purchase.

There are those who reason that certain types of paintings remain undervalued because their equivalents from other countries bring much higher prices. These observers compare the prices achieved at auction by the French versus American impressionism. They reason or opine that great examples of the impressionist aesthetic by American artists will eventually sell for millions and representative works by these master American impressionists will someday routinely bring hundreds of thousands of dollars just as the French do presently.

Although I do not believe American impressionism to be a totally derivative art form, I do not feel this painting style executed by Americans will ever reach the financial numbers achieved by Monet, Van Gogh, and their contemporaries. The value of paintings by American impressionists should increase with time but may very well not exceed that of growth stocks, money instruments, real estate, or commodities, and should also be considered illiquid investments which I will discuss again later. Collect paintings for aesthetic pleasure and leave the profit motive for other activities. Can you realize a large profit with art? You can but I only suggest to you that it not be your major consideration or a means to an end of your collecting. There are other and superior benefits.

The multiple considerations of auction prices for paintings may not provide you a clear strategy for any particular course of action. However, you should decide within yourself the value of any particular work to you. You should then offer this at auction in whatever manner you feel most comfortable with.

Depending upon your assessment of your own self-discipline, you may wish to avoid the open competition and "hype" associated with the live auction itself. You have the alternatives I have discussed and another important one.

Absentee bidding in writing or through a factor may obviate the perils of auction mania. Avoid the mistakes you could make by having a plan. Never depend upon intuition in this instance — you are engaged in a serious activity and it involves money, not pride and honor.

Another little-known method of acquisition which offers interesting possibilities — that is to very selectively purchase "buy-ins" or "passed" works. Conventional wisdom fosters the idea that unsold paintings are not good ones and are thus not suitable for collectors to acquire. These works are dismissed due to condition problems, that they represent poor examples of the artist's work, are "too dark," "too stiff," or of questionable authenticity. Each of these circumstances represents valid reasons for the "did not sell." If these reasons obtain, then you should not attempt a post-sale purchase of these paintings. If, however, a painting did not sell because the pre-sale estimate was unrealistic, the reserve was too high, the painting was too large for most collectors, or the subject matter does not have general appeal, then the painting may still be appropriate for you.

High estimates in the pre-sale catalog sometimes discourage potential bidders to the point they simply do not enter the process. High reserves (usually about 80% of the low estimates) may create the illusion that a painting has sold at the auction when it, indeed, has not met the reserve. Large paintings even of museum quality may not be practical from a space consideration for most collectors or dealers, but you may have a specific collection or space in which they will fit nicely.

Whether a particular subject is appealing to you or fits your collection is a personal consideration. For example, some of us have a penchant for nocturnes which seem to have limited appeal to the general collecting public, J.A.M. Whistler nothwithstanding. Because of this contrarian logic, I have been able to purchase at auction outstanding noctures by recognized artists such as Robert Henri, Edward W. Redfield, Leon Dabo, and George Elmer Brown for very reasonable sums. These form my nocture and tonalism collection that has been the subject of a traveling exhibition and monograph and give me a wonderful feeling of affirmation.

Most collectors are either unaware of the post-auction process or do not understand it. They also may feel a bit intimidated by dealing "one-on-one" with the auction gallery staff and through them with the consignor of the painting. Another deterrent is the incorrect assumption that the price they should offer is the highest bid that was achieved on the auction floor. Actually the only relevance the auction bid has to the post-sale transactions is that it may influence the expectations of the consignor. If this figure achieved at auction is far below the reserve, the consignor may become much more flexible and accept a lower post-sale offer from you.

Sometimes a consignor will indicate to the auction house how eager they are to sell a painting. Museums, as previously noted, are often anxious to complete a deaccession because of the difficulty they encounter receiving approval from their museum board or deaccession committee before the sale to even offer the work to the public. Also, their cost basis is often low as the painting may well have been a donation to them. They often deaccess paintings because of legitimate space and exhibition theme considerations and the consigned paintings are the result. For museums, taking a painting back is a complex procedure and one they go to great lengths to avoid.

Private consignors such as collectors vary greatly in their reasons for deaccession of paintings so you are best guided by the consignor's understanding with the auction gallery staff. This is much more rewarding than attempting to deduce by Jungian logic the consignor's mindset. The auction house wishes to make a sale, usually knows what the painting is actually worth, and wants to have a satisfactory transaction from the perspective of both parties. They are in reality advocates for both sides but legally represent the consignor at this point.

Private galleries generally consign two types of paintings: those they cannot sell for various reasons, and "blockbuster" paintings they believe will fetch "super retail" prices due to the open competition at auction. The latter is a fairly recent and sometimes transient phenomenon, but the dealer's expectations for those paintings will usually mean that you will have little chance to acquire them after the sale. The dealer will let them "bid in" to await another day or offer them again in their gallery.

The fact that a dealer cannot sell a painting does not always condemn the work. Most dealers have a specific clientele and may specialize in a particular period, subject matter, group of artists, or those from a specific region. But the piece they consign may represent none of these criteria, so they arrange for a quick deaccession at auction. Again, what you wish to avoid is a "shopped" painting; one that has been around the trade and is "tainted" by this history. An analogy from real estate is a house that has been on the market repeatedly or has had a "for sale" sign in front for an unreasonable length of time.

Acquiring paintings after the sale may represent an opportunity for you. The same criteria of quality should be employed as with any other method of acquisition. You can expect the auction gallery staff to be helpful and discreet. After all, they are probably dealing with a disappointed consignor and a circumstance in which the process has not been successful. Often your price of acquisition can be reasonable as the "high but unsuccessful bidder" during the auction is no longer a part of the process. Thus, you should offer initially what you feel personally comfortable with in acquiring the work. If this is not accepted by the consignor, you can always increase the offer or discontinue the negotiation. A counteroffer may often reveal the true expectations of the consignor. If the staff of the auction house feels your offer represents fair market value, they may indicate this to the consignor. Auction houses make great efforts to avoid having paintings repeatedly offered by them or by rival auction houses, as they become "trade pieces" that have been declared by this process "used goods." Avoid these paintings because among other things, they are often quite problematic for exhibitions, illustrations in publications, or later deaccessions.

In a rather fast-paced world, many collectors allot limited time to consider their acquisitions. The preview of auctions may be hurried or cursory, the gallery staff available for only a short period of time, and the number of paintings under consideration almost overwhelming. Thus, a post-sale transaction may well represent a more studied and careful form of acquisition. This method of purchasing art is a little appreciated one but in the context presented, quite viable.

Auctions are a reasonable forum for you to acquire paintings if you follow at least some of the suggestions in this chapter. The auction floor is also interesting if you enjoy "people watching" and like to observe dynamic, human behavior. On the other hand you just might be rewarded with a bargain for your independent scholarship and if you follow the guidelines discussed, you probably will avoid paying too much or acquiring a painting you will never enjoy. This is as close to the "free marketplace" as you may get in the art world. Prior preparation and discipline are the characters of your successful performance and subsequent pleasure and satisfaction.

A Tradition — The Picker

If you wish to acquire paintings and at the same time participate in a true adventure, use the venerable picker as your source of paintings. Pickers come in all varieties, from those who have a doctorate in art history or a BMFA from some celebrated university to an individual with a superb eye and decades of experience who never spent much time in class but whose OJT makes them a portable art library. There is also the picker who describes everything as a "picture" leaving you to discern whether you are viewing a print, pastel, watercolor… or none of the above.

Pickers are essential elements in the painting supply chain. They are a major source of paintings for dealers. Most dealers rather than specifically admit they acquired the work from a picker, will employ a euphemism that the work was "acquired privately." The picker will often tell you "it came out of a house." Of course, if it was not purchase from Winslow Homer's easel in some sunlit field near Prouts' Neck, then it probably did come from a house.

Provenance is a standard part of the assessment of a painting's value just as are the identification of the artist and determination of condition. Pickers characteristically avoid provenance or indicate that they have insufficient time to uncover or document the provenance. In most instances this is true and reflects their style of doing business. Just as a dealer would when obtaining a painting from a picker, you may have to acquire the provenance after the sale by independent research. We did this recently with a Childe Hassam watercolor, painted in Havana in 1895, sold in St. Louis in 1897, and matted and framed in New York.

But who are these pickers and from where do they come? Pickers seem to possess the common trait in that they are independent operatives who avoid fixed schedules and revel in the chase. They do not usually employ the technology to uncover signatures. With most pickers, the action is the message. Pickers thrive upon the activity and most enjoy a rapid turnover. Buy, turnover, buy again; a process in which the driving force is the acquisition characterizes the style of many pickers.

The accessibility of the picker to the collector is often tenuous and problematic. Remember the primary client of the picker is the dealer because they are predictably in one place and by their nature represent the potential for repeat and ongoing business. Most pickers have some type of informal relationship with a number of dealers to present paintings to them on a fairly regular basis. These dealers represent a fairly predictable income stream for the picker and methodology of painting flow and distribution that should be respected by the collector. However, many paintings acquired by the picker may not fit the usual inventory of any particular dealer or the asking price of the picker may not leave enough margin for the dealer to realize enough profit to meet their overhead expenses. Many, if not all, dealers avoid unsigned paintings. As a collector you may wish to position yourself as an alternative client for the picker in this situation.

One should have very realistic expectations when acquiring paintings from what might fairly be described as a nontraditional source. First, there will be little warranty as to the authenticity, provenance, and condition of the painting. The transaction might occur in any number of locales from the back of a van, to a motel room near an antique fair, a booth in a mall, or in the confines of the collector's home.

One efficient location of exchange is near an antique show or antique fair. Often the picker will pay the "early shoppers" fee on "set up" day because this is the most common time for exchange of goods among dealers and between the dealers and the most avid collectors who have paid the early fee. A collector, in dealing with pickers, should establish some predictable time and place of interaction. If the collector is realistic they will have already accepted and factored in the lack of safeguards of the transaction. Their major challenge

will be to have the picker believe they are an ongoing source to dispose of their acquisitions. Providing the picker a ready method of communicating is a first step. Acquiring several paintings at most offerings is another. Giving the picker the particulars regarding time period, genre, and even size of paintings they should present to you is helpful as is providing them with an artist list. After a period of time your picker may even tell you they acquired a painting because they knew they could sell it to you.

Pickers are not collectors or art scholars, they acquire paintings to sell and depend upon their skills to acquire ones that will sell more quickly. They usually have limited capacity for storage of works in a protective and secure environment. Thus, if they present you with a painting about which you are not certain of its suitability for you, understand this may be your only opportunity. Realize there will be other chances to acquire similar works. I have purchased the same painting offered first to me by a picker subsequently from a dealer or at auction — for a substantially higher price but with certain additional guarantees as well.

Pickers do, indeed, represent a spectrum of styles and challenges. One of my pickers is a conservator (restorer), another a certified appraiser, and one of the more interesting sells from racks in his house and makes "house calls." Some have no phone and no fax while others carry a beeper or can be reached on the Internet. They have discovered eBay or Yahoo or Amazon.com, but most ride around in used vehicles much like the itinerant medicine man or circuit preacher of days of yore.

Part of the excitement of dealing with them is the variety of personal interactions and the opportunity to acquire a painting at a favorable price. If you have some expertise in judging authenticity and condition and are reasonably current regarding values, this is an interesting alternative mode to acquire works for your collection. Understand that your exposure is great and your best safeguard is knowledge.

Works on Paper

Considerations of collecting works on paper are the same as any other combination of medium and support except that these paintings may be considerably less expensive than oils.

When you collect visual images of any medium placed on the support the principle criterion for acquisition should be painting quality. If you cannot afford a good example of any genre or artist, do not buy it. If a painting seems like a bargain, be careful.

There are alternatives to the usual expenditure required for collecting major paintings by certain acclaimed artists. One can achieve this by acquiring major examples by the students of the most famous artists, and paintings which are characteristic examples of the famous artists that can be refurbished or restored.

I would also recommend that works on paper be considered as a collecting strategy, especially if the goal is to have technically as well as aesthetically good examples of acclaimed artists.

Conventional wisdom has been that works on paper are less than the substantial effort required to create an image in oil. Some collectors mistakenly believe that works on paper represent studies in prepa-

Botanical Study, *Anna Heyward Taylor,* 20" x 16", *watercolor.*

Birmingham, *Arthur Beaumont, 1924, 12½" x 16", watercolor. James Southern collection.*

ration for more important oil on canvas versions of the same image.

The common statement by collectors "all I have is only a watercolor pastel, pen, and pencil drawing" by a named accomplished artist is a telling comment and reflects an unjustified bias.

Watercolors by Winslow Homer, John Singer Sargent, or Maurice Pendergast are works of monumental value. Certain artists who have since become almost unaffordable and are rare may be still available as works on paper and at prices many collectors will be able to manage.

This may no longer be the case for all. One can understand the auction house and private dealer comment "good paintings are very expensive; lesser examples are difficult to sell." In effect, this says that you can get a "bargain" in an undesirable painting, but the validity of this statement depends upon one's definition of a bargain.

If the image of the painting does not represent the qualities that made that artist desirable, then the example before you is not a bargain at any cost of acquisition because it violates the first principle — the absolute insistence upon quality.

In recent years the canons of prudent collecting have been relaxed, and I think correctly so. I can recall when the pastels of most artists sold for only a small fraction of their oils, even of the same subject. They were simply

Female Profile, *Clara Weaver Parrish, 26" x 23", watercolor.*

Tobacco Warehouse, *Aaron Bohrod, 16" x 12", pen and ink.*

considered such lesser examples of his efforts that few collectors (hence dealers) manifested little interest in them. By conventional wisdom, a pastel on paper was not believed to be as desirable as an oil.

Edmund Tarbell did a number of pastels, and would it not be logical to collect the works of pastelists Glen Cooper Henshaw or Mary Cassatt and not have some inkling that Tarbell's pastels might also demonstrate his draftsmanship and painterly qualities that made him an acknowledged leader of the Boston Museum of Fine Arts School?

Frank Weston Benson it was said by several well-known dealers and scholars, several years ago, to have almost never composed pastel works. This statement reflects the fact that they had either not seen one, dismissed the examples shown to them out of hand as forgeries, or simply failed to reason that Benson may have completed or sold only a few pastels.

A cache of "rare" Benson pastels has been subsequently uncovered. It was conceded that he indeed did pastels and that they are desirable, especially for someone entering the "pricey" market of the Boston Museum of Fine Arts School.

Henri at Macbeth's, *Christopher Murphy, Jr., 14" x 12", charcoal. Murphy was from Savannah, Georgia, and studied under Henri at the Art Students League in New York. James collection.*

Young Female, *Muriel Morrison, 29" x 23", watercolor.*

The watercolor, to many collectors, is considered not to be a serious undertaking because it cannot be extensively reworked and refined, as can an oil painting. The corollary to this, in the minds of many, is that the artist attempts to make the effort simple in order to minimize the chances of an untoward result — the "do little" plan of painting.

However, painterly qualities are demonstrated quite effectively with watercolors, and mixed media or gouache will allow not only the juxtaposition of color contrasts but the embodiment of texture as well.

If the watercolors of a Maurice Pendergast demonstrate his talent, why cannot those of other less expensive or less well-known artists? I personally would rather own a William Merritt Chase watercolor landscape than his oils depicting carp.

Paintings executed on location with pen and ink, watercolor, or pencil on paper are often more effective and more spontaneous than a reconstruction of the image by the artist in oil (or whatever medium) at some later date.

The Civil War was documented by wonderful visual images on paper, and those are highly collectible — a fact well accepted between scholars, collectors, and dealers. The recognized value of documentary works on paper is now translated to a more generic appreciation of these images.

The Lament, *Thomas Anshutz, 10½" x 6¾", pencil drawing on paper. A leading teacher at the Pennsylvania Academy of Fine Arts. Farmer/James collection.*

Shacks Outside Charleston, *Elizabeth O'Neill Verner, 20" x 24", pastel, exhibited at Knoxville Art Museum (1992), University Club (1993), Cosmos Club (1994), and Chapel Hill Art Museum (1998).*

I should interject a caveat related to conservation and restoration. Just as pastels and watercolors are difficult to rework, one is constrained by what can be done in restoration with a work on paper that is in poor condition or has been damaged. You may be very cautious in your acquisition if you have reservations about the condition of the work on paper you are considering.

Conservation or restoration of these works will require an individual specifically trained for this purpose; known as a "paper conservator."

Some conservators will refuse to accept works on paper, and prior to acquisition you should seek an opinion if there is any doubt regarding condition of the work on paper and the projected cost of restoration.

You should acquaint yourself with the basic environmental insults that can affect works on paper. You should know the multiple varieties of mold that find this such a wonderful culture media. You should know what "foxing" is.

Conservation of works on paper is a very specialized circumstance and it will be quite productive for you to become aware of the basics. I have been very pleased with the results of removing acid stains or a bit of brown discoloration on a modest purchase that became a major work but have been disappointed when

Snowy Egrets & Spanish Moss, *Athos Menaboni (1895 – 1990), 24" x 18", oil on gessoed paper, signed lower right. Courtesy of Knoke Galleries of Atlanta.*

House Near Newbury-port, Massachusetts, *H.C. Ahl, watercolor and stencil.*

we were unable to remove foxing and still preserve the color of the image.

As a collector, works on paper should be regarded not as a compromise but as an alternative — one that I believe has the potential for significant rewards.

Fancy Lady, *Mabel Pugh, 12" x 19", pen and charcoal. Pugh was a highly acclaimed artist from Raleigh, North Carolina. Farmer/James Southern collection.*

The Banjo Player, *Rufus Zogbaum, 12" x 10", pencil drawing, private collection.*

Abstract, *Will Henry Stevens (1881 – 1949), 19½" x 15¼", pastel on paper, signed lower right, dated 1946. Courtesy of Knoke Galleries of Atlanta.*

Drawing, Civil War, watercolor, Center for Study of the American South, University of North Carolina at Chapel Hill.

Still Life Flowers, *Helen Turner, 26¼" x 14", pastel, mixed media.*

The Locomotive General at Big Shanty, 1862, *Wilbur Kurtz (1882 – 1967), 16" x 27", gouache & watercolor on artist board, signed lower left and dated 1966. Courtesy of Knoke Galleries of Atlanta.*

Lillies, *Mayna Avent, still life.*

Mississippi Mansion,
Arthur Carles, 20" x 16",
watercolor.

Civil War drawing,
Center for Study of the
American South,
University of North
Carolina at Chapel Hill.

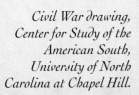

It's in the Frame

Paintings are commonly viewed as merely the representation of pigment distribution on the image layer placed on the support (canvas, board, panel…). For descriptive purposes we usually characterize paintings as portraits, landscapes, or even "cow paintings." However, we should be mindful of the entirety of the composition and include the frame as an inherent part of the whole. Frames can be an art form by themselves and one that has not been appreciated by either acquirers or sellers.

Eli Wilner, the authority who has done much to help American collectors appreciate frames, expressed, "I see a frame as a sculpture, a handcrafted object that can exist on its own artistic merits. It is not a process of subordinating the frame to the painting. The correct frame on a painting creates a harmony and resonance." In the marketplace there is a direct correlation between the value of a painting and the frame in which it is contained. Frames now have a market of their own. A 1915 handcrafted frame by Charles Prendergast sold for $75,000 and the Eli Wilner Company offers many valued above $25,000.

In recent years there have been several exhibitions of important frames and an excellent small text on the subject (*Antique American Frames*, Eli Wilner, Avon Books, New York). These important efforts, however, have only marginally raised the awareness of the intrinsic value of the frame in the mind of the average collector. While we are aware of the aesthetic improvement provided by a complementary frame, we usually do not properly regard its implications for the value and quality of the painting as a whole.

Among the most attractive features of Old Master paintings are the truly extraordinary frames that are a part of the compositions. They are often intricate works of craftsmanship rivaling the pictorial content of the painting and some represent architectural refinements in their own right (Figure 1).

Figure 1: *Sixteenth century Italian tabernacle frame, carved, polychromed, sgrafitto, and gilded. Courtesy Eli Wilner & Company.*

Many times the painter and framemaker of eighteenth and early nineteenth century paintings were one; but in almost all instances, the design and construction were for that particular work. In fact, the frame may have been completed before the painting.

Now Dr. Rebora Barratt of the Metropolitan Museum of Art offers the opinion that "the collaboration between craftsmen, artists, and collectors resulted in American frame designs that parallel the shifts in painting styles as well as changes in architecture and interior design." A vivid example is the arts and crafts frames (Figure 2) with emphasis upon simplicity in design and craftsmanship. (These frames can still be acquired with some degree of regularity.)

Certain artists of the nineteenth century were as famous for their frame design as for their ability to create paintings. Hermann Dudley Murphy and Charles Prendergast are examples. Thus, if you have a documented Murphy frame, the painting contained therein becomes signifi-

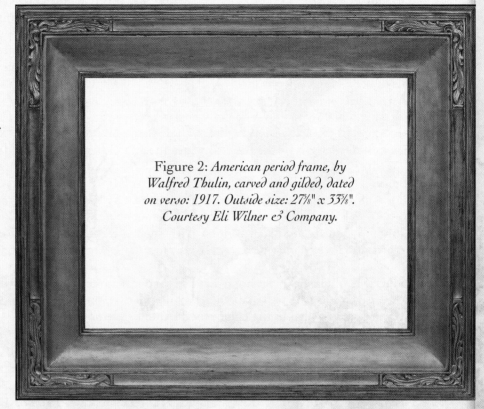

Figure 2: *American period frame, by Walfred Thulin, carved and gilded, dated on verso: 1917. Outside size: 27⅞" x 33⅞". Courtesy Eli Wilner & Company.*

cantly more valuable because of the frame. I have sometimes purchased an undistinguished work, at a modest price, to acquire an important and valuable frame. Only a few years ago you might acquire at auction an excellent antique frame for hundreds or only several thousands of dollars. This is no longer true, but period frames still remain undervalued.

I remember acquiring at auction an unimportant New England landscape by an undistinguished painter and standing in line after the sale waiting to retrieve my purchase. The director of the auction house said to me, "You must know something about that piece we do not." I did not justify my purchase but removed the nails anchoring the painting. I then handed the painting to the attendant and walked away with only the frame replying "I do." That gesture probably kept me from acquiring my next frame purchase from that auction house inexpensively, but made a point.

Several companies in the nineteenth century had a successful business making custom frames for artists, museums, galleries, and

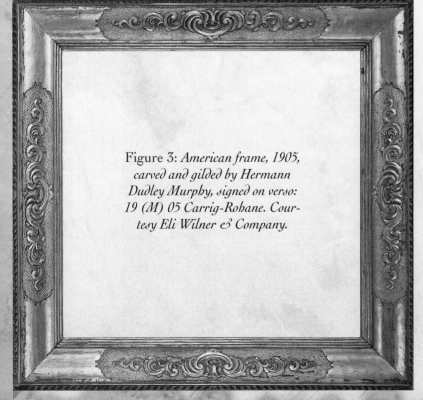

Figure 3: *American frame, 1905, carved and gilded by Hermann Dudley Murphy, signed on verso: 19 (M) 05 Carrig-Rohane. Courtesy Eli Wilner & Company.*

even important collectors. Boston was the center of early frame making at the turn of the century (Figure 3). Murphy formed Carrig-Rohane and had Charles Prendergast as his associate. On Boylston Street, he went into business with Walfred Thulin. Murphy later sold his business to Vose Galleries in 1917.

New York's best-known frame company was Newcomb-Macklin which also had an office in Chicago and supplied many well-known western artists. They also made frames of the designs of the legendary architect, Stanford White, after his death in 1906. In Bucks County, Pennsylvania, Frederick Harer frames were made famous by being seen on the paintings of the New Hope School. In California, Arthur and Lucia Matthews made a substantive contribution with their unique method of flat-relief carving and designs shaped by the influence of J.A.M. Whistler.

Reproductions of classic styles are available from a number of contemporary frame companies. While not inexpensive, the value added to the composite of frame and painting will usually justify the commitment. The traditional frame moulds and patterns if patented have been acquired by contemporary firms and are available. If your dealer's frame their inventory with these frames, you will pay cost plus a markup when you acquire the painting. It is often worth it provided you did not have an original frame you could or should have restored.

Occasionally, someone will describe a "Hassam" or a "Stanford White" or "Whistler" frame to provide specific identity to a particular pattern, but Stanford White was better known as an architect and J.A.M. Whistler and Childe Hassam as artists. However, each made a significant contribution to the design of frames.

More generic terms for frames may reflect a more generic contemporary architectural fashion of the time such as an "arts and crafts" frame. In the American Renaissance period of the 1870s and 1880s frames evolved to become more linear and subdued. One style leading the way was the so-called "Eastlake frame" named for the influential English tastemaker who wanted his frames only to confine the view of the spectator to the frame's physical limits. These frames are available (Figure 4) and often at modest prices, especially when compared with 1870s composition frames.

Figure 4: *Eastlake style, circa 1970s, painted faux finish, incised corner decoration and gilded inner liner. Outside size: 12" x 14". Courtesy Eli Wilner & Company.*

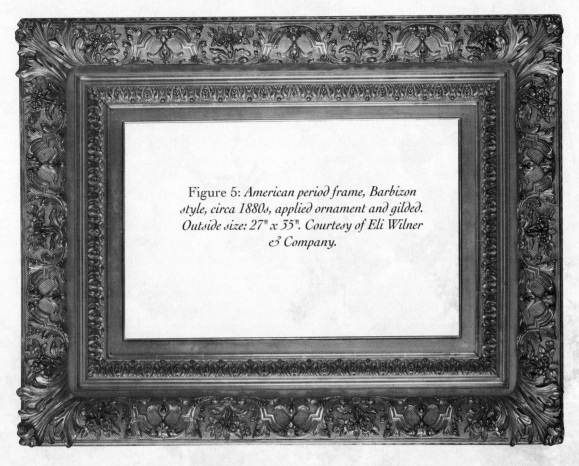

Figure 5: *American period frame, Barbizon style, circa 1880s, applied ornament and gilded. Outside size: 27" x 35". Courtesy of Eli Wilner & Company.*

In the 1890s, Stanford White was probably the most influential frame designer in America. This was an obvious adjunct to his role as an internationally acclaimed architect. During this period until the turn of the century with the emergence of American wealth, the great collections were being acquired by persons of the mould of Thomas Lang Freer, William T. Evans, George A. Hearn, Mellon, Carnegie, and others. Barbizon painters like William Morris Hunt returned to America and popularized the Barbizon style frames which they placed on their paintings (Figure 5). With international travel, Islamic, Moorish, and Oriental motifs were also introduced producing an even greater variety of choices.

Giving a proper name to a frame achieves at least one significant end — it increases the importance of the frame as an element of the composition and the value will be increased commensurably. If a frame happens to be signed and dated, it may be worth thousands of dollars. In collecting frames, I would offer a caveat. Should you become too enthralled with the acquisition of important frames, measure them before your acquisition. Your painting should properly fit the frame or

your stretcher should be easily modified to do so and not compromise the image of the painting. There are standard sized stretchers (12 x 16, 16 x 20, 20 x 24, 24 x 30, 25 x 30, 30 x 36…) and you will eventually find a painting for a frame of these dimensions. If the size of the frame is not standard, you might reduce its dimensions by a bit of cosmetic surgery. Certain frames because of their corner design, or from other structural reasons, cannot be cut down. Most lovers of frames have a collection stored in the attic, basement, or under the bed as a testament to either their resolve or bad judgment, depending upon your bias.

I have been quite impressed with what can be achieved in the repair and restoration of frames in this regard. Just a simple waxing can restore the luster of a frame. Do not regilt (regild) a frame until you have considered whether or not the original gilt may be intact under a dull layer of varnish or, heaven forbid, "radiator" paint. Reapplying gilt, however, is not so expensive as most collectors believe but something to be done by an expert. Is there gild underneath the gold paint and grime? You might just moisten your handkerchief with a bit of saliva and rub a small area. You will see the gild if it's there; and if the gold comes off, it is probably acrylic gold paint. Acetone will remove varnish, but it can also remove your purse or pants lining.

Molded corners can be reproduced using the intact corners of the frames as a template. This often can make a somewhat damaged corner appear intact. If you enjoy "healing," the satisfaction can be enormous. Simple toning of the color of a frame will often improve its contribution to the aesthetics of the composition. Even the cleaning and waxing of a frame may dramatically improve its appearance and its contribution to the whole visual image.

Sometimes dealers, in an effort to give a fresh or what they believe is a more impressive appearance to a painting, will discard the original frame and add one that appears brighter, and they believe more enhancing. Often a liner will be added as well. Despite all good intentions and even if this exercise results in an improved image, I personally lament the lost opportunity to have brought the entire work back to its original state (appearance) as a composite. Another reason to keep the original frame and stretcher is that the exhibition labels are often attached there. Even more interesting might be a note by the artist in their own hand.

Antique frames are not for everyone and obviating this sequence of described events to replace the old is probably common. Recently I donated a painting to an institution which had a wonderful arts and crafts frame on it. Several weeks later the curator called me to ask if they could reframe the work with a more "important" frame which I agreed to and inquired what they intended to do with the period frame which they indicated was of no interest to them. I retrieved a 25 x 30 "derelict" in excellent condition worth about $1,500 – 2,500 which they had replaced with a $600 – 800 reproduction. They were pleased, I was pleased, and their framer was very pleased.

The legacy of the American framemaker is a testament to our native craftsmanship and I believe that appropriate homage should be given to this art form. Thus, when you next consider an acquisition, factor in the contribution or potential contribution of the frame, it may be the package in which the artist's "gift" to you is wrapped.

Frames are part of the composite. Examine the frames in museums, learn the classic period designs, and factor this as part of your successful acquisition.

Ornate, inexpensive Victorian frame.

*Barbizon frame, 1880 –
1900. James collection.*

*Mid-nineteenth century ornate
portrait frame, Rococco style.
In good condition these
frames are quite valuable.
They can also be repaired.
James collection.*

Stanford White (Whistler) frame, Mammy & Child, Wayman Adams (circa 1900).

Barbizon frame (1880 – 1900). James collection.

Arts and Crafts frame.

Simple period frame, cira 1890 – 1910.

Condition of Oil Paintings

The collection of paintings is a very pleasurable activity and the enjoyment is significantly enhanced by the later realization that your choices affirm your good judgment at the time of acquisition.

One of the great disappointments for a collector is to subsequently realize the painting they have acquired is not in the condition they judged it to be at the time of purchase.

Oil paintings should be thought of as a series of layers moving in directions analogous to the earth tectonic plates. After application by the artist, these layers of the painting will individually expand and contract in the particular material's response to drying or added moisture from the environment; thus causing a shearing force to develop between the layers. This phenomenon will be visually manifest as a general "weblike" pattern of thin lines in the pigment layer. This appearance is often termed as "crackle" or "crackleur."

Since this is part of the natural aging process, if the lines in the pigment layer are very thin and are closely opposed, it will not significantly devalue the painting. The process can also be stabilized. If the opposing edges of pigment become raised or the separation of the individual pigment areas is large enough to allow the fibers of the canvas or those of a mounted support to be seen, then the problem is a significant one. The treatment of this painting may require inpainting and, if extensive, this repair compromises the authenticity of the work.

In this circumstance, valuation of the painting as well as its appearance becomes an issue. Is a 60% John Singer Sargent truly a Sargent? What is the value of an A.P. Ryder with 40% inpainting?

Visual inspection will usually give you an idea of the severity and extent of the "crackleur" but a so-called raking light inspection will provide a more accu-

Cracking (crackleur) — usually due to failure to control temperature and humidity in the environment of the painting.

rate evaluation of this process. As the light hits the surface of the pigment layer from an angle, due to the obliquity of source, any elevation from the flat surface of the painting will be delineated. You can stimulate a raking light examination by using a hand-held penlight or a small flashlight in a partially darkened room. Certainly this method will detect gross elevation of the edges of the opposed pigment.

If there is "cupping" or curling at the edges of the separation, then the pigment layer will need to be stabilized and re-affixed to the support or it may totally separate resulting in an area of the painting devoid of pigment.

With oil on canvas paintings a "reline" is often the treatment of choice. If the painting has already been relined, you should determine whether it was wax relined, a second canvas was glued on to the obverse of the original, or whether the canvas support was fixed with a press or vacuum machine. Glue relines, while simple to perform, are difficult to reverse or take down. Removal of the reline can further damage the original canvas and in so doing, the pigment layer containing the image. The glue can be very adherent and when it is separated it may physically pull or damage the pigment layer.

A wax reline is an attempt to stabilize the pigment layer from its undersurface without providing

Stabilization and refixation of the pigment layer during the restoration process.

Oil placed behind glass and then in sunlight. Effects of heating — paint separation and loss.

the challenge of an additional structure that might later require removal. Sometimes the canvas support is stabilized by mounting it on a more rigid surface. In the past 50 years there have been a number of "fashions" in this procedure with the use of such varied rigid supports as masonite, aluminum, fiber-board, tongue in groove wood panels, and other compositions.

If a painting is mounted on a rigid surface, it will in general become more difficult to later rework or restore. An oil on canvas has the greatest potential for restoration. With this combination you can elect to repair the limited area that has been damaged or you can patch a simple puncture. You can also take down a restoration if you do not achieve the desired result with your first attempt. If you are considering acquiring a painting that has already been mounted on a rigid structure, then be conservative in your

Small areas of painting loss. Necessary to stabilize and then inpaint. Post collection.

Replacing chips of paint that have become separated from the canvas. Courtesy of Turkey Strummel.

expectations for any future planned restoration or refurbishment and cautious in your initial acquisition cost. Your conservator will probably be more reluctant to assure you of a favorable outcome for the effort expended if you acquire a painting that has been mounted or even significantly restored. Your ultraviolet (UV) or "black light" inspection will assist in this later assessment. Areas of added pigment will fluoresce when exposed to the proper UV wavelength. A word of caution; some very dark pigments will also appear to fluoresce, giving you a false positive. Thus compare the visual appearance of the pigment distribution with the findings of the black light examination.

Paintings in addition to atmospheric challenge can suffer direct trauma especially when they are being moved or stored. You may see this as punctures or rips in the image layer or the support. These are dramatic in their appearance but can represent an acquisition opportunity for you as a collector.

If the canvas fibers can be opposed by simply placing the torn area together, then you might have only to place a localized patch in that area on the under-sur-face of

the canvas. If the fibers have been stretched and there is a great deal of pigment loss, both a reline and inpainting may be required.

Most collectors see the stark appearance of the injury and fail to recognize that the cure may be local as the rest of the painting may be completely intact. In fact, a localized puncture, while dramatic, is much easier to repair than significant overall crackling and much easier to treat than generalized paint loss. The inpainting may be so localized that you will have over 95% of the pigment having been applied by the original artist.

If a painting is in severely damaged condition or the support has been significantly compromised, then the decision not to acquire that example of the artist's work should not be particularly difficult if the major criteria is condition.

However, if the condition is such that a restoration can still be car-ri-ed out,

Female portrait following repair.

Scrape near left shoulder of sitter due to incorrect storage.

Girl in Blue Dress, Ruth Ogden Lanier, 24" x 20".
Note "blooming" of varnish in upper part of painting.

then one must render a judgment as to whether it is a reasonable purchase from its artistic importance, the value of the artist's works, the desirability of subject matter, and the subsequent time and expense of undertaking a restoration.

The quantification estimate in this circumstance depends upon your or your advisor's knowing what is possible and the anticipated expense. For example, if a canvas has rested in water for a time, the lower part of the painting may be devoid of pigment and more than likely the signature has been lost. Unless the work is by a major artist, which can be documented, and you can acquire it for a sum much less than its potential value — pass on the so-called opportunity. If it depicts an important event or demonstrates a genre particularly well, then you might wish to expend the energy and cost required.

Pickers and dealers who have high turnover will not take the time to evaluate "problematic" paintings and will often sell them to you at a very favorable price. We once acquired a painting of a young girl with a partial signature that was very well painted. The picker told us about acquiring it from a private party along with three to four major paintings in the collection and since this was "unsigned" he paid very little for the work. He had never properly examined at the signature because he felt it was not likely to be important. He had not used a black light or even tried evaluating the signature with a penlight. His reasoning was that he had already acquired a substantial profit from the sale of other items in the transaction and that this painting was essentially "a freebie."

We were intrigued with the fact the painting obviously needed cleaning and there was evidence of at least a partial signature that merited further investigation and acquired it to see if we could determine who could have rendered that technically competent work. Under magnification a "Geo…W. Bello" signature with several missing letters could be seen. After cleaning, the painting was even more appealing than before and the signature sufficiently recognizable as to strongly attribute the work to George Wesley Bellows.

Although Bellows's prizefight scenes and some of his coastal landscapes have sold in the millions, his "Henri like" works of young females represent major acquisitions for most collectors and this did for us.

Sometimes you may be presented with a canvas that is not even on a stretcher and is so fragile that your restorer will either have to mount it on another canvas or a rigid support before they can even clean it or begin whatever inpainting that may be required. Most of the time you will have to make a personal decision how important this specific painting is to you.

While working on a text with the widow of Eugene Healon Thomason about his life in New York with "The Eight" and Ashcan School, I discovered in her storage area a large canvas of a woman in a kimono. Thomason's widow related a very interesting story about the painting. It seems the sitter was a "friend" of both George Luks and Thomason, and the painting was a joint venture as well. It had originally been a nude but at Lib

The conservator insisted he could minimize the inpainting if he could mount the canvas on a rigid structure, which he did. While "the Kimono" is approximately 15% inpainted, it has been in three exhibitions and is now a loan in a major public space. The condition of the work is not ideal, but the painting is stable and its story remains a wonderful one.

I cannot present criteria that will be so quantifiable and specific that they will identify the exact state of health of every painting and implications for restoration. However, these general guidelines added to your own judgment and experience should help to prevent you from making unfortunate choices. The importance, rarity, and appeal of any particular painting will certainly be factors as well as the physical integrity of the work in your decision regarding restoration.

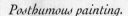

Posthumous painting.

Thomason's insistence the female form had been covered with a kimono by her husband over a decade after he and Luks painted the original version.

Lib wanted me to have the painting restored, but I was concerned that before stabilizing the image layer, most of the pigment might be separated from the canvas. I was intrigued by the story and bought the painting from her so if the restoration was unsatisfactory it would only be a matter between the conservator and myself.

Obverse of posthumous remembrance painting.
Due to improper canvas restoration the image is
clearly seen on "back" of painting.

Determining Condition

Radiographic Techniques

Growing public appreciation of the visual arts has led to recent community efforts to develop new museums and to reevaluate works of art in collections that already exist.[1] With the introduction of certain new radiographic methods, especially computer-assisted techniques, radiography may be of greater value in evaluating the qualities of paintings than previously.

Paintings contain materials that are subject to continuous deterioration. From the moment a work is completed, the painting will change in response to many natural phenomena and handling methods. Not only the composition materials chosen by the artist, but also the hazards associated with handling, framing, and display, affect the condition of the painting. Nondestructive radiography has been useful to assess these effects.[2, 3]

Paintings are composed of at least two layers, but often more.[4] Generally pastels and watercolors have only two layers, whereas oil paintings may contain many, even up to seven in some instances.[2] X-ray techniques can be successfully employed to analyze the various layers with regard to their individual composition as well as their combined relationships[5] (Figure 1). I would ask your indulgence in some technical background for the next two sections.

Support Materials

Each type of support has properties that influence vulnerability to deterioration. Metal, ivory, stone, plaster, wood, fiberboard, papers, and fabrics all have been used as carriers or support for the design layer. The x-ray attenuation properties of each of these materials are of course different and visual inspection and/or consultation is needed to select the proper radiographic technique.

With fabric supports, a stretcher or strainer is used to fix the fabric for handling. However, fabric can be mounted on board or masonite and aluminum. Mounting often fixes the design layer, smooths out the painting, and assures the stability of the work. It is prudent to avoid permanently mounting the canvas to the rigid material. The composition and

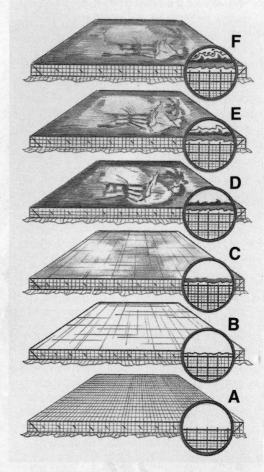

Figure 1: *Layers of typical oil painting. A. Support; B. Sizing; C. Ground; D. Paint or pigment layer; E. Varnish; F. Accumulated dirt, soot, dust, etc.*

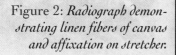

Figure 2: *Radiograph demonstrating linen fibers of canvas and affixation on stretcher.*

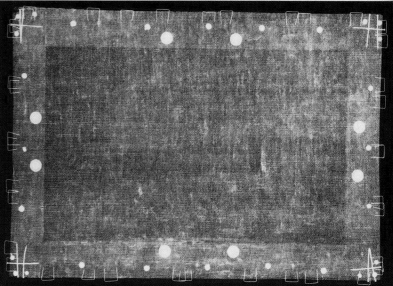

integrity of the support or carrier can be evaluated by a variety of special radiographic imaging methods. For instance, fissures and separation in wood can be noted on standard emulsion film radiographs or by xeroradiography before they will be detected by visual or raking light inspection.

Paintings can be considered as objects in motion. They expand and contract as the composition materials constantly absorb or release moisture. Thus, they may warp, oxidize, or decompose. Warp in a wood support is caused by realignment of the wood fibers with change in their relative orientations and distance from each other. Warp is well delineated by low-kilovoltage radiography or xeroradiography. General fiber loss leading to decomposition of a canvas can also be predicted by an assessment of the appearance of the individual fibers (Figure 2).

The paintings most often radiographed are oil on fabric. The supporting fabric usually is linen which, much as other fabrics, is subject to deterioration from mold, insect, or vermin damage, and rot. Mold destroys the individual fibers of the fabric in much the same manner as rot. Rot can be assessed in the early stages by low-kilovoltage radiography or xeroradiography. This can be done with magnification techniques.

Most support fabrics are initially coated with a sizing of water-soluble gelatin to seal the threads against the penetration of the paint medium. The fabric threads may swell with moisture and contract with dehydration causing paintings to go "slack" or to become "taut." With such movements, the layers can separate from the support, necessitating resizing or waxing for stabilization.

Paint Layer

The paint layer (the design or "picture" layer) can be readily evaluated by radiographic techniques. The medium is composed of pigments mixed with a fluid vehicle acting as a binding material. The binding material characterizes the paintings as watercolors, pastels, or oils. The pigment is applied in such a way as to adhere to the material over which it is spread. The degree of adherence may be assessed by simple visual inspection, light "raking," ultraviolet analysis, and by radiographic methods. Pigment is finely divided coloring material that has been reduced to a powder particle form, usually by a grinding process. These pigments are more or less radiopaque depending on the atomic composition, particle size, and application density.[6] Inorganic pigments may be natural earths, treated minerals, or byproducts of human manufacture, whereas the organic pigments are usually animal or vegetable dyes or, if of more recent origin, synthetic chemicals. Radiographic techniques are especially useful in evaluating the design layer because they may accurately determine the pigment and its distribution. Oil paint is produced by mixing ground pigments with some type of drying oil, the most common being linseed. Oil paints may be further diluted with benzenes, kerosenes, turpentine, and varnishes.

Certain groups of artists have adopted unique styles of pigment application. For example, the impressionists often used heavy application of light pigments in thick layers (impasto) alternating with thinner applications. The areas of thicker pigment attenuate the x-rays and are more clearly delineated than the parts of the canvas on which less pigment has been applied (Figure 3). This very thick pigment layer, however, will

Figure 3: Georgette, *Will Low,* oil on canvas. *Pre-Raphaelite work demonstrates thin pigment application, as clearly demonstrated in low-kV film radiograph.*

not penetrate the canvas fibers and the layer tends to sit on the surface.

The "visionary" artists used multiple layers of pigment interspersed with varnish, a compositional arrangement causing continuous movement of layers. This motion will cause shearing, the depth of which is an important determinant of the condition of a painting. Radiographic techniques, especially magnification, can be used to document these changes (Figure 4). Several exposures at different kilovoltages may allow selective layer visualization. The various layers can be detected by the changing pigment patterns on the serial films

with the change in radiographic exposure. Newer techniques such as digital radiography offer promise in this particular type of evaluation. Mask subtraction using a time-interval difference could theoretically allow serial changes in the pigment design to be recorded.

Almost all paint films will crack with time. Specialized radiography may allow recognition of the cause, whether it be age, drying, or mechanical stress. In age cracking, one will see fracture lines penetrating all layers of the painting (Figure 5); whereas, if this process is due to drying of the suspending medium or "traction," these processes will show fissures confined to a particu-

Figure 4: The Old Oak, *Henry Hammond Ahl, oil on canvas. Film radiograph shows total absence of correlation of the pattern of radiographic density with the visual image. The visual image represents the projection from multiple layers of interspersed pigment and varnish, while the radiograph demonstrates the accumulated attenuation of the pigment layers.*

Figure 5: *A*. The Creek at New Bedford, *Ralph A. Blakelock, oil on wood panel. Film radiograph shows multiple cracks.*

lar layer. You may wish to study various photos in these chapters to better grasp these concepts.

Mechanical localized cracking is most often a result of a sudden traumatic event, such as a direct blow or jar to the surface of the painting. Visual inspection or raking light will demonstrate the characteristic "cobweblike" pattern or "feather lines" of this type of cracking. Survey radiographic images can be used to determine the extent of the cracking process. Xeroradiography is valuable and magnification (Figure 6) will allow a more specific analysis regarding depth.[7,8] Radiography also can be used to identify those areas that should be selected for microscopic analysis; in general, it remains the method of choice for evaluation of a small, well defined area of the painting subject to inquiry.

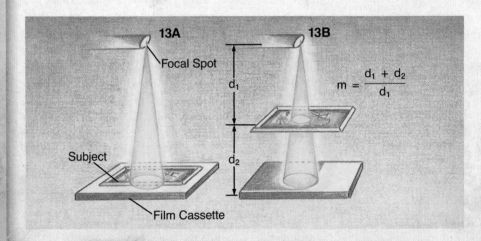

Figure 6: *The principle of radiographic magnification. A. In conventional radiography, in which the subject is in close apposition to the film, the radiographic image is only slightly enlarged. B. Magnification radiography, in which the magnification factor is the focal spot to image distance divided by the focal spot to subject distance.*

Any separation between or within the various layers of a painting is described under the nonspecific descriptive term of "cleavage." This process usually begins as cupping (curling) at the edge of the defect and may end in flaking and paint loss from the surface to the support. Frank loss of the full thickness of a composition from varnish to ground can be readily assessed by visual inspection. Significant curling and cupping is readily evaluated by raking light examination. However, radiography can detect these processes in the early stages, when preservation techniques might be most effective. By examining the width and regularity of the lines of cleavage, one can determine the level of the separation phenomenon.

Authentication

X-rays are not confined to the evaluation of condition of paintings but may be used in classification and authentication as well as discovery of a hidden work below the visual image. Unlike ultraviolet light inspection, which causes fluorescence from the varnish surface, radiography can determine the internal composition of a painting. At times, there may be superimposition of the design layers or changes in the various other parts (Figure 7). If the painting was constructed by multiple layers containing pigment, the images on the radiograph may not correlate well with that observed visually. Thus the correlation of the appearance of a painting by visual inspection, raking

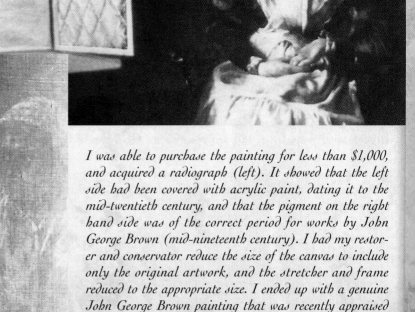

Figure 7: Woman in Chair, *John G. Brown. This painting was consigned to a major auction house, where inspection showed that the technique and composition were not uniform. On the right-hand side was a rendering of a woman in a rocking chair, with detail and style characteristic of Brown. On the left was an open window revealing a landscape. The technique on this side was somwhat impressionistic, with brighter colors, and a composition that appeared contrived. An examination with a shortwave black light showed that the pigment on the left side was much newer than that on the right, leading me to believe that the left side of the painting had either been seriously overpainted or finished by a later artist.*

I was able to purchase the painting for less than $1,000, and acquired a radiograph (left). It showed that the left side had been covered with acrylic paint, dating it to the mid-twentieth century, and that the pigment on the right hand side was of the correct period for works by John George Brown (mid-nineteenth century). I had my restorer and conservator reduce the size of the canvas to include only the original artwork, and the stretcher and frame reduced to the appropriate size. I ended up with a genuine John George Brown painting that was recently appraised at $12,500.00.

light, ultraviolet examination, and radiography often provide a more complete concept of the work.

I might ask not only to assist in evaluation of a painting for proposed conservation/preservation but also to assess the condition before acquisition by a gallery or museum. Repairs made by "inpainting" can usually be seen to fluoresce by ultraviolet inspection. However, white lead filling material has in the past been used to repair large areas of paint loss. Repairs of this type will be revealed readily on radiography, as the lead attenuates the x-rays much more than the other substances commonly used for this process (Figure 8). Gesso used in the filling of the defect of the painting will not be as readily demonstrated, as the compositional elements in gesso are not sufficiently dense to be clearly delineated.

The choice of film type and film/screen combination is a challenge and requires a team approach and dialogue among the conservator, curator, physicist, radiologist, and technologist. Some knowledge regarding the expected materials in the composition, measurements of the thickness of the work, and consideration of the imaging alternatives will properly initiate the diagnostic process.

Application of New Imaging Techniques

Conventional radiographic methods have proved very useful in examining the composition of the various layers of paintings. New developments such as digital techniques, neutron activation analysis, nuclear magnetic resonance, and x-ray fluorescence offer promise for additional information in the evaluation of paintings. We have had the opportunity to use several. Some will be treated here and with some overlap in the next section.

Computed tomography can sensitively measure the density difference in tissues or materials.[9 – 11] Density differences of 0.5% in the materials used in paintings are usually depicted by this method. Since density differences are recorded digitally as numeric measurements, the display could be manipulated by the observer to "enhance" density differences at a chosen specific density level. For example, one can actually

Figure 8: *Detail of a film radiograph of an anonymous eighteenth-century painting in poor condition (right). Radiograph indicates a loss of pigment but retention of canvas support (lucent area). Edges of defect illustrate cupping and curling. Density (upper center) is result of repair with heavy metal pigment. Edge enhancement (below) allows differences in pigment to be clearly identified.*

choose a numeric measurement corresponding to the density thought to be contained in the pigments that compose the design layer of a painting. An example might be elements of known density including lead, bismuth, or zinc. The selection process could allow those chosen elements to be optimally displayed in the image by "windowing" the attenuation numbers of those elements on the density scale.

Digital radiography has recently been applied to achieve improvement in density detection.[12, 13] One technique is to subject the painting to a beam of x-rays while collecting transmission data with an array of detectors. The data obtained in this manner are displayed as black and white images on a television-type display in which the brightness of the individual picture point or pixel is proportional to the density of the corresponding point in the painting.

Computer-controlled enhancement of the digitized image may allow one to emphasize the low contrast found in the radiographs of many paintings. An advantage of this method is that it is possible to change the energy of the x-rays over a wide range and still produce excellent images, because the electronics of the detector array can be optimized for the particular x-ray energy being used. We have been able to portray figures and objects in paintings by digital techniques that were not depicted with conventional radiography. In addition, by certain "postprocessing" techniques, one can better evaluate the individual artists' styles and manners.

A second method is the use of a special image digitizing system optically connected to an image-intensifying tube. Digital images of small regions (25-cm-diam circles) can be obtained with very good spatial resolution. The image is a single exposure similar to standard film systems. This type of imaging device has a more limited dynamic range than the scanning system in x-ray computed tomographic instruments but has a higher spatial resolution and, therefore, is useful for digital processing of images for the examination of fine detail, such as small cracks in the painting and brush stroke patterns.

Digital radiology has added a significant dimension to the evaluation of paintings. The sensitivity and flexibility of this technology may allow the detection of small changes in composition; this will be treated in depth in the next section. The ability to amplify various selected densities by energy subtraction will allow specific delineation of the various pigments in the design layer while the overall density image is received on a television screen. Images emphasizing certain densities can be selected to evaluate certain areas for overpaint, repair, cracking, and cleavage.

Medical imaging has benefitted from improvements in engineering techniques that can be applied to the evaluation of works of art, especially paintings. With these should come better understanding of the composition of paintings and changes that may occur over time. The ability to evaluate both large and small areas by nondestructive inquiry is a great advantage, appealing to curators and conservators and offering interesting diversification for radiologists.

References

1. Keck, C. *The Care of Paintings*. New York: Watson-Guptill, 1967.

2. Bridgman, C., Keck S. *The Radiography of Paintings*. Rochester, New York: Eastman Kodak Co., 1961.

3. Ruhemann, H., Kemp, E.M. *The Artist At Work*. Baltimore: Penguin, 1952.

4. Coulam, C..C., Erickson, J.J., Rollo, F.D., James, A.E. *The Physical Basis of Medical Imaging*. New York: Appleton-Century-Crofts, 1981.

5. James, A.E. Rao, G.U., Gray, C., Heller, R.M., Bush, M.R. "Magnification in Veterinary Radiology." *J Am Vet Radiol Soc*, 1975; 16:52–64.

6. James, et al. *Radiographic Evaluation of Paintings*. Eastman Kodak Co., 1989.

7. Osterman, F.A., James, A.E., Heshiki, A., et al. "Xeroradiography in Veterinary Radiography: A Preliminary Study." *J Am Vet Radiol Soc*, 1975; 16:143–150.

8. James, A.E. "Selected Promising Radiological Imaging Techniques." *Radiology*, 1977; 17: 144–148.

9. Hounsfield, G. "Computerized Transverse Axial Scanning (Tomography). I. Description of System. *Br J Radiol*, 1973; 46:1016 – 1022.

10. Brooks, R.A., Dichiro, G. "Theory of Image Reconstruction in Computed Tomography." *Radiology*, 1975; 117: 561 – 572.

11. Mistretta, C.A., Crummy, A.B., Struther, C.M. "Digital Angiography: A Perspective." *Radiology*, 1981; 139: 273 – 276.

12. Roehrig, H., Nudelman, S., Fisher, H.D., Frost, M.M., Capp, M.P. "Photoelectronic Imaging for Radiology." *IEEE Trans Nucl Sci*, 1981; NS-28: 190 – 204.

13. Erickson, J.J., Price, R.R., Rollo, R.D., et al. "A Digital Radiographic Analysis System." *Radiographics*, 1981; 1: 49 – 60.

14. James et al. "Radiographic Analysis of Paintings." Eastman Kodak, 1989.

15. James et al. "X-Rays of Paintings," *Southern Antiques*, 2001.

Digital Radiography

Conventional film has several disadvantages as an image-recording medium for the radiography of paintings. The x-ray attenuation characteristics of any given paintings are unknown before several radiographs are exposed, developed, and evaluated. Thus, several trial exposures must frequently be made before a radiography of optimal density is obtained. Further, it is not always possible for the observer to perceive the entire density range from a single radiograph. Several films obtained at differing exposures may be required to display the complete spectrum of density differences providing maximum radiographic information obtained from a single painting. Finally, the inherent radiographic subject contrast of many paintings is quite low. Thus, important image details may be difficult to perceive in film radiographs because of the subtle gradations in density. Digital imaging techniques overcome many of these difficulties. Our experience with certain of these computerized methods is summarized here.

Digital Fluoroscopy

Digital fluoroscopy is accomplished using a modified version of the standard radiographic system in which the image is produced by passing x-rays through an object (in this discussion, a painting) to fall on an image intensifier tube acting as the receptor (Figure 1). In conventional systems, the output of the image intensifier is viewed by a video camera for display or by a film camera system for permanent recording. In the digital fluoroscopy system, a video camera designed for maximum fidelity and minimum noise and distortion is required if the full advantages of digital technology are to be gained. The output of the video camera is converted from its analog electrical signal (voltage) to a digitized format which is stored in the computer.

A major advantage of this technique is the instantaneous display of the radiographic image on a television screen. This means that the image may be evaluated for proper exposure and positioning factor while it is being obtained. A second advantage is the very fine spatial resolution that is possible with this imaging device, which is important if one is interested in small details in the images of the paintings. Current image intensifiers have the capability of showing details as small as 0.25 mm in size, allowing the display of the fine details in individual brush strokes in the painting. The major difficulty with the use of this imaging modality is the limited area that can be imaged at one time. The largest image intensifier currently available is only 14 inches in diameter. Thus, the examination of larger areas would require multiple exposures. This system is thus useful for the detailed analysis of a small painting or a portion of a large one, while other digital techniques described subsequently may be used for overall analysis of works of major size. The digital imaging technique offers new nondestructive ways to evaluate a painting as well as to compare the components of the work, the artistic technique employed, and the condition of the work.

The digital fluoroscopic image in Figure 2 shows an example of one of the more common techniques of computer image processing, known as subtraction. If two radiographic images of the same subject are obtained under different conditions and one is subtracted from the other, only the differences between the two images are displayed. This image was obtained by slight movement (called "pixel shift") of the painting between the two exposures. When one of this pair of images is subtracted from the other, the result provides enhancement, or the exaggeration of contrast bound-

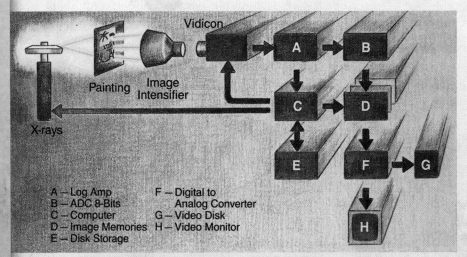

A — Log Amp
B — ADC 8-Bits
C — Computer
D — Image Memories
E — Disk Storage
F — Digital to Analog Converter
G — Video Disk
H — Video Monitor

Figure 1: *Schematic drawing of a digital fluoroscopy system. The attenuated x-ray beam, after passage through the object, is detected by the image intensifier. Output from the camera which views the intensifier is amplified and passed through the analog to digital converter (ADC) to provide digital information for computer storage. At display time, the image is converted back to the analog video signal through the digital to analog converter.*

aries (Figure 2). Thus, this method makes perceptible some features of the radiographic images that were totally invisible to the unaided eye.

Other possibilities for this subtraction technique include energy and temporal subtraction. Energy subtraction is based on the well-established fact that the attenuation properties of all materials are functions of the energy of the incident x-ray beam. The ability to perform subtraction using digital radiographs obtained at two different x-ray energies may provide additional information in the analysis of paintings. For example, two different pigments may have attenuation characteristics which are nearly identical at a given x-ray energy, making it difficult to differentiate between the two on the basis of contrast in a single image. However, the energy dependence of the attenuation of the two pigments may differ, allowing enhanced contrast by energy subtraction.

Figure 2: *Subtraction radiograph obtained by the pixel shift method provides edge amplification for improved visualization of boundaries or abrupt changes in density.*

Figure 3: *Schematic of a scanned projection system. In the scanner, the fan-shaped x-ray beam is stationary, striking a linear array of electronic detectors positioned along an arc of a circle such that all are equidistant from the source. The painting is then passed linearly through the beam at a constant speed while the computer samples each detector at frequent, uniform intervals. Again, the analog signal is digitized and stored in the computer for future display.*

Temporal subtraction involves the use of two images obtained at different times, within the interval ranging from seconds to years. It may be used to study the deterioration of paintings with time, since only the changes in the attenuation pattern will be displayed in the subtracted image. Further, it could be useful in the authentication of paintings. A digital image of a painting obtained and stored could at some later date be subtracted from a similar image of a suspected copy. Any difference between the two would be exaggerated, making identification of the painting from which the later image was obtained relatively simple and quite precise.

Scanned Projection Radiography

One of the outgrowths of modern computed tomographic (CT or CAT) scanning instrumentation is a method for performing digital radiography which has many of the features of an ordinary radiographic study but in which each data point ("voxel" or small rectangular portion of the painting) is recorded in a discrete, finite manner. This technique is often called the "scout view." At present, it is available in any hospital radiology department with computed tomography equipment. The method consists of placing the x-ray tube and detector assembly in such a position that the painting may be moved linearly through the x-ray beam (Figure 3). As it is moved, data are collected by the computer from the detector array, and the image of the painting is thus stored in computer memory for subsequent manipulation and display.

The collected image with or without digital processing is displayed on a video monitor. In this image, the intensity of each individual point ("pixel") in the image is proportional to the quantity of x-rays passing through the corresponding point in the painting. The spatial resolution of this system is acceptable but not as good as that obtained by digital fluoroscopy.

A major advantage of the scanned projection technique is that x-ray energies over a wide range may be used. This is possible because the electronics of the detector array can be optimized for the x-ray energy

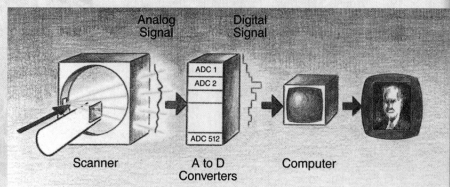

Analog Signal   Digital Signal

ADC 1
ADC 2
ADC 512

Scanner   A to D Converters   Computer

being employed. This calibration procedure is not available for either conventional radiography or digital fluoroscopy. Large field-of-view are also possible (Figure 4). The equipment is expensive ($800,000 to $1,200,000) but is widely available in major medical centers. We have had the opportunity to evaluate several of these systems and feel that they offer great promise in the evaluation of paintings.

The scanned projection images in Figure 4 demonstrate a second common technique of digital image processing known as "windowing." Image intensity or "brightness" using this equipment is measured on an arbitrary scale in units called Hounsfield units (HU). For the typical machine, the dynamic range is 1024 – 1024 (or more). HU, where -1024 is assigned to the attenuation of air, 0 to water, and 1024 (or the equipment maximum) to the densest material in the subject. If the entire dynamic range of image intensity is displayed simultaneously, the contrast resolution is low, as in film radiography. However, the windowing technique allows the viewer to select only a portion of the dynamic range for display at any one time. These static images can never demonstrate the information display capacity of this technique. It can be accomplished in "real time," that is, the display can be altered as the window level and height are changed, providing for a continuously varying image that almost resembles a moving picture as it displays the various features of the painting.

Scanned Point Source System

A third digital radiographic method is the "flying spot" or scanned point source system. In this system, the x-ray image is formed by scanning a fine pencil beam of x-rays over the area being imaged. After passing through the object, the attenuated x-ray beam is detected by a large scintillation crystal whose light output is measured, digitized, and stored in computer memory. The formation of the pencil beam of x-rays is accomplished by a mechanical system of collimators which block the beam and move in such a manner that the beam is scanned over the imaged area in a rectilinear raster. The time required for imaging a painting of moderate size (16 x 24 or 20 x 24 inches) is of the order of five seconds.

This technique has not been generally available because, until recently, the imaging time was of the order of fifteen seconds, and the spatial resolution was significantly less than with other methods. Although these time and resolution limitations are not so important in radiography of paintings, they are in clinical circumstances. Thus, these machines have not been widely employed in medical facilities. At present, images can be obtained with resolution of about two line pairs per millimeter. In addition, images can be stored and repeated images of the same area can be summed to provide higher quality pictures. Data can be manipulated to change contrast and other characteristics as for the other systems of digital radiography. This technique has not as yet received sufficient use to permit us to evaluate it and to compare it with the other two more widely accepted computer methods.

Acknowledgement

I thank art conservators Colin Post of PostRestorations, Cynthia Stow of Cumberland Restorations, Shelly Reisman of the Tennessee State Museum in Nashville, John Pettery, William Gerdts of New York University, and Caroline Keck in Cooperstown, New York, for encouragement. Ron Price and associates and Gary Novak and GUV Rao as well as George Holburn in Radiological Sciences, General Electric, Inc., Xerox Corporation, Siemens Corporation, and Technicare for special equipment; and Eastman Kodak and the DuPont Corporation for film-screen combinations. S. Julian Gibbs edited the text for some of this book.

   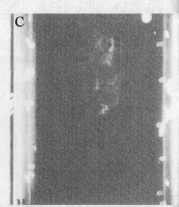

Figure 4: *Self portrait, Cornelius Hankins, oil on canvas. Scanned projection radiographs windowed at different levels. See text for details. In A, the image is processed to display details of the canvas painting support (arrows). In B, processing is aimed to show the distribution of pigment. In C, the wood and metal supports of the painting are demonstrated.*

A Theme in Collecting

Collectors have significant difficulty in deciding about the first or the first several acquisitions, and while this is an important decision, it is not a permanent and irreversible one. If you will share your feeling of insecurity with experienced collectors, who by now you think have all the answers, your confessions of anxiety will be met with great compassion and quite possibly you will be regaled with their tales of inappropriate choices, even acquisitions of fakes, and multiple changes of direction.

Think of this as a learning process. Thus, as an initiate you have comfort in numbers and you will come to realize that most collectors have experienced these same bouts of insecurity and fear. These manifestations from your "acquiritis" will not give you colitis or a noticeable chronic palsy. But can you benefit from the history and love of collecting and avoid some of the perils suffered by others? While there exists no better instruction in art collecting than personal experience, the tuition may be very dear. I would recommend a collecting style that tends to minimize your risk and, more importantly, enhance your knowledge about what you are doing and provide you with confidence and pleasure as you progress. This style is collecting the various aesthetics, singly and specifically, for at least a significant period of time.

Books and articles about collecting art will predictably extol the virtues of acquiring personal knowledge about the kind of acquisitions you plan to make. This, as I have previously stated, can be done by visiting dealers, reading the academic offerings in the field, spending time in the appropriate museums, and exchanging ideas with other collectors.

The acquisition of information, however, tends to be random, and, like all random data, is difficult to encode in one's memory and recall system. As an embellishment process, you can become competent and knowledgeable in a reasonable time frame by systematically studying the various aesthetics (like, for example, Impressionism). In so doing, you will not only learn the traditional artistic canons of any particular art form, but about individual practitioners of that particular technique (and the expected resource allocation to acquire an example). You will also come to know the physical characteristics that must be in evidence to represent a quality example of that particular artistic style.

As you move through the various aesthetics (such as impressionism, tonalism, realism) you may discover the ones you prefer and you can then concentrate on a particular artistic movement and even specific artists within that genre. This choice will be made based upon a variety of alternatives now known to you and with some confidence that you are responding to a synthesis of your personal desires and tastes. It will become clear that, while these choices may have been made in consultation with others, you have largely relied upon your own judgment. Reaching this level of collecting is truly rewarding and every accomplished collector will tell you so if asked. Without resorting to an encyclopedic litany of examples, several personal experiences in my collecting of American paintings might prove illustrative of this thesis.

Until the mid-nineteenth century, the preponderance of American art was portraiture or modified portraiture. Early in our history and in the rural areas, documentation of one's existence, appearance, and station in life was deemed important enough to have likenesses fashioned by all manner of artists — from itinerant limners to the studio-based, academically trained masters of New York, Boston, Philadelphia, and other urban centers. While sophisticated renderings of well-known figures have always been relatively expensive, the less well-documented portraits by unknown hands and the primitive works by self-taught artists have not. More recently, these stark, often decidedly two-dimensional images have been caught up in the general increased appreciation of Americana and folk art. Still, these "tokens of genealogy" remain of good value if you would like to acquire a survey collection. Having several dozen in one's domicile or a half dozen in one's office would be problematic from the visual perspective. Thus, this genre probably should be only a subset of your collection and not the theme.

By mid-century, Americans were coming to recognize the incredible grandeur of their native land, and this was celebrated on canvas by practitioners known as the Hudson River School. This thin application of of pigment in a flowingly academic style of such notables as Church, Bierstadt, Moran, Cole, and Durand represents a body of widely acclaimed, eminently desirable work that many feel represents America's greatest artistic statement. While a representative example of these artists will be quite expensive (in six to seven figures), but still of lasting value, there were many other practitioners of this aesthetic who created representative examples that can be acquired for a much smaller allocation of your resources. In studying this aesthetic and the related one, luminism ("American Light" as John Wilmerding describes this phenomenon), you will come to appreciate a significant aspect of American artistic tradition. If neither of these aesthetics can be afforded by you, the academic self-discipline and information will still have been meaningful. Don't we all look at the Palm Beach real estate offerings or the exotic cars in the Robb Report knowing that this is an exercise in fantasy?

Certain art forms may be "good buys" or the subject of a survey or theme collection only if they appeal to you. Tonalism, which I will subsequently discuss, represents a technique in which the overall hue of the work is depicted through a thin veil of color from the lower key register. This is an aesthetic that has proved too evocative, moody, and, at times, too serene for the general public to collect. This, along with the Barbizon mood of pastoral, wooded scenes of browns and greens, has been avidly collected, however, by some of the great patrons of American art such as Thomas B. Clark and Charles Lang Freer. One of the more celebrated of the tonalists was James Abbott McNeill Whistler. Those artists more closely associated with the American tonalist aesthetic were Dewing, Tryon, Dabo, Crane, Ranger, and Murphy. Ranger also sought to establish an "American Barbizon" in Old Lyme, Connecticut, at the turn of the century. A modified tonalism resulted in landscapes representing "paintings of quietude" and were more generally accepted by the public. Any survey collection will be enhanced by several Barbizon and tonalist offerings. I once put together a theme collection of these works, wrote a small monograph, and had a traveling exhibit. This was very well received partly because the public had not been often exposed to these aesthetics, recognized the scholarship, and appreciated the validity of the theme.

Bursting onto the American art scene in the last decade of the nineteenth century and the first decade of the twentieth century was the most universally admired technique of all, impressionism. The opportunities for acquisition of impressionism are multiple. If you want to collect the leaders of American impressionism such as William Merritt Chase, John Henry Twachtman, Theodore Robinson, Edmund Tarbell, Julian Alden Weir, Willard Metcalf, Frank Weston Beston, and others, the best examples will cost you hundreds of thou-

sands or even millions of dollars. However, you should still study their paintings and the technical characteristics of these masters to be able to appreciate the benchmark qualities by which the merit of any impressionist work should be judged.

As I have discussed elsewhere in this text, literally hundreds of American impressionists have been uncovered, discovered, rediscovered, and introduced to the collecting public in the past decade and a half. These artists represent all manners of experience and training — from those studying directly with the masters to pupils of the great ateliers, artists who belonged to colonies like: Old Lyme, Connecticut; Bucks County, Pennsylvania; Rockport, Massachusetts; Woodstock, New York; or Brown County, Indiana; some who stayed in France for long periods of time; and others who remained in obscurity by personal choice.

Some of these lesser-known artists produced works of such quality that they remain undervalued to this day. If a collector has a discerning eye and an appreciation of the desirable qualities of the impressionist aesthetic related to other art forms, excellent and informed choices can be made. The relative values can only be established by disciplined scholarship on your part but as I have and will emphasize later, the rewards can be great. They enliven a survey collection and offer a pleasing contrast to the portraiture, tonalism, Barbizon, and unembellished landscape paintings. My response to the values of the Chase, Tarbell, or Benson offerings has been to collect extraordinarily good examples by their students.

Obviously, my discussion could take us through the various movements in American art since the turn of the century through the Ashcan School, realism, modernism, regionalism, and the other "isms." These would also require some diligence on your part and more effort to understand them all. As the complexity of American life has increased, so has American art. This does not invalidate the methodology I have suggested guiding one's collecting activity but simply makes it more interesting. Any focused scholarship will enhance the pleasure of the acquisition process and enable you to derive greater pleasure and satisfaction from your choices. A survey collection in a disciplined manner will have led you through a number of passages which you will by now be comfortable with. You can then enlarge upon a specific interest if you choose, but if not, you will have a body of work that is interesting and visually pleasing. The message is that your collection should make a statement about the genre you have chosen to acquire.

American Barbizon

Barbizon painting embraces an aesthetic first practiced by French artists working in the forest of Fountainbleu near Paris and in the Dutch lowlands. They created a body of works collectively described as the Barbizon tradition. Well before mid-century, artists including Corot, Millet, Daubigny, Rousseau, and Diaz depicted rural tableaus as their principal emphasis; peasants at work, farm animals, and the virtues of agrarian life. This visual expression was truly a social statement opposing an increasingly industrialized and urban European society.

The Barbizon artists, while developing a clearly identifiable style, followed the tradition of the English landscape painters such as John Constable and the seventeenth century Dutch painters, van Rujsdael, Hobbema, and van Goyen. These painters created pastoral images in a dark matrix of russet and golden browns. They often superimposed flecks of yellow and orange. Tinted glazes and multiple varnishes produced a lustrous sparkle to their works, subjects were perceived through an almost tonalist (monochromatic) veil of earthen hues.

Their landscape compositions were involved with a personal view by the artist rather than the heroic and awe-inspiring vistas of the American Hudson River School or the formal academic court painters of Europe. The toil of the laborers, despite having an element of melancholy, also projected a sense of nobility and dignity. These works were composed with low key palette, which had historically made it difficult for many collectors to be attracted to the Barbizon aesthetic. Many initially find these paintings uninspiring and are more attracted to other contemporaneous styles such as the more dynamic impressionism. However, the Barbi-

The Forest at Fontainbleau, *William Morris Hunt, 21¾" x 16", oil on canvas. Hunt, a Boston Brahmin, was a member of the Circle of Writers and Scholars. He was an early Barbizon artist.*

zon tradition is an important movement in art and a genre of great present value both aesthetically and from an investment viewpoint.

One of the first American artists to embrace the Barbizon aesthetic was the Bostonian, William Morris Hunt, who studied with Jean Francois Millet as early as 1853. Hunt was an influential Boston Brahmin who developed a small following of artists and collectors. He was tragically found dead at the artist's colony on the Isle of Shoals but the legacy of his work has endured, as has his influence.

George Inness, Sr., one of America's premiere intimate landscape painters, was also exposed to Barbizon painting in France in the last half of the nineteenth century and employed elements of this technique in the late 1880s. He subsequently turned to a more subjective interpretation of natural phenomena. Inness was a very important painter because he influenced an entire generation of landscape artists to follow certain elements of this genre. In fact, Robert C. Minor, George Inness Jr., Charles Warren Eaton, and Elliott Daingerfield, and others have been described an "Inness-like."

In the late 1880s and 1890s, Henry Ward Ranger made several trips to the Barbizon area in France and to the low country of Holland as well. He was not only a highly respected American landscape artists but an engaging personality possessing great leadership qualities as well. His friends and followers were legion.

By 1899, Ranger was convinced that he thoroughly understood the Barbizon painting technique and could form a true American Barbizon along the Long Island Sound in the lovely town of Old Lyme, Connecticut. He described the gentle landscape, the seasonal rhythms of nature, the elegant gnarled old oaks, the estuaries and tributaries of the local rivers and creeks, and the tree-lined streets of the old village as the "land of Millet."

Returning to Old Lyme and the conviviality of the Griswold Mansion in 1900, Ranger spent the next three years persuading a large number of his fellow artists to summer there and create works of the surrounding countryside employing Barbizon artistic techniques. Artists in the early days of Old Lyme using old master techniques created images in which light pene-

Coming Home, *George Inness, Jr., 22" x 26", oil on canvas.*

trating the surface could be reflected back to the observer. The emphasis was upon a romanticization of common labor and a subjective depiction of nature.

Although the Barbizon aesthetic was an important influence in American landscape tradition for decades, as a definitive movement in American art, it was short-lived. In Old Lyme, with the arrival of Childe Hassam and J. Alden Weir in 1903, the Barbizon mood which they derisively referred to as "brown gravy" painting came to be rapidly replaced by the light, bright, flickering images of impressionism. In 1904, a disappointed Henry Ward Ranger moved eastward a few miles to Noank. Later with some of his colleagues Ranger formed the Old Mystic Colony, which practiced the Barbizon manner as the primary technique.

Paintings representing the Barbizon aesthetic are traditionalist, somewhat monochromatic, and subtly convey a mood of tranquility, pensiveness, and are sometimes melancholy. They do not create the visual excitement of impressionism nor the dramatic social statement of the Ashcan School or abstract expressionism. In some measure, the Barbizon tradition has been relegated to museum exhibitions and like tonalism, not widely collected.

The influence of the Barbizon aesthetic was profound and has been appreciated by art scholars for decades. Collectors are now sharing in this realization of the value and subtle beauty of Barbizon works. Juxtaposed against American life at present consisting of chronic unpredictability and inconsistency, the images of the Barbizon mood may be appealing in their simply portrayal of timeless values.

These images are both sufficiently reductive and visually understandable to increase their contemporary appeal as the world continues to increase in complexity. They will never surpass impressionism in public interest but certainly mix well with paintings of this aesthetic in a public exhibition or in one's private collection. Barbizon paintings are particularly attractive in a more intimate format of display in a private place and this has come to appeal to the more discerning collector.

My Studio (near Noank, Connecticut), *Henry Ward Ranger, 10½" x 13½".*
Ranger founded Old Lyme art colony in 1899. With coming of Impressionism
he left in 1903 and was founder of a colony in Old Mystic.

Coming Home, Lloyd Branscom, 24" x 28", oil on board. Branscom was a member of the Knoxville group that included the Wiley sisters and members of the Art Institute of Chicago (AIC) that painted there in the summer.

Barbizon Landscape, J. Conn, 20" x 24", circa 1890.

Barbizon Landscape, *S.W. Griggs*, 14" x 23", oil on canvas. Private collection.

Man Plowing, *Abbott Graves*, 28" x 22", oil on canvas. Farmer/James collection.

Connecticut Landscape,
*Charles H. Davis, 25" x 30", oil
on canvas. Davis, primarily a
Barbizon artist, painted at Old
Lyme. Private collection.*

Landscape, *Albert
Pinkham Ryder, 22" x
28". Cowan collection.*

The Picnic, *George Inness Sr., 23¼" x 28", circa 1893, oil on canvas. The late tonalist works by Inness were very desirable. He was very influential among contemporaries and students including his son. Farmer/James collection.*

The Lawn Party, *Maurice Gerberg, 16" x 21", oil on board. Given to Preservation North Carolina.*

Preparing Dinner,
Charles Gruppe, 18¼"
x 14½", oil on canvas.
Private collection.

Trees Beside River, *Washington Girrard, 14" x 28", oil on board. Private collection.*

Field in East Tennessee, *Bertha Herbert Potter, 21" x 24", oil on board. Regional Artists of mid-Tennessee include a number of Chase students.*

Woman and Dog in Landscape, *Ida Crawley, 20" x 24", watercolor. Southern Women Artist collection.*

The Old Church Yard, *Henry Ward Ranger (1858 – 1916), 12" x 14", oil on board, signed lower right. Courtesy Knoke Galleries of Atlanta.*

Barbizon Landscape, *Charles Gruppe, 20" x 22", oil on canvas.*

Landscape (Cape Cod), *Robert Swain Gifford, 16" x 20". Private collection.*

Autumn Landscape, *J.F. Murphy (1853 – 1921), 13" x 19", oil on canvas, signed lower right. Courtesy Knoke Galleries of Atlanta.*

The Nurse, *Waldo Pierce, 28" x 21", oil on canvas. Farmer/James collection.*

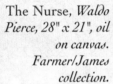

Old Oak, *Henry Hammond Ahl, 25" x 30", oil on canvas.*

Woman by Road, *Walter Shirlaw*.

Studio, Arkville, New York, *J. Francis Murphy, 16" x 20", oil on canvas, "America Beautiful Collection 1840 – 1950."*

Tonalism and Nocturnes

Tonalism

Tonalism of the many technical movements in American art in the late nineteenth and early twentieth centuries remains one of the most obscure and under-appreciated. There are the giants of tonalism such as James Abbott McNeill Whistler and Thomas Wilmer Dewing that only a Charles Lang Freer can afford to collect and then there are many artists who practiced this aesthetic only sporadically during their career. Many American tonalists were best known as Barbizon artists and others painted in the characteristic mono-chromatic hue to render their nocturnes. Henry Ward Ranger composed a number of compelling tonalist works yet he is best known as the founder of the Amer-ican Barbizon colony at Old Lyme, Connecticut. In 1903 when impressionism began its ascendancy there,

Ranger moved to Old Mystic and influenced others to continue to paint in the Barbizon manner.

Leon and his brother T. Scott Dabo were tonalists throughout their careers. Henry Ossawa Tanner, the expatriate black artist, rendered many paintings with a predominant hue in which elements of tonalism are quite apparent. Granville Redmond and Rollo Peters, two artists practicing in the western states, provide many examples of American tonalism. Many of the paintings by the impressionist John Henry Twatchman have tonalist elements of prevailing mist hovering above a small stream filled to its natural edges by melting snow. The indistinct edges of his works containing structure, such as his depictions of the Bush-Holly House at Cos Cob, are almost classically tonalist in composition.

Village at Dusk, H.W. Ranger, 25" x 30", oil on canvas. Private collection.

The natural atmospheric phenomena with the still pools and bayous of the South readily lend themselves to accurate portrayal employing the tonalist manner. The fog of morning and the mist of late evening and dusk have inspired many artists in the South including Joseph Ruisling Meeker, Knute Heldner, Walter Thompson, Sydney Buman, Roger Millet, George Inness Jr., at times William Aiken Walker, and very late in his career (1891 – 1894) George Inness Sr.

Despite the writings of Wanda Corn and Robert Preato and the collecting emphasis of such luminaries as William T. Evans, George A. Hearn, and Charles Lang Freer, there is little public appreciation of this aesthetic and the works are relatively undervalued. Thomas B. Clark was a very influential collector who considered tonalism to be a truly American art form. He loaned many of his tonalist works for exhibitions at the World Columbia Exposition, the Pennsylvania Academy of Fine Arts (PAFA), the Metropolitan Museum, the National Academy of Design (NAD), and the St. Louis Exposition. Despite these advantages and fortunate events, the subtlety of this aesthetic has hampered its general public acceptance.

Swamp in Georgia, *Sydney Buman, 16" x 20", oil on canvas. Buman was part of the Savannah art colony. She was noted for her portrayal of local scenes. Southern Women Artists collection.*

Louisiana Bayou, *Wil Owsley, 14" x 23", oil on canvas, inscribed as to composition and place on reverse. Purchased "unsigned," uncleaned, and unframed. Cleaning revealed Louisiana artist Will Owsley. Framed, lined, and cleaned, included in exhibition "The South 1850 – 1900."*

Tonalism is an intimate style of composition which expresses themes in a limited color scale; there is often an even hue to the image. Structure in tonalist paintings are dissolved in an ill-defined penumbra and indistinctly perceived in a uniform light. The mood of nature is expressed by an intimate style of composition employing a limited color scale using the prevailing hue in an evocative manner rather than a proactive manner. Tonalism is aesthetic rather than analytic art; a cerebral and reflective attitude of painting.

Tonalist compositions are rendered by the use of varnish as the suspending medium for pigment. Colors are not mixed on the artist's palette but primarily on the canvas itself. As with the Barbizon aesthetic glazing is important to achieve the diffusion of light in tonalist paintings. Glazing also allows the softening of the edges of the compositional elements in these works. Light

On the Mississippi, Henry Moser, 22½" x 24¼", oil on canvas. Moser was noted as an accomplished genre and upper Mississippi artist.

Tonalist Landscape, W.S. Richter, 24" x 30", oil on canvas. Richter painted and taught at Burnsville and Little Switzerland.

becomes the expressive protagonist in tonalist paintings where in impressionist works, light is the force of the work and in these the light may have the movement suggested by the use of broken color.

A part of the appreciation of the heroic landscapes of our Hudson River School is the representation of nature with great at times almost microscopic exactitude. The reference departure of a recognizable structure is not available to the viewer in tonalist compositions and the technical virtuosity is often not fully appreciated by the viewer. However, the value of this manner of painting should not be dismissed because of its lack of general public acclaim. One grows in appreciation of these works as they are viewed over a period of time.

While the impressionists had their landmark exhibition of 1874, "the Ten" in 1898, and "the Eight" in 1908, the tonalist painters only coalesced as a group briefly in 1896 at the Lotus Club in New York. They also exhibited with the Barbizon artists in 1899 at

Connecticut Landscape, *Leonard Ochtman, 25" x 30". Private collection.*

Early Morning Fog in the Garden of Dreams, *William Posey Silva, 8" x 10", oil on board, 1928.*

Knoedler and Company, the American Art Gallery both in New York, and at the Art Institute in Chicago.

Tonalism as a movement in American art never achieved notoriety or widespread recognition yet it influenced American painting to this day. The works of Whistler and Dewing have come to demand incredible prices and the ones of their followers have increased in value substantially. Among the collectors of Southern works paintings by Meeker, Herman Herzog, Louis Remy Mignot, and Heldner are expensive and those by Millet, Walter Thompson, Sydney Buman, Alice Smith, Lawrence Mazzanovich, Adolph Shulz, and Dawson-Dawson Watson have achieved substantial sums recently.

Tonalism is more likely to be an attractive genre to the experienced collector than the initiate. Other aesthetics will have become familiar to the accomplished collector and this subtle technique can be appreciated in context of a number of acquisitions. Tonalism should be valued for the importance it should be accorded and acquired after thoughtful consideration of its technical components.

House at Daybreak, *James Augustus McClean, 31" x 24", oil on board. McClean began his career as a realist dealing in regional subjects and later became a modernist.*

Tonalist Lowland Landscape, *Eliot Candee Clark*, 40" x 30", oil on canvas, signed lower left, circa 1910.

Florida Sunrise, *John R. Wilcox, 1910, 8" x 16", watercolor on paper, signed lower right.*

Nocturnes

Noctures are an aesthetic, if collected as a group, require a very specialized taste but as embellishments to a collection offer singular opportunities of pleasure and an artistic statement. They are a pleasurable contrast to other genre such as the bright palette of impressionism, the bold, sometimes brutal reality of Ashcan works and other forms of realism. Nocturnes very much complement Barbizon paintings and are in much the same spirit of tonalism.

More art historians consider nocturnes a subset of tonalism. In fact, nocturnes are usually compared in the same manner as tonalist renderings. All of the great tonalists produced excellent nocturnal works during their careers and to a lesser extent the Barbizon artists did as well.

I can remember vividly seeing my first tonalist exhibit. It was organized by the Grand Central Galleries in 1982. From talking with the late Robert Preato, the organizer, I found that a seminal publication had been written on the subject by Wanda Corn for the California Palace of the Legion of Honor in San Francisco a decade earlier. This monograph was out of print, but Robert gave me one of his two remaining copies.

The Harbor at Night, *George W. Whittaker, 25" x 30", oil on canvas. Private collection.*

Griswold Mansion,
B.K. Howard, 31" x 25".

I found that I was attracted greatly to this aesthetic for a number of reasons. It confronted nature as an extremely personal experience. It captured the most suggestive moments and presented shapes and forms under the magic pall of night illuminated by the monochromatic light of the moon. Individuals and defined architectural structures are portrayed in nocturnes in the same indistinct penumbra as the bodies of water and the sentinel foliage.

The interpretation of these artists of nature was achieved by "tone." Van Dyke characterized this quality as the prevailing color or intensity of a painting. The general color scheme should be tinctured by an overall hue that sets the viewer's visual response to composition. The French called it an envelope of atmosphere. Nocturnes obscure the sharp edges and abrupt contrasts and has the effect of viewing nature through the veil of moonlight and stars.

This is an intimate style interpreting themes in limited color scales, especially blue and gray producing a low key, evocative moodiness. Nocturnes possess misty atmospheric qualities produced in the monochronicity of available light.

While this is indeed a cerebral genre and has never achieved

The Docks, *George Elmer Brown, 36" x 30",
oil on canvas. Private collection.*

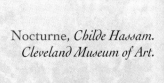

Nocturne, *Childe Hassam.
Cleveland Museum of Art.*

widespread public acclaim nor a general unfulfilled desire of a great number to collect these works, certain members artists rendering nocturnes can be very expensive. Works by the expatriate and certainly enigmatic American, James Abbott McNeil Whistler, are in the millions and Thomas Dewing, a Bostonian, often approach these figures. Interestingly, the legendary collectors, William T. Evans, George A. Hearn, and Charles Lang Freer collected these artists.

However, other accomplished artists produced very compelling nocturnes that can be acquired at reasonable sums. Henry Ward Ranger, a principle figure in American art and originator of Old Lyme Colony, was primarily a leader in the American Barbizon move-

ment. Our best Ranger nocturne appealed so much to my colleagues in the Cosmos Club that they added it to their collection. Ranger's remain reasonable considering his competence and importance.

Colonies that were known to emphasize other genre also produced tonalistic nocturnes that are very collectible. Among our collection are those of Alexander Harrison at Woodstock, Edward Willis Redfield at New Hope, Wilhelm Richter at Little Switzerland, George Whittaker of the Rhode Island School of Design, and George Elmer Brown of the Provincetown School.

Harbor at Night, *Eliot Clark, 25" x 30", oil on canvas. Private collection.*

Nocturne, *W.A. Coffin, 24" x 29½", oil on canvas. Private collection.*

While the works of Leon Dabo are certainly within the thousands, his brother T. Scott Dabo also inspired by James Abbott McNeill Whistler, have similar qualities of this analytic style. They interestingly enough gave lyrical titles to their compositions much like Whistler believing that description of tone and mood more appropriately lent themselves to the harmony of musical metaphors than visual. They described their paintings as musical poems. Two western artists who painted outstanding nocturnes were Charles Rollo Peters and Xavier Martinez. Both were trained in Paris and were influenced by Whistler. They are both reasonably expensive.

During the period 1880 – 1910 there was great interest in artistic circles in light and atmosphere and their capacity to affect the viewer's perception. Many artists were drawn to paint nocturnes as a personal experiment in this regard. The nocturne painters were, without apology, interested in the poetic and subjective. They de-emphasized the effect of daylight for dusk, night, or predawn.

San Souci Ferry, *Jack Campbell, Indiana, 24" x 30", oil on canvas.*

The Fete, *John F. Carlson, 25" x 30".*

The right light was the expressive protagonist of their work. While these artists, however, produced other works more interesting to the general public they thought their reductive works endured the psychic alienation from the values of their contemporary gilded age. These paintings were not composed en plein air but represented thoughtful compositions in their studies as works of reflections and remembrance. They were often constructed on the surface with elusive imagery reflecting the interior quality of dreams.

Certain terrains were particularly appropriate for nocturnal paintings; the swamps and bayous of the South and sailing scenes on open water.

Nocturnes were often composed by the visionary artists, most notably Ralph A. Blakelock but A.P. Ryder, Robert Newman, and Eugene Higgins as well. The visionaries were such individualists that their production never achieved the cohesion of a movement; their physical contact with each other was intermittent, if at all. However, their physical affinities resulted in the

production of a body of works that embraced the tenant's tonalism. They expressed these through nocturnes.

In summary, the general public has come to accept the virtues of nocturnes and tonalist works. However, the avidity for collection is and will probably forever be much less than for the bright, vibrant examples of impressionism. Nocturnes for many have a cerebral, analytical quality that are compelling and collectible.

Glouchester Harbor, William Partridge Burpee, 16¾" x 21½", oil on canvas. Burpee, from Maine, was an outstanding tonalist. Farmer/James collection.

Tonalist View (near Pinehurst), George Cook, 24½" x 29¾", oil on canvas. Cook was largely an expatriate who settled in Southern Pines and painted in that area from the 1920s to the 1940s. James collection, The South, 1840 – 1940.

Impressionism

Impressionism is generally recognized as the most widely appreciated painting style. The elements of pleasant subject matter, light bright pigments applied in such a manner as to represent vibrancy and movement, and the summary treatment of form to stimulate the imagination have given impressionism widespread public acclaim for over a century.

While Monet, Pissaro, Degas, and their equals have been beyond the resources of most collectors for many decades, America's Childe Hassam, William Merritt Chase, John Henry Twachtman, Frank Benson, Willard Metcalf, and Edmund Tarbell have been "unaffordable" since the mid-1970s.

Landscape with Lake, *Lawton Parker, 18" x 24", oil on canvas. Parker, a prominent post-Impressionist, created valuable genre and scenic works. Gift to Johnston Center for Undergraduate Excellence, University of North Carolina at Chapel Hill*

Brown County Landscape, *Edward K. Williams, 25" x 30". American Roentgen Ray Collection, gift.*

The interesting and well-illustrated texts on the subject have increased our awareness and appreciation of American impressionism. Concomitant with this knowledge has been a general increase in fervor of acquisition as well as a significant increase in the price of the impressionist works.

The paintings of artists who would be characterized as "second line" impressionists, such as Frederick Frieske, Lawton Parker, Richard E. Miller, and Louis Ritman, have recently fetched hundreds of thousands of dollars, making their acquisition by the major-

ity of collectors problematic. However, this does not mean one should feel they cannot collect subsets of this genre. I will share with you some of my experiences in collecting impressionism.

Conventional wisdom has been that all American impressionism is derivative. Most scholars feel that American impressionism is based upon the stylistic legacy of the Europeans. The value of works by even the

Grace, *John J. Enneking, 30¼" x 25", oil on canvas. Enneking of Boston was described by Patece as "the first Impressionist." Enneking (1841 – 1961) went to Paris (1872 – 1876). The background exhibits broken color and the shimmering effects of the Impressionist technique.*

Western North Carolina Landscape (Foothills), *Nena Morrow, 16" x 20". Morrow trained in New York City and painted in Southern Pines. Chase student.*

more important artists of American impressionism will not approach that of Monet and his colleagues. Despite the incredible increases in value, the American impressionists generally can still be acquired for less than the cost of their European counterparts. However, do not acquire poor examples by any artist because they are below market price. A viable and more practical alternate for collectors is the Impressionist colonies such as Old Lyme, Connecticut; Brown County, Indiana; Woodstock, New York; or New Hope, Pennsylvania.

The impressionist work from Griswold Mansion at Old Lyme not only embellished the image of notables such as Childe Hassam and J. Alden Weir but greatly increased collector (and investor) interest in the lesser-known figures of this group such as Edmund Greacen, Walter Clark, Elmer Livingston McCrae, William Chadwick, Will Howe Foote, Henry Rankin Poor, Charles H. Davis, William S. Robinson, and Clark Vorhees.

Additionally, the value of the tonalist and Barbizon works by Bruce Crane, another of the Old Lyme artists, were further increased by Charles Teaze Clark's article on the Barbizon artists in *Antiques* magazine. The paintings I then owned by many of these lesser artists were technically excellent and they increased greatly in value without any effort by me.

There is a certain amount of "fashion" in any type of investment. Junk bonds and dot-com stocks were poignant examples of this phenomenon.

Cape Cod, *Dennis Miller Bunker, 16" x 20". Bunker died at age 29. Private collection.*

Spring Meadow, *John F. Carlson (1875 – 1945), 18" x 24¼", oil on canvas, signed lower left. Photography courtesy of Vose Galleries of Boston.*

With the numerous exhibitions featuring impressionism as an aesthetic, the relationship to Claude Monet and the environment at Giverny to the American counterparts have been greatly emphasized. Those American artists who lived in the village of Giverny and painted in close proximity to the "father of impressionism" are now very much in vogue, and the value of their paintings has escalated markedly as a response to this mind set.

The works of Frederick Frieseke, Lawton Parker, Theodore Earl Butler, and Richard E. Miller are well into the six-figure range, with major examples over $500,000. A little-known member of that group, Louis Ritman, achieved $418,000 auction in the 1980s when collectors suddenly realized the magnitude of prices

Landscape, *E. W. Redfield, 30" x 25".*
Courtesy of Chapellier Galleries.

Wellsley Hills,
Marion Howard, 30"
x 26", oil on canvas.

commanded for the others and that the best works of Ritman had the characteristics which made them desirable such as light palette, dappled sunlight, with the subject of ladies in flower-filled gardens.

Many collectors/investors believe that the publication of Bill Gerdts's and other texts on regional schools of American art will continue to increase the demand

for paintings from such impressionist colonies as Brown County, Indiana; Old Lyme, Connecticut; Rockport, Massachusetts; Carmel, California; the Broadmoor in Colorado; Burnsville, North Carolina; and Provincetown, Massachusetts.

There is simply no question that texts of these types can enhance, if not create, a demand. I will discuss several of these colonies that I have collected in my interest and emphasis of regionalism.

Although the impressionists had their first collective exhibition in 1874, it was several decades later that this technique of painting became the dominant one in America. A number of American artists traveled to Paris to receive training in the 1880s and 1890s where they studied in the salons of the Academic Julian or the Ecole des Beaux Arts.

September Afternoon, Road to Milton, Massachusetts, *Joseph R. Decamp (1858 – 1923), 20" x 27", oil on canvas, circa 1895, signed lower left. Courtesy of Vose Galleries of Boston.*

Anisquam River, Autumn, *Anthony Thieme, 25" x 30", oil on canvas, signed lower right. Courtesy of Knoke Galleries of Atlanta.*

Upon their return to the United States, these artists wanted to duplicate the experience they had in Europe and did so by founding and changing the format of training in various American art schools, such as the Boston Museum of Fine Arts School and the Arts Students' League in New York. They also formed art colonies, such as Shinnecok on Long Island and Old Lyme in Connecticut in direct response to this legacy. Other colonies followed.

The Boston Museum of Fine Arts School had a rigorous and lengthy schedule in which draftsmanship was emphasized. This school flourished under the leadership of Edmund Tarbell and Frank Weston Benson and later under William McGregor Paxton and Joseph R. DeCamp. Some of their students went on to become

acclaimed artists in their own right, while others who were quite accomplished have not, to date, received the recognition they deserve.

Tarbell, the acknowledged leader, specialized in interior genre scenes and modified portraiture as did many of his students, especially the women who were referred to as "Tarbellites." A major example by Tarbell

Study for Mother and Child in a Boat, Edmund C. Tarbell, 14" x 17". Courtesy of Vose Galleries of Boston.

Brimstone Corner (Boston), A.C. Goodwin, 21¼" x 23¾", oil on canvas, circa 1900 – 1910. Boston Museum of Fine Arts, chronicler of Boston scenes.

will now be priced well over $100,000, yet a good quality painting reflecting the same technical competence by one of this students may be acquired for several thousand and certainly under $25,000.

Certain of the major works by these students remain with the descendants and in estates in the Boston area offering a good acquisition opportunity. You can certainly find them on Newbury Street with a bit of effort and time. They appear from time to time up on the North Shore and at the ubiquitous New England country auctions.

The artistic legacy of Boston and its immediate environs is a very important one for the collector. From the early portraitists to the landscape artists of the mid-nineteenth century, the luminists and marine painters as well as the more recent impressionists, artists receiving their training, artistic experience, or having a residence in the Boston area have been among the leaders in American painting.

A majority of "The Ten" American painters had some connection with the Boston area even if it were a summer spent painting at Rockport, Gloucester, Ogunquit, or at Provincetown.

The contributions of the early Boston sea and landscape painters such as Fitzhugh Lane or Martin Johnson Heade

Near Tryon, *signed Lawrence Mazzanovich, 11½" x 14¼", oil on canvas. A member of the Art Institute of Chicago, Mazzanovich captured the atmospheric condition in western North Carolina. James Southern Collection 1850 – 1950.*

Winter Sun, *Robert Emmett Owen (1878 – 1957), 30" x 40", oil on canvas. Courtesy of Knoke Galleries of Atlanta.*

are universally recognized and their work expensive. Visit the collection at the Boston Museum of Fine Arts especially the Karolik bequest. Then visit Newbury Street. This will orient you to both quality and price of this particular school.

Boston's artistic statement was embellished by the fact that many of these artists were friends with the other intellectuals of Boston society. As a group, they became "arbiters of taste" with national and international influence. William Morris Hunt and his brother Richard number among their closest friends Henry and William James and Lilla Cabot Perry. The poets and philosophers were also a part of this circle of great cultural influence.

In this scholarly and sophisticated milieu were very few women, and these were included by circumstances of birth or marriage such as Ellen Day

Hale of that distinguished Hale family. However, Boston was one of America's cities where women could study painting in a formal setting during that period. Housing or proper housing was not available in Europe for those aspiring female artists. This meant that many of the BMFA students were local and this is where their works have remained.

Women artists in Boston could, indeed, receive adequate formal training in several recognized schools

The Yellow Shawl, *Charles W. Hawthorne, 20" x 24", oil on canvas. Private collection.*

Landscape, *Phillip Little, 28" x 24", oil on canvas. Boston Museum of Fine Arts School. Private collection.*

of the city. The most well known, however, was the Boston Museum of Fine Arts School (BMFA). Following their experience in Paris, Tarbell and Benson returned to Boston and carefully organized a curriculum at the BMFA School that would duplicate their experience in France. They were particularly interested in their students receiving adequate fundamental training in draftsmanship and composition to enable them to produce interior genre works, which they favored, with competence but still lifes and the landscapes of their native New England as well.

Certainly, students of the BMFA like Lee Lufkin Kaula, Mary Brewster Hazelton, Marguerite Steuber Pearson, and others created works that not only reflect the training at the BMFA school and impressionism but also demonstrates remarkable individual artistic skill. Much of the portraiture by these women became the modified portraiture characteristic of the works of Paxton and DeCamp who were the leaders of the BMFA School after Tarbell and Benson. These artists have been regarded as followers; in fact, a number were wives of other artists in the BMFA school. Their work has been traditionally judged as reflective of their mentors or derivative only of their experience.

Shrimp Boat Dock, *Claude Howell, 23" x 29", oil on board. Howell was trained at Woodstock and painted at Rockport. He lived and taught in Wilmington, North Carolina. Southern collection.*

Springtime in Western Maryland, *S.E. Whiteman, 27" x 32", oil on canvas. Whiteman was chair of the art department of Johns Hopkins for over two decades. James Southern collection.*

More recently, with the increased awareness of regionalism and public exposure of these students through exhibitions, monographs, and texts, the more unique quality of the artistic statement of these artists of the BMFA School have been appreciated. This has resulted in their inclusion in museum exhibitions and a rather marked escalation of the price of their works at auction as well as in the private sector. They still remain good values if they manifest quality in the context I have discussed. I have seen and acquired works by Lee Lufkin Kaula, Ellen Day Hale, Gretchen Rogers, and Marguerite Pearson that would reflect a Tarbell, Benson, or DeCamp.

Probably the most influential Boston female impressionist was Lilla Cabot Perry. She was a remarkable and resolute woman in every regard, managing to be a very supportive wife, mother of three girls, and an artist of great influence. In

fact, this artist's contributions in popularizing impressionism for a conservative and skeptical American public have been widely appreciated, almost obscuring the fact that she was an accomplished painter in her own right. You will probably not be able to easily or inexpensively acquire a major work by her, some are privately held and there is always the rare opportunity. I acquired two paintings by Perry from her descendants but only after a great deal of "leg work."

Sometimes her small intimate landscapes turn up at auction and represent very good value. They are or can be as appealing as her modified portraiture. Hischl and

Forest Interior, *Lilla Cabot Perry, 21½" x 23", oil on canvas.*

Landscape with Church in Normandy, *Stephen Parrish (1846 – 1938), 7½" x 13", oil on canvas. Courtesy of Vose Galleries of Boston, collection of Frances Morris.*

Adler handled at least some of her estate and published a monograph. Mongerson Gallery in Chicago had a number of her works. She was treated to a retrospective by the National Museum of Women in the Arts. My two examples were included and were published in the text.

William Merrit Chase was not only one of America's great impressionists, but as a teacher and leader, inspired a large number of artists to achieve success. Chase's paintings have simply reached acquisition costs far beyond the means of most collectors as have the examples of certain of his students.

Other pupils, however, can still be obtained at a rather modest outlay of funds. The pupils from the Art Students League in New York and Chase's Summer School at Shinnecock created works of art that have many of the desirable qualities and aesthetic appeal of their mentor. With some diligence you can still acquire good examples for only a few thousand dollars.

Chase was a figure of such importance that his students have been reasonably well documented by the late art historian Ron Pisano and others so that they can be properly identified with little effort on your part.

Thus, if a painting you are considering appears to reflect the qualities, style, and subject matter of one by Chase, then matching the signature with a student list will often permit documentation of the relationship. The Nashville artist Edith Flisher studied with Chase. I had seen a number of works by her that were competent but not exciting. A St. Louis dealer, however, showed me a still life that was magnificent and so

Still Life, *Edith Flisher, 30" x 25", oil on canvas. Flisher was a William Merritt Chase student from Nashville, Tennessee.*

Winter Landscape, *Robert Emmett Owen, 16" x 12", oil on canvas, Estate represented by Vose Galleries of Boston.*

Chase-like that Chase must have been holding her hand when she composed the work. I acquired the painting at once.

Besides the formal schools such as the Pennsylvania Academy, the Art Students League, the Chicago Art Institute, and the Boston Museum of Fine Arts School, there were impressionist art colonies active in the last decade of the nineteenth and first several decades of the twentieth centuries. Certain of these colonies were under the leadership of a single famous artist like Chase's School at Shinnecock while others represented a gathering of kindred spirits.

Even in the colonies of the later type, certain artists were dominant, influencing the lesser-known members. The close interaction and critique between the artists in these colonies elevated the general quali-

ty of paintings that were created in this environment. These colonies are very important to collectors and will be discussed again.

American impressionism, in my opinion, actually embraced a rather wide spectrum of styles and is not just a derivative adoption of the sunlit fields or flower-filled gardens depicted by the French. In the 1910 –

Strolling Along the Beach, *Russell Patterson (1896 – 1977), 19½" x 25½", oil on canvas, signed lower left. Courtesy of Knoke Galleries of Atlanta.*

Train Station, *Anne Goldthwaith, 20" x 24", oil on canvas, artist from Montgomery, Alabama.*

1920 era, the color contrast employed by these artists became a bit more pronounced and the brush strokes more delineated than the French practitioner of this genre to construct the images of realism.

This has also been given the rather all-inclusive term of "post-impressionism." Examples of this variation of American impressionism have been traditionally less expensive than the more painterly works. This difference is not as great at present as it was just several years ago especially since the European post-impressionists have achieved such high auction prices.

A phenomenon that often causes fluctuations or rather escalation of the price of paintings is the public's fickle desire for a certain "look." As noted previously, among the most highly sought-after paintings have been the ones that reflect the "Giverny look," often described as "a female in a garden surrounded by flowers." The scene is often illuminated by dappled sunlight.

Artists such as Frederick Freiseke, Lawton Parker, and Richard E. Miller have become very expensive because their body of work has this appearance. Almost any painting of this subject matter, executed with bright color, and employing a high key "blonde" palette should increase in value.

Many lesser-known American impressionists created paintings with the characteristics demonstrated

Woman in Flower Garden, *Abbott Fuller Graves. Courtesy of Vose Galleries of Boston.*

Lake Scene, *Lawton Parker, 20" x 25". Johnston Center for Undergraduate Excellence, University of North Carolina at Chapel Hill.*

by those in Monet's circle. These paintings can often be acquired in the $10,000 to $15,000 range but should increase in value over time. As long as these works were executed in a painterly fashion and the perspective is good, the universal appeal of the subject matter makes these paintings desirable and a very good acquisition both aesthetically and commercially.

An example of how a specific subject can be "in vogue" and affect collecting tastes and value is the price achieved by many of the "kimono" paintings. The use in paintings of "things Oriental," stimulated by a growing appreciation for Japanese wood block prints, became popular from the last decade of

the nineteenth century through the early 1920s. Especially popular was the Japanese female dress.

In the 1980s, several articles appeared describing the virtues of these images. The La Femme exhibit arranged by Grand Central Gallery heightened public

The Languid Pool, *Will Henry Stevens, 20" x 24", oil on canvas board. Stevens, a successful Southern Impressionist, led the Modernist movement in the South.*

New England Autumn, *Ernest Albert, 1938, 30" x 36", oil on canvas. Courtesy of Knoke Galleries of Atlanta.*

awareness of these works just at a time when Japanese buyers became interested in impressionism. This subject matter had obvious appeal to them. Thus, the stage was set for a sharp break in the slope of the acquisition price curve.

"Kimono" examples in our collection are by Marguerite Pearson, Howard Hildebrandt, Clifton Wheeler, William Chadwick, Lee Kaula, and Katherine Dreier; all of these works follow the same visual theme and have increased remarkably in value.

You can sometimes anticipate trends in art and employ intuitive knowledge of their development to acquire capital for what you believe to be prudent acquisitions. I have used American impressionist paintings to acquire other genre. Upgrading your collection is a journey with no ending and "in vogue" styles can be used as resources.

American impressionism is an excellent investment if you appreciate this art form, have an interest in learning about it and the "art world," guard against hysteria and fads, and are patient in your acquisitions. Some of my impressionist works have

Noank, *Walter Clark,* *22" x 28", oil on canvas.* *Exhibited at Connecticut* *Impressionism 1979,* *Storrs, CT; Dikon* *Gallery; Vanderbilt* *University Club.* *Farmer/James collection.*

Welsley Hills, *Marion Howard,* *30" x 32", oil on* *canvas. Farmer/* *James collection.*

increased in value dramatically without any anticipation on my part.

Can you still acquire examples of American impressionism that are aesthetically pleasing, representative of the qualities of the famous practitioners of this aesthetic, and represent works that may someday greatly enhance in value? With some understanding of the American impressionist movement as well as alternative methods of acquisition and a small token of courage, this can certainly be accomplished.

There is no absolute success formula in acquiring American impressionist paintings inexpensively. Auctions are hazardous and require adequate preparation which I have discussed. Dealers sell for retail unless the work is not attractive for

their particular clientele which probably means you should not acquire it as well.

Having enumerated the many downsides, should one invest in paintings of this genre? The answer is a

Beach at Ipswich, *Henry C. Ahl, 25" x 30", signed "Ahl Jr."*
Farmer/James collection.

Woman in Garden,
Louis Ritman, 23½" x
27¼", oil on canvas.

modified affirmative if you enjoy the process, are willing to engage in some independent scholarship, derive pleasure from the possession for aesthetic reasons, and accept the illiquidity of this particular commodity.

Some investors in American impressionism will experience an incredible financial return on their investment, while, for others, the pleasure may be largely emotional. The aesthetic appreciation of impressionism is almost guaranteed. The rather substantial prices are also.

Your challenge is to acquire these examples at a price you can afford. I have and will discuss several techniques in this text by which you might well achieve your goal.

Haying, *E. Harkness McRea*, 30" x 34", oil on canvas. Private collection.

Backyard, *Lloyd Branson*, 20" x 16", oil on canvas. Private collection.

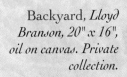

Haystacks on the Marsh, *Henry Hammond Ahl, 30" x 25", oil on canvas. George Watts Hill Alumni Center, University of North Carolina at Chapel Hill.*

The Orange Fan, *William Chadwick, 28" x 22", oil on canvas. Private collection.*

Stream in Winter, *30" x 36", Alberta Shulz. Excellent example of impasto.*

Harbor, *Haley Lever, 20" x 24", oil on canvas. Private collection.*

Greenwich Harbor, *Walter Clark, 30" x 25," oil on canvas. Farmer/James collection.*

Washday in the Quarter, *Robert W. Grafton, 24" x 16", oil on canvas, circa 1916. The Roger Ogden collection.*

Below Quebec City on the St. Lawrence River, *Rupert Scott Lovejoy, 12" x 14", c. 1926, oil on board. Private collection.*

The Swing, *William Starkweather, 25" x 30", oil on canvas. Exhibited "America the Beautiful," Hickory Museum. Private collection.*

Color Perception

Visual perception has rarely been considered in relation to a creative artistic style such as impressionism. I will consider the physiological implications of the painting style impressionism which had its origins in an emphasis upon color and light. This artistic movement grew from an effort to depart from the academic, salon-based techniques of the earlier part of the nineteenth century.

Impressionism is a sufficiently generic term that a myriad of descriptive characteristics has been proposed to describe this technique in the art literature. Impressionism has been variously presented as a technique of painting whereby the sense of nature, as perceived by the artists, is transferred by the application of pigment in a particular brush stroke pattern. It is a manner of painting that eliminates line and detail in favor of a generalized treatment of subject matter. Form is created in part by color.

The primary colors of yellow, blue, and red are emphasized with concomitant elimination of black as a pigment. These light (often referred to as "blonde") palette colors are applied in such a manner that they tend to be fused by the observer, thus creating the "sense" of form and structure. Juxtaposition of contrasting pigments ("broken color") allows representation of the quality of light and a motion effect upon the appearance of the painting.

Impressionism is a form of painting representing the tendency in the nineteenth century to de-emphasize classical line as the premiere element in a painting for a much more "painterly" style. The emphasis upon creating form from the use of color allows an artist to represent subject matter in a different fashion, depending upon the available natural sunlight, the time of day, and the season of the year.

The quintessential impressionist style, in which line and form are almost totally disregarded was embraced by only a few of the American impressionists. A more realistic approach, with evidence of draftsmanship and some attention to structure and form, was adopted to depict the "nature" of America. The colors employed to represent the American landscape were not the same as those used for European scenes. This was due to differences in natural light and foliage in the different locations.

Winter was the subject of many American paintings. The whiteness of snow creates a similar visual response to color, offering a sharp background contrast for objects in the composition.

Impressionism never suffered the fate of tonalism, the Barbizon School, or luminism. It has continued to be a painting method most enjoyed by the public and the preferred method of painting by several generations of artists. This may be partially explained by its effect upon the human visual system.

When we view a painting, the optic lens system projects an image of the visual field onto the retina. There photosensitive cells convert the pattern of intensity and color into the equivalent of electrical signals which are transmitted by the optic nerves to the brain's visual cortex.

The properties relating to the perception of paintings can be divided into brightness, contrast, color, resolution, and pattern recognition. Each is related to some aspect of impressionism. Brightness is the subject determination of intensity of a stimulus. The human visual system can adapt to a broad range of intensities. The range from threshold to the extreme glare limit is a factor of ten billion.

Two types of photoreceptor cells in the eye are involved in determination of brightness of a painting at low light levels, the rods in the retina are primarily involved in the visual process. The rods respond only to brightness whereas color is the province of the cones.

Threshold intensities are wavelength (color) dependent. The maximum sensitivity of the rods is in the central portion of the color spectrum. If ambient light intensity is sufficient, the cones transmit information concerning both intensity and color which is described as photopic vision. The vision of paintings is almost always at photopic levels. Photopic vision provides us with the ability to discriminate the same relative difference in luminance, regardless of the overall intensity level of the stimulus reflected back from the surface of a painting.

Since we cannot perceive the enormous range of luminance levels, we accommodate to a given level by adaptation. This phenomenon may occur quite rapidly when viewing a painting in a gallery or museum. Another factor in the human adaptation phenomenon can be accomplished by varying the diameter of the pupil of the human eye. Normal pupil diameter varies from about 2 mm under under bright light to approximately 8 mm with total dark adaptation. This accounts for a factor of 16, the ratio of the pupil areas in a large adaptation potential.

Most adaptation is achieved as a function of the biochemistry of the retinal photoreceptors and of processes in the visual nervous system. Only a limited range of brightness levels can be finely discriminated by the physiology of human vision at one time. Adaptation from threshold to greater luminance is accomplished rapidly, while dark adaptation is a relatively slow process, often requiring several minutes.

Impressionist works may have a spontaneous and immediate acceptance by the public for this reason, whereas tonalist paintings require a more studied and slower response. Granted, this perception is much more complicated psychsocial phenomenon, but basic physiology is, without doubt, an important factor.

A related phenomenon to the photopic response is brightness constancy. The perceived brightness of a given surface is usually evaluated in its relation to the brightness of other surfaces in the same environment or area. The overall light palette of impressionist paintings tends to de-emphasize contrasts between neighboring surfaces, yielding greater homogeneity and unity to the scene as a whole.

Many impressionist painters were attentive to the manner in which the perceived brightness of other specific points on the overall surface of the same object. A collection of discrete but similar points (brush strokes) could be used to represent a connected and homogenous perception center, visually integrated and unified by the eye of the observer. This is one of the basic tenets of the impressionist methodology.

Broken color and pointillism are two well-described techniques of pigment application which can be employed to have color produce form and movement as well as vibrancy. Broken color, or the juxtaposed application of contrasting pigment in a short stroke or hatched pattern, is effective as the visual integration and, at some distance, will produce a vibrant pattern of form stimulating movement. The light palette and the scintillation effect of pigment application in impressionist works are felt to make them emotionally uplifting.

The movement or shimmering quality of certain paintings has a basis in human visual response. When a sharp boundary between areas of greater and lesser luminance is encountered, a bright line is perceived along the lighter side of the boundary and a line of lower color registers along the darker. Broken color, if used with identifiable strokes, can produce these lines known as Mach bands, which actually represent an artifact of the human visual system that enhances contrast.

Mach bands also occur when a boundary is not sharply defined. In the purposeful use of broken color, the boundaries are not meant to be well defined. The artist intends for them to be fused by the viewer to create the impression of structure which accompanies spontaneity in the painting. Because boundaries of structures in impressionist paintings are ill-defined, Mach bands will also occur in complex patterns which are unavoidable. The artists in the development of a painting must utilize nature's image perceived by his visual system.

Mach bands may be explained physiologically by the phenomenon of lateral inhibition. When a neuron (nerve terminus) in the retina transmits impulses at a rapid rate, it inhibits impulses from adjacent neurons. This phenomenon creates the impression of a dark line along the edge of the darker area of the surface and a bright line at the edge of the lighter field. The broken color application of pigment of an impressionist painting offers the observer opportunities to experience this phenomenon.

In color perception, two factors in addition to brightness are involved and are significant in our perception of paintings. Hue is the aspect of perception that varies with wavelength of light, which is also the property of light primarily responsible for our perception of color. Saturation relates to the amount of white light that is added to pure monochromatic light as we perceive it and initially on the artist's palette. White light is defined as a uniform mixture of all wavelengths (colors). Pure monochromatic light is totally saturated, and as more white is added, the saturation can actually become less.

Fascinating use of unsaturated colors can be seen in the works of many of the impressionist artists, especially Monet, Pissaro, Sisley, and Americans such as Childe Hassam and John Henry Twachtman. The Indiana impressionists referred to this as the "white light or glare aesthetic." This physiological phenomenon is partially responsible for the "blonde" palette associated with impressionism.

True color discrimination is generally defined as the ability to distinguish color on the basis of wavelength alone, which is almost entirely limited to the human retinal cones. Current experimental evidence indicates that there are three classes of cones in the human retina (trichromacy). Color discrimination derives from differences in the relative activity of two or more classes or cones with different action spectra. Thus, if one color produced a large response in cone A and little response in cone B, while a second color produced a large response in cone B and little response in cone A, then these two colors would appear different and easily discriminated. A third class of cones with a third action spectrum, as in the normal human eye, reduces potential ambiguities. The possession of three classes of cones provides sufficient information for visual discrimination among a large spectrum of colors. Even with this capacity, the human color reception is not infallible. Certain color harmonies in pigment application will produce minimal viewer effect because of the properties of the human visual perception mechanism.

The additive color mixtures with different spectral components can occur either optically or visually by neural integration of spatially or temporally neighboring points of light. Visual color mixture by spatial integration of adjacent colors is an important aspect of many impressionist paintings. Pastel pigments of similar brightness but different hue were frequently interlaced in the same region of canvas, yielding a heterogeneous pattern of discrete patches when viewed closely, but an apparently homogeneous blend of an intermediate hue when viewed from a distance. Our visual spatial color mixture phenomenon is altered by the fact that spatial resolution is poor with light patterns varying only in hue but not brightness.

The poor spatial resolution of hue as a property of the human visual system is not readily apparent under the viewing conditions in which paintings are normally exhibited, because colored patterns usually vary in both hue and brightness, providing the use of both properties to achieve an accurate spatial localization of different colors. Impressionist painters often capitalized on this subtle but significant characteristic of the human visual process by choice of pigment to convey the sense of nature without depicting it in exacting accuracy.

In color perception as with brightness, our visual system considers the overall environment in which the pigment pattern exists; this phenomenon is an attempt to achieve hue constancy. In general, the perceived hue of an object remains reasonably constant even though the hue of the illumination may be changed considerably. Our visual system responds to related differences in hue, rather than the absolute hue itself. The pleasing homogeneity of impressionist works as well as the naturalness of the appearance of individual objects within them is partially explained by this phenomenon.

Another very basic element in our visual perception is the capacity for spatial resolution. The study of spatial discrimination, or resolution, of an optical system is expressed as the modulation transfer function (MTF). This is the ratio of contrast in the image to contrast in the object as a function of varying light intensity.

The greater the value of the modulation transfer function (MTF) at each spatial frequency, the more faithful is the reproduction of the original object by the perceived image. The larger the spatial frequency at which the modulation transfer function remains high, the greater the resolution by the human visual apparatus. Our visual system can insert form into a relatively formless impressionist painting by focusing our attention to the boundary of changes in brightness of the applied pigment. We are able to localize such differences in brightness to a much greater degree than we do differences in hue alone.

Bias as a psychosocial phenomenon is an important factor in our perception of paintings. We tend to select familiar patterns in our perception and that is why impressionism often does not seem formless, although the technique does not apply the boundaries; those we perceive result from the non-linearity of our perception.

One of the basic characteristics of visual perception is that the recognition of organized structures in complex optical patterns is shaped by prior knowledge, expectations, and interests. Thus, what we see in any painting is not a simple response casually determined by an objective physical stimulus. This is particularly true in impressionist works. Rather than a cause-effect sequence, perception involves the selective recruitment of available information in the environmental and emotional bias of the viewer's activities and interests.

The physical pattern constructed by the painter offers opportunities for the variation in our perceptual organization of information, depending on the degree of contrast between neighboring colors, the distinctness of lines and forms, the global consistency of formal organizations, the relative position and perspective of the viewer regarding the object, and even upon the continuities and contrasts in the painting.

The artist communicates with the viewer by shaping pigments to present the perceptual opportunities they wish. The distinctness of form and unanimity of organization in classical paintings made the perception between the object and the observer virtually inevitable and predictable, leaving little room for the viewer's imagination. The faithful re-creation of familiar structures with exacting precision virtually eliminated the function of observer creativity. Impressionism greatly reduced the clarity of contour and form inviting more active participation by the viewer.

This brief, non-technical discussion of the basics of visual perception and impressionism will lead to an improved understanding and appreciation of the genre of impressionism. The old cliché, "beauty is in the eye of the beholder" remains true. Thus, it seems apparent that artists, critics, and art historians might profit by being familiar with the beholder's visual perception mechanisms. The techniques of applying pigment, use of hue and color, and de-emphasis of line and form in impressionism can well be considered in visual response terms.

The Ashcan School

American art can be characterized by a number of significant movements. Among the more short-lived but influential was that realist aesthetic begun by several newspaper artists in Philadelphia led by Robert Henri. These painters, after moving to New York, became the "Immortal Eight" and later were placed in the general context of artistic history as the "Ashcan School."

The thesis of Henri, John Sloan, George Luks, and others was that American art should reflect the current social phenomena of this vigorous nation depicted in a bold, realist painting style. They sought not to capture the beauty of sunlit gardens, the vistas of the American West, or interior genre scenes of women in elegant attire engaged in genteel, leisurely activities. Instead, they chose to depict the images of urban construction, city streets teeming with vendors, tenements, and celebrated the struggle of those just arrived to the land of opportunity.

The leaders of this group had been newspaper artists covering the instantaneous happenings in the city of Philadelphia, while at least one other (George Luks) had followed the fortunes of Americans in the Spanish-American War. They learned to create works rapidly by the technique of blocking in the "sense" of the images with large summary strokes and later completing them by adding the corpus of the picture. For the subject matter of interest, they chose darker pigments at the lower end of the color register rather than the light, "blonde" palette of impressionism or the warm luminosity of traditional American landscape painting. The detail of the Barbizon artists and the subtle moodiness of tonalism were lacking in these much more bold, provocative works. This was true realism, about very real contemporary events of American life.

The exhibition of The Eight in New York City (1908) shocked the public — not only in the painting style but in the artists' choice of subject matter. In a review of the exhibition, one famous critic, pronouncing the work as "dreadful," stated that the theme appeared to be a demonstration of "clotheslines and aschans." This phrase was so often repeated that "ashcan" came to be associated with the painting style espoused by several of The Eight, their own students, and their followers.

The Picnic, *Paul Bartlett, 24" x 20", oil on canvas. Bartlett, known mainly as a sculptor, was an accomplished artist. He trained with Henri and members of the Ashcan School. This example shows the influence of Henri and Sloan. James Southern collection.*

Henri was the acknowledged spokesman of the group. His insightful lectures and essays often served as the collective statement of The Eight. Henri also regarded himself as a leader in artistic progress that was to celebrate contemporary American life and its major social statement. His portraits and figure caricatures were meant to capture the phenomena and effects of urbanization, capitalism, and the influx of European immigrants to America. The other member of The Eight closest to Robert Henri in style and purpose was John Sloan. In a similar, realistic manner often employing grays and other darker pigment tones, he would portray city life in New York and the commerce and movement of the expanding numbers of the people.

George Luks was the only member of The Eight whose colorful personality and flamboyant lifestyle rivaled that of Henri.

Luks was ribald, sometimes charismatic, and thoroughly unpredicatble. He was a frequent of bars, the burlesque, and a friend of the street people as well as the champion of the suppressed. His paintings were often summaries of draftsmanship in which the essentials

City Park (Washington), *Edgar Nye, 25" x 30", oil on canvas. Nye was noted for his realistic landscapes.*

Street in Baltimore, *Harold Wrenn, 24" x 20". Ashcan street scene from the 1930s. James Southern collection.*

were hastily rendered and enough detail was added so that the viewer gained the "essence of the composition leaving room for the imagination." Luks was greatly admired as a teacher, especially due to his lively demonstrations. He also attracted enemies and died rather mysteriously in 1933.

Another member of The Eight was enamored with

American life surrounding the theater. Everett Shinn was an actor of sorts and painted stage sets, theater interiors, and the actors themselves. He was later to illustrate 28 books, 94 stories for *Harper's*, and was the art director for Metro-Goldwyn-Mayer. Although his subject matter was different from that of Henri, Luks, and Sloan, his technical style has definite similarities. Collectors are often attracted to his subject matter.

The "Immortal Eight" was never a true marriage of artists but only a liason of convenience, as other members of the group were not similar in their painting style nor in their choice of subject matter. William Glackens has often been called (and with some justification) "the American Renoir." His personal New York was the elegant ladies and their prosperous men, boating parties, and picnics in the

Beach Party, *William Glackens, 12" x 14", oil on canvas. Private collection.*

Western North Carolina Landscape, *Augustus McClean, 25" x 30", oil on canvas. McClean utilized a subdued palette for his realistic landscapes.*

lovely surrounding areas on Long Island Sound. These works were visual representations of public fantasy and very popular. Maurice Pendergast was a unique mosaicist who captured the urbanites at leisure. He has often been described as a "neo-impressionist" and is well known also for the 200 monotypes he did to develop subjects by variations in color rather than the visual subject.

Another member of "The Eight," Ernest Lawson, was by most standards an impressionist who studied with John Henry Twachtman at Cos Cob, Julian Alden Weir, and with Laurens and Constant at the Academie Julian in Paris. Lawson portrayed New York in a bold, bright, heavy

impasto technique, creating images that had the scintillating qualities of "crushed jewels." Arthur B. Davies was a versatile artist whose media ranged from watercolor to oil, wood, ivory, marble, and wax, lithographs to etchings, enamel to glass, or Gobelin tapestry to finely woven rugs. Davies was a mystic and a romantic whose

Anticipation, *Ernest Lawson (1873 – 1939), 25" x 30", oil on canvas, signed lower left. Courtesy of Knoke Galleries of Atlanta.*

Shipwreck, Together with the Father, *Arthur B. Davies, 6¼" x 9½", watercolor. Davies, a versatile artist, was an organizer of the Armory Show (1913). James collection.*

favorite image was a landscape occupied by nymphs and allegorical figures. Thus, his association as a member of this group was more intellectual than asthetic.

The Ashcan School could be best characterized as the style of Henri, Sloan, Luks, and those artists like George Wesley Bellows, Isabel Cohen, Eugene Thomason, Eugene Higgens, Guy Pene Du Bois, Leon Kroll, Walt Kuhn, August Lundberg, Jerome Meyers, and Walter Pach, who all followed a similar style and a sensitivity for common, everyday life as subject matter. These realists saw themselves as expressing American life and as capturing the social forces of their native land in visual images. Their departure from the rigid, conservative tendencies of the National Academy of Design and the painterly, bright images of "The Ten" and the Society of Landscape Artists begged for a reaction, which was indeed forthcoming from both their fellow artists and the public.

Progress to the art establishment is often represented by merely an accumulation of the lessons from the previous artistic experience. There is also a tendency to equate artistic insurgence with political radicalism. Change can be viewed in a negative context rather than as progress. "The Eight" saw their exhibition as the beginning of their ascendancy to the most influential positions in the structure and conscience of American arts. Little did they know that as a clearly identifable movement, this show in 1908 may well have been their zenith, for by the famous Armory Show of 1913, modernism had emerged as the favored direction of American art. The modernists saw themselves as expressing fundamental artistic principles, and their statements were such departures from artistic norms that they captured the imagination of the public. The Ashcan School was in decline.

The Wrestlers, *Eugene Thomason, 36" x 30", oil on canvas. Thomason trained at ASL and shared a studio with George Luks. Private collection.*

Going Home,
*Eugene Healan Thomason,
24" x 20", oil on canvas.
Farmer/James collection.*

By the time of the Armory Show, only Davies was involved in the governance hierarchy of the exhibition. However, the influence of the Ashcan School remained signficant throughout the 1920s and 1930s.

Their legacy can be seen in the emergence of the regionalists such as Thomas Hart Benton and Grant Wood and to some extent among the most accomplished of the WPA artists whose realistic works reflect this artistic influence. Many of the more popular instructors of the Art Students League taught for several decades after the Armory Show the realist style espoused by the Ashcan School. Thus, their aesthetic's life was greatly extended.

The importance of "The Eight" and the Ashcan School in American art cannot be underestimated, as they were largely responsible for establishing the legitimacy of everyday American life as an appropriate subject for visual art. Whether or not you are attracted to the bold images with their direct social statements, to collect them is quite another determination. Several are monumentally expensive, while others the primary determinant is the subject matter.

Carolina Coast, *B. R. Holsclaw (a WPA artist).* Note the elongation of the arms and emphasis on physical aspect of the labor. James Southern collection.

Landscape, *Callie Braswell, 16" x 20", oil on canvas. WPA artist.*

Collecting Regional Art

Many historians have regarded the art colony phenomenon as the wellspring of regionalism, as often the major attraction for the artists was the compelling geography and the lifestyle they could enjoy in a particular setting. The type of environment often provided by the art colonies created circumstances in which pupil and mentor might often paint side by side rather than in an impersonal classroom setting. The skilled, but lesser-known artists might be directly influenced by the leading figures of a particular school because of the daily intimate contact and prevailing spirit of collegiality. The lesser artists benefited greatly by this intimate arrangement.

The personal interaction with the great and famous was also inspiring. The opportunity for advice, counsel, and one-on-one instruction from more accomplished artists tended to ensure that the quality of work by the lesser-known regionalist was good and often reflected the skill of the more accomplished artists. These lesser-known members often produced works that mirror the quality as well as the creativity of their mentors. The length of treatment of the individual colonies will reflect my experience and not necessarily their relative importance.

The New Hope Colony

The relationship of the New Hope Colony to the Pennsylvania Academy of Fine Arts is due to a single artist, Edward Willis Redfield. His concept of painting en plein air in the snow and the "use of white as a color" influenced a generation of followers. Many members of this group, such as Daniel Garber, Rae Sloan Bredin, Elmer Schofield, Fern Coppage, and Walter Emerson Baum are very collectible as are examples of Redfield's early works which are still affordable. They tend to be somewhat tonalist renderings rather than pure impressionism. The artistic merit of these examples sometimes offers greater value than paintings by his followers that are as expensive.

Redfield was a major figure in American art because he influenced an entire generation of painters and introduced the idea of painting outside in the snow. The towns around New Hope are quaint and the Bucks County area is blessed with scenic beauty.

Woodstock, New York

Another colony of artists who emphasized snow scenes was the Woodstock group led by John Carlson as well as Alexander and Birge Harrison. This regional movement was largely a product of the Art Students League in New York City. Among the students of this group was John Bentley. His portrayals of snow scenes in a realistic style are a good example of the quality and subject matter that make the Woodstock group collectible. Bentley and the Harrisons are still quite affordable. Carlson's estate is handled by the Vose Gallery.

Woodland Brook, Big Indian, New York, *John F. Carlson (1875 – 1945),* 18" x 24", *oil on canvas, signed lower right. Photograph courtesy of Vose Galleries of Boston.*

Old Lyme, Connecticut

Just before the turn of the century, H.W. Ranger, attempting to found an American Barbizon, persuaded a group of artists to join him during the summer in the village of Old Lyme. These painters sought to establish an intimacy with the understated, agrarian landscape of the Connecticut lowlands and inland countryside. Many of the artists lived at the Griswold Mansion with "Miss Florence" Griswold. They used the mansion as a home base from which they would venture forth to the nearby rolling hills, the adjacent seashore, or the banks of the Lieutenant River. Back in the mansion they lived in apparent conviviality, engaging in lively discussions of all types of subjects including art, playing charades or pitching horseshoes, and always painting. This intimate contact between the artists seemed to enhance the quality of the paintings they created.

The Old Lyme group is especially collectible for several reasons.

Winter, Bruce Crane (1857 – 1937), 25" x 30", oil on canvas, signed lower left. Courtesy of Knoke Galleries of Atlanta.

Those lesser-known artists living at the Griswold Mansion greatly benefited by the immediate presence of their mentors such as the leading proponents of impressionism, Childe Hassam and Alden J. Weir. The relationships of the artists were quite personal, and one can see the direct influence of the more famous members upon the lesser-known artists' works. The works are characterized by the uniformly good quality of the paintings. These less famous artists were not only technically competent but demonstrate a flair in depicting the phenomena of nature related to the coastline of Long Island Sound and the inland hills.

Because of the presence of Hassam and Weir, the activities of the Old Lyme group were fairly well documented during the first decade of the twentieth century. Several recent retrospectives and exhibitions (especially the one of Connecticut impressionism) have increased the exposure of works by the lesser-known artists and have increased the availability of examples. Auction houses and dealers have persuaded the descendants of these artists to offer portions or entire estates for sale. When a large body of paintings became available the technical skill and consistency of the painter could be appreciated. William Chadwick was an excellent example.

The Hoosiers

The artistic heritage of the state of Indiana is truly remarkable and, to many, unexpected. The legacy in the visual arts in that state has historical precedent. Before the 1893 Chicago Colombian Exposition, the Indianapolis School of Art had existed for over a decade. A number of native sons such as T.C. Steele and William Forsyth had been to Munich for their formal training and returned to establish a school of landscape painting in the state capital. A significant and influential art publication, *Modern Art*, was begun in Indianapolis in 1890. It was considered one of the most influential American art periodicals for that day.

The Indiana painters were well represented in the monumental 1893 Colombian Exposition. Steele's landscapes were particularly noted, and the influential critic, Hamlin Garland, commented favorably about the "Hoosier School." He praised them for their glorification of the countryside of the heartland of America. Garland had repeatedly called for a truly Americanized response of impressionism and opined that the Indiana movement was closer to achieving this goal than any group or colony existent at that time.

In examining the historical precedent of the Indiana art movement, one cannot help but be impressed with the fact that it not only involved Indianapolis by mid-century with its beginnings of urban development and its amenitites of the state capital, but the small towns and villages as well. The artistic style was Munich inspired by tradition, but once these painters

Tinker Place, *T.C. Steele, 21" x 25", oil on canvas.*

Flying a Kite, *Adam Emory Albright (1862 – 1957), 31" x 38¾", oil on canvas.*

returned to their native state they adapted whatever technique they felt was best to portray the natural beauty that surrounded them; many embraced a form of modern impressionism.

By the time Steele, Forsyth, and their colleagues arrived in Munich, Frank Duveneck and William Merritt Chase were gone. Rather than the cosmopolitan experience of that Bavarian city, they chose the rural existence of Schleisshiem, a nearby village. Completing their training, they returned to Indianapolis but soon began depicting the open landscape that still occupied the areas within the limits of their state capital, such as Pheasant Run, and sought as a challenge to capture the surrounding countryside of Brookville.

These works began as broadly painted tonal landscapes with distinctive Barbizon influence often depicting peasant genre by Steele, Forsyth, Otto Stark, and J. Otis Adams. These painters later developed a modified impressionist style which they felt enabled them to best depict the beau-

Winter Landscape, *George Herbert Baker, 30" x 40", oil on canvas.*

ties of rural Indiana. What began as introspective, mood-producing interpretation of nature became a vibrant and scintillating application of pigment with loosely formed brushstrokes. The subject was the landscape of Indiana, and the occasional figures were almost accessories which provided animation to the composition.

Otto Stark in 1895 traced what he felt to be the evolution of style of the "Hoosier School."

"Paint was first applied in the Munich manner with predominance of black and brown later to be modified by tonalism." This was described as the gray movement of an almost monochromatic palette. Recognizing that many of the elements they wished to portray were not captured by this limited color range, several of their group turned to the high key, "white" movement — described by some as the "glare aesthetic." Stark noted that the final stylistic form of many of the Hoosier School was that of the "impressionism of sunlight." Several art historians have stated that the Indiana painters were the first regional group in America to work in the impressionistic aesthetic.

Sugar & Spice, *Wayman Adams, 20" oval, oil on canvas.*

Following the full spectrum of exposure of the leaders of the Hoosier group in 1893, there was a well organized, well orchestrated exhibition of their work held in the Dennison Hotel in Indianapolis in 1894. They expanded the collection of paintings which then traveled to Chicago, where the exhibition was quite well received both by the public and art critics. Indianapolis was declared the most significant reservoir of art after Chicago in the Midwest. It was noted that "light floods the Kankakee marshes as well as the meadows of Giverny and that the Muscatatuck has its subtleties of color as does the Seine." Indiana artists were active in organizations as well. They were among the founders of the Cosmopolitan Art Club in Chicago (1895) and the influential Society of Western Artists (1896).

In 1897 Steele and his colleagues purchased the Butler house in the Indianapolis suburb of Brookville just beside the Whitewater River. Here they were able to create a native pedagogical form of outdoor landscape instruction not unlike that of their contemporary and fellow Indianian, William Merritt Chase, at Shinnecock on Long Island. Under the mentorship of Steele, these artists were concerned with the presentation of that which was distinctly Indiana; the local color was their raison d'etre. They were the first group in the western United States to use the local conditions in pure, clean color to delineate its natural charm. These Hoosier artists achieved a level of professionalism that went beyond the provincial and produced a sufficiently uniform but distinct style of painting that could be characterized as a school.

In 1895 the art patron John Herron's estate became available and from that a full-fledged art school and repository for works of Indiana artists became possible. By 1906 the present Herron Museum had been constructed. An ambitious and important collaborative project was begun by the artists in Indianapolis in the mid-1890s. This was a group effort to paint murals in

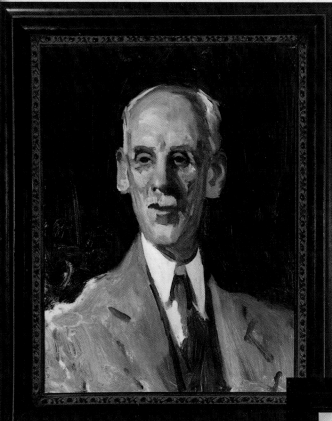

Portrait of Fellow Artist, *Wayman Adams, 22" x 18", oil on canvas.*

Brown County Landscape,
*Adolph Robert Shulz, 32" x 40",
oil on canvas, signed in lower
right corner, original frame.*

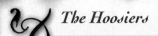
the various public areas and the wards of the Indianapolis City Hospital. Not only did the project interest the public in the work of these painters but it galvanized the resolve of the artists to have a distinct Indiana school.

As has been previously emphasized, the artistic movement in Indiana was characterized by activity throughout the state. Many of the artists had come from the rural towns and villages. Suprisingly these isolated areas had an active community organization such as the Federation of Women's Clubs to support the arts. Richmond, a town of 25,000, founded an art association in 1897, and Bundy had an active school of instruction at the turn of the century. Bundy, Baker, and Eyden achieved state and modest national fame for their work.

The Brown County Art colony could be properly characterized as a phenomenon of nature. The nature was the allure of the undulating hills and the slow moving creeks of that locale. Adolph Shulz discovered Brown County and the village of Nashville at the turn of the century. Shortly after 1900, T.C. Steele arrived with his second wife, Selma, purchased over 200 acres west of the county seat, and built

Sunset in the Pines, *Adolph Robert Shulz, 30" x 30".*

Stream in Brown County, *Adolph Robert Shulz, 34" x 46".*

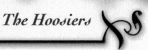

Brown County Landscape, *Alberta Shulz, 25" x 30", oil on board.*

a home, studio, and cottages for fellow artists. Adolph Shultz and his artist wife, Ada, came in 1907 to permanently settle.

Most of the artists lived in the county seat of Nashville. They enjoyed the collegiality of residing in close proximity with others of like interest and activity. The Brown County Artists Guild became quite active in the early decades of this century and remains a viable entity at present. The landscapes around Nashville consist of wooded rolling hills. In the valleys are meandering creeks. In this farming community, fences, barns, and wooden outbuildings abound. At certain times of day in the spring and summer a haze rests just above the tree line. This atmospheric phenomena has repeatedly been portrayed by the group of Brown County landscape impressionists.

A number of the better known landscape artists of the Brown County colony are included in this chapter. Several painted there revealing the natural beauty that has captured the minds of both artists and collectors for over half a century.

Study for Mural, Indianapolis City Hospital: Children's Ward, *Otto Stark, 12" x 22", oil on board.*

Covered Bridge, *V.J. Cariani,*
25" x 30", oil on canvas.

Woman by Stream, *William*
Forsyth, 22" x 20", mixed media.

Indiana Landscape,
*George Mess, 25" x 30",
oil on canvas.*

Lady in an Arbor,
*Clifton Wheeler, 20" x
24", oil on canvas.*

Autumn Harvest, *Anna Hasselman, 20" x 24", oil on canvas, signed in pencil on reverse.*

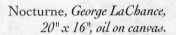

Nocturne, *George LaChance, 20" x 16", oil on canvas.*

Indiana Woodland: Forest Interior, *William Arnold Eyden, 30" x 40", oil on canvas.*

Peonies, *Sybil H. Conglin,*
25" x 30", oil on canvas.

Self Portrait, *L.O. Griffith, 22"*
x 30", oil on canvas.

Colonies of the South

For years the paintings by nineteenth century Southern artists were generally unappreciated outside the South. Many art historians were of the opinion that indigenous artistic expression in the South was limited to a few native portrait painters, migrant artists who depicted subjects of the region, or self-taught genre painters. Only as a documentation of Southern manners and lifestyle were some of the "Southern" works deemed important.

The South (and in some respects, the nation) has been more aware of this genre by the exhibitions arranged by the Virginia Museum of Art in Richmond; Artists of the South; The Robert Coggins Collection; as well as the founding of the Morris Museum of Art in Augusta, Georgia; and the Roger Houston Museum in New Orleans. Historians Jesse Poesch, Michael McCue, and Buck Pennington have published excellent texts and certain dealers such as Rob Hicklen, Robert Mayo, Nowell Guffey, Jim Williams, and Dave Knoke, have had exhibitions,

prepared brochures and catalogs, and published monographs that have greatly increased awareness as well.

Examples of the work of these Southern artists reflect regional tendencies and have universally desirable qualities as well. Even more compelling are those images that particularly depict some unique characteristic of the life and time of the South. As art collectors

Southern Landscape,
*artist unknown, 25" x 30",
oil on board.*

Congaree Swamp, South Carolina, *21" x 24", oil on canvas. Sherman changed his march to Columbia because of the physical barrier. James Southern collection.*

have become more aware of the quality and importance of the nineteenth and early twentieth century Southern artists, many have incorporated representative examples into their collections.

In the nineteenth century it was fashionable for aspiring Southern artists to study at the Art Students' League, the National Academy of Design in New York, or the Pennsylvania Academy of Fine Arts, before returning to their native South to ply their trade.

The South never enjoyed the phenomenon of established schools of national and international acclaim (The Corcoran is an arguable exception).

There were no art colonies that would rival those at Old Lyme, Woodstock, Shinnecock, or New Hope. There were, however, a number of artists living and painting together in Savannah, New Orleans, and Charleston. These artists benefitted from the shared knowledge and sometimes diverse experience of the members of their group. Some traveled widely to acquire their skills, such as Hattie Saussy who trained at the New York School of Fine Arts, the National Academy of Design, the Art Students' League, and the Academe Julian in Paris. Others remained at home, such as Christopher P.H. Murphy of Savannah, who was a ship's chandler and a very accomplished watercolorist.

The Charleston artists were never an official group but the leaders Alfred Hutty, Elizabeth O'Neill Verner, Anna Heyward Taylor, and Alice Ravenal Huger Smith shared their knowledge.

Florida Scene, *William Lester Stevens, 1888 – 1969, 21" x 24", watercolor.*

Southern Mansion, *A.C. Howland, oil on canvas. Private collection.*

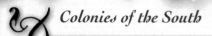

Other artists working contemporaneously in Charleston include Edward Harleston a free, black artist, Virginia Chisolm, Rufus Zogbaum, Charles Bryan, Emma Gilchrist, Mae Paine, and Eola Willis. Often they improved their work through mutual critique and analysis without the benefit of formal training.

A number of artists painted portraits on commission for their livelihood while executing other paintings of different subject matter, such as landscapes and genre works, as evidence of their own self-expression. Many taught in the fledgling Southern art schools.

During their vacations, they painted while traveling

Florida Landscape, *George Higgins, 10" x 14",*
oil on canvas. Loan to Center for School Leadership
Development, University of North Carolina.

Robert E. Lee, *C.W. Cox, 20"*
oval, painted from life (ca. 1860s).
James Historical collection.

throughout the South. In the summer they might join artists from other schools, such as the Art Institute of Chicago, in Asheville, Tryon, or Burnsville in the North Carolina mountains. Most of these artists painted traditional landscapes, but a few embraced elements of both luminism and tonalism. The latter method of pigment application was particularly well suited to the depiction of atmospheric conditions of the lowland South with its unique moist humid climate, moss-laden trees, and the mixture of diminished sunlight and fog in the swamps and bayous.

Some Southern artists of the nineteenth and early twentieth centuries maintained residences in both the North and South. Their work in each location often reflected the environment and the colleagues with whom they were associated.

The Glory Road,
Rachael Hartley,
24" x 20", oil on board.

Trailer Park, Hendersonville, North Carolina, *James Pearce Wharton (1893 – 1963), 25" x 30", oil on board. Wharton was born in Waterloo, South Carolina, and trained in Paris. He was an artist for the* Atlanta Journal *and chair of the art department at University of Maryland. This is an example of regional subject matter. James Southern collection.*

Chopping, *Francis Dobbs Speight, 25" x 30", oil on canvas. Private collection.*

Bayou, *Knute Heldner, 16" x 20", oil on canvas, c. 1925. Courtesy of Roger H. Ogden, New Orleans, LA.*

French Quarter Tenement House, *Clarence Millet, 26" x 22", oil on canvas, 1935. Courtesy of Roger Ogden.*

Florida Scene, *George Higgins, 11½" x 14", oil on canvas.*

Southern Women Artists (1840 – 1940)

In the past several decades, there has been an increasing realization of the contribution and legacy of Southern women artists painting in the late nineteenth and early twentieth centuries. Several recent exhibitions of Southern paintings have demonstrated the skill and creativity of these women painters who, for many reasons, went relatively unacclaimed in their lifetimes. The establishment of the National Museum of Women in the Arts in Washington has also increased our knowledge of the contributions of these skilled women and well-trained painters. Despite these events, Southern women painters have still been and remain among the accomplished and yet relatively unappreciated. Certain advantaged Southern women artists trained at the Pennsylvania Academy of Fine Arts or the Art Students League or in the colonies at Shinnecock on Long Island or Woodstock, New York.

Multiple social factors were operative in the South during this time period (1840 – 1940) that negatively influenced the opportunities for women artists. Some were cultural, others economic and political but none were operative alone. This section is intended to demonstrate the abilities of these Southern women artists and to propose that they are to be admired and very collectible.

Elegant Lady, *Marian Lane, 23½" x 18", oil on canvas, Washington, D.C., on loan U.S. Department of State Art in Embassies Program.*

Due to the responsibilities thrust upon them by the War Between the States and its aftermath of reconstruction an entire generation of Southern male leadership was either eliminated, physically and emotionally compromised, or diverted from their occupation and industry for the years before, during, and after the Civil War. The women of the South were thrust into this void and became the administrators of the land and the managers of Southern businesses. Often the impoverished families depended upon the women to earn what little money they could to sustain the entire household. Maria Howard Weeden, as an example, sold her paintings and poetry to support her widowed mother and sister. Today there is a museum in Huntsville, Alabama, celebrating the work of this artist.

The imposed loneliness, struggle, and heartache of the War and Reconstruction for the remainder of the nineteenth century seemed to provide the source that might decades later be manifest in their poetry, fiction, and occasionally the fashioning of visual images. The sense of place and homage to tradition is evidenced by some of these works. Some represent memories of people and events from decades

Still Life (Roses), *Marjorie Phillips, 30" x 25", oil on canvas. Marjorie Phillips was the wife of collector and scholar Duncan Phillips.*

In Repose, *Isabel Cohen, 20" x 16", watercolor. On loan to U.S. Embassy, Helsinki, Finland.*

earlier. As these circumstances become more stable, the environment began to provide additional opportunities of expression for women and the creation of the paintings was a venue taken by some Southern females in the post-Civil War era as well as the early decades of the twentieth century to express their creativity.

The women of Southern cities such as Charleston, New Orleans, Savannah, and Washington were the leaders. Although not ever achieving the organization of a proper colony or school of painting often symbiotic relationships advanced the skills of the individual artists as well as their recognition. They fed upon group creativity. It allowed sharing of whatever academic training that some of the women artists had received.

The Southern women artists selectively recalled memories of the black/white relationships and often emphasized the quaintness of black attire and the

characteristic manners that represented the separateness of the somewhat stylized black and white

My Aunt, *Ella Hergeshimer, 20" x 16",*
oil on canvas, Gallatin, Tennessee.
James Southern collection.

Lillies, *Mayna Avent,*
24" x 18", pastel.

lifestyles. This imagery will be discovered. These images created by women artists were not meant to be dramatic social statements but rather an expression of sadness for an era that was a more tranquil and pleasant period of their world. Artists such as Celine Baekeland, Elizabeth O'Neill Verner, Mary Cabiness, and Mayna Avent, early in the twentieth century painted universally compelling images of the lifestyle of Southern blacks. Comparable paintings by their male counterparts, William Aiken Walker for example, are highly acclaimed throughout the United States and in Europe yet only Verner has achieved even regional fame. The works of fellow Charlestonian Alice Smith have become very desirable and expensive.

Certain of the Southern female artists remained in the North after training or in Europe and had their work appreciated nationally and internationally before returning to the South. Some also returned periodically to New York or Philadelphia and exhibited with their mentors who were acclaimed and famous.

Church on Hill, *Kathleen Bartlett, 24" x 20". Kathleen Bartlett was the wife of Paul Bartlett, who studied with Henri and Sloan. She painted in an Impressionist manner. Farmer/James collection.*

On the Wando, *Fannie Mahon King, 20" x 24", oil on canvas. Private collection.*

A traditional interest of women of the South has been that of gardening and flower arrangement. Some are noted for their scholarly botanical studies and many for their still life paintings. Paintings celebrating the fauna and flora of the South are common subject matter for the women artists. This subject had such an attraction and a ready made audience of collectors that artists such as Isabel Cohen, who trained in New York City with Robert Henri and John Sloan of "The Eight," upon returning to the South changed both their subject matter from the urban scenes of city streets to flower gardens and their technique from the broad brush strokes and somber palettes of post-Achcan realism to bright landscapes rendered in an impressionistic manner. Other Southern women artists modified their technique only slightly to accommodate the reentry into their native environment.

A number of the Charlestonians had relatives in Philadelphia, making this a popular city in which to have the young, aspiring women artists study. The knowledge of their experience outside the South was brought back to South Carolina, enriching the art world in their native city. Emma Gilchrist studied in Philadelphia and was exposed to Martha Walter, and her sun-filled beach scenes with colorful parasols and attire reflect the subjects that earned national and international acclaim for her mentor. This sort of circumstances occurred a number of times in the South.

Travel to Europe for extended periods of time was something many aspiring Southern women artists could not afford. The living conditions were considered improper as well as problematical. Living in a communal loft in Paris was not a socially acceptable option for the women. Men were much more likely to acquire some income from temporary employment than their female contemporaries were. Thus, foreign study was much more difficult for the women.

In Alabama, *Anne Goldthwaite, 25½" x 30", oil on canvas. Private collection.*

Most of the teachers of art were men providing an inherent gender bias. It was generally considered that the women following their training would not pursue their art as a career. Often their efforts were not taken seriously. Exhibiting their works in important venues was also difficult for the women. The selection committees were dominated by men, as were the juries. A number of the women had very successful exhibition records but they were the exception, especially if you consider the most prestigious exhibitions.

A few women artists, although not natives of the South, painted in the Southern cities and to some extent the countryside or in nationally well-known vacation areas such as Florida. Charleston proved an especially attractive venue for these women artists. Several made their reputation outside the South. However, a body of work was created by these women which provided a clearly identifiable contribution to the knowledge and experience of native Southern culture.

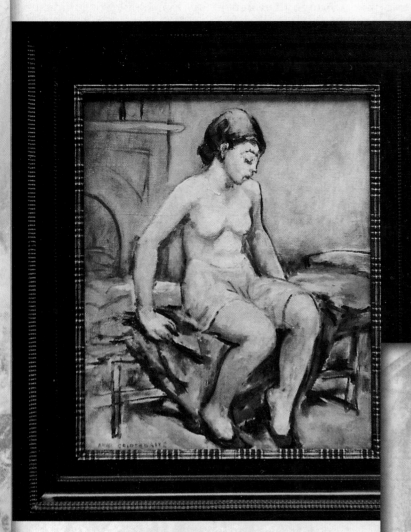

Nude in Interior, *Anne Goldthwaite (1869 – 1944), 22" x 18", oil on canvas, signed lower left. Courtesy of Knoke Galleries of Atlanta.*

Young Female, *Hattie Saussy, 20" x 18", oil on canvas. Private collection.*

The women artists of the South (1840 – 1940) have always been involved with making images that were intimately woven into the fabric of Southern society. Their contributions in other areas of Southern culture probably enhanced their stature as artists. Whatever the reason, their belated success has now contributed to an atmosphere in which Southern women artists are encouraged to fashion images that will provide lasting evidence of the continued legacy.

Bridge in Gardens, *Mae Payne, 30" x 38".*

Brevard, *North Carolina, Elizabeth Chant, 12" x 16", oil on canvas. Farmer/James collection.*

Motherhood, *Anne Goldthwaite (1869 – 1944), 20" x 16", oil on canvas, signed lower left. Courtesy of Knoke Galleries of Atlanta.*

Western North Carolina Landscape, *Nena Morrow, 16" x 20", oil on canvas. Farmer/James collection.*

French Quarter Court-
yard, *Alberta Kinsey, 19½" x
15½", oil on panel. Courtesy
of Roger Houston Ogden,
New Orleans.*

French Quarter Courtyard with
Standing Cistern, *Julia Massie, 11¼"
x 16¼", oil on canvas, circa 1890, signed
lower right. Courtesy of Roger Houston
Ogden, New Orleans.*

Cabin and Well (West Virginia or Virginia), *K.A. Smith, 22" x 26".*

Southern Shack, Rachel Hartley Grandaughter, *George Inness, 25" x 22½", oil on canvas.*

English Garden, *Mabel Pugh, 24" x 20", oil on canvas. Pugh won a traveling fellowship to study in Europe. This work was from that experience. Farmer/James collection.*

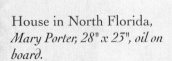

House in North Florida, *Mary Porter, 28" x 23", oil on board.*

Isle of Palms, *watercolor, Alice Ravenal Huger Smith. Private collection.*

Farm Cabin, *Eunice Clayton Pritchett, 23½" x 21", oil on board.*

Landscape, *B. Symmes,*
19½" x 14½". Private collection.

Isle of Palms, *Iola Willis,*
29¼" x 21¾", oil on canvas.
Farmer/James collection.

Western North Carolina Landscape, *Freda Ledford, 20" x 24", oil on canvas.*

Landscape,
*Virginia
Chisholm, 22" x
29½", oil on
board.*

The Portrayal of African-Americans in Southern Painting (1850 – 1950)

Art in the South for the most part, from the pre-Civil War period through World War II mirrored images generally fashioned throughout America. However, because of the Southern sense of place and the intimacy of black-white relationships in the region, there were certain identifiable differences from contemporary paintings fashioned in other parts of the country.

From mid-nineteenth century until Reconstruction, blacks were largely dehumanized in American works of art. It was as if blacks were not given individual identities by the artists but were illus-

Mythological Figures, *Robert Loftin Newman, 8½" x 11", oil on canvas. Private collection.*

Pickets Mill, New Hope Church, Georgia, *Wilbur Kurtz (1882 – 1967), 21" x 15", gouache on artist board, signed, dated 1915 lower right. Courtesy of Knoke Galleries of Atlanta.*

trated more as caricatures. Their skin color was usually depicted as coal black and the thick African-American ruby lips were supported by a protruding set of overly large teeth. This created an almost subhuman primate appearance. The contrived and exaggerated physical features and the activities engaged in by the blacks in these paintings cast them as primate like buffoons and not true members of the American social establishment.

Sambo, Top Hat, and Zip Coon were cultural generalizations imposed upon blacks by white society and served as the inspiration and partial justification for black images seen in paintings rendered during this time period. These restrictive stereotypes relegated blacks to dehumanizing roles and added to the justification of the white denial of their humanity.

As one might imagine, during the Civil War or as some term, the War of Northern Aggression, much of the social fabric of the United States was undone and rearranged. In the early years following the Civil War, changes in depiction of blacks in paintings did occur. However, by the mid-1870s the hardships and frustrations brought about by the unanticipated complexity of reconstruction were often expressed in art by an idealized nostalgia for the pre-war relationships and structure between the races as whites chose to remember it. The images during this period depicted the pre-Civil

Bull Durham ad. Private collection.

Top Hat, Maria Howard Weeden, *water-color with pen. Weeden was an artist and poet from Huntsville, Alabama.*

War years as a time of harmony and tranquility between whites and blacks. While this characterization was certainly not entirely accurate, it did have a measure of truth and was a popular myth in the South as well as to a lesser extent in the rest of the country. Memory was unintentionally selective and certain symbolic black-white relationships were given more prominence than they deserved.

Artists painting in the South, like William Aiken Walker, presented a meticulous but one-sided imagery of black life, pre and post Civil War. His carpetbagger blacks became an icon provoking an unexpected death of social commentary after the regression of the post-war nostalgia. Walker's later nostalgic images were rare and equally as popular among whites in both the North and South. His larger depictions of plantation life have fetched vast sums from museums and collectors despite their often simplistic and inaccurate portrayal of black life.

Very little changed in the depiction of blacks in art from the time of reconstruction until the urbanization of America. The response from existent contemporary social change did not begin until the last decade of the nineteenth and first decade of the twentieth century. The alterations of the social structure by the urbanization movement in America from an agrarian base to industrial/urban life led to changes in the status of blacks.

Boy Sniffing Rose, *W.A. Walker, 16" oil on plate.*

Black Male, *W.A. Walker, 10¼" x 7¼", oil on panel (board).*

The images depicting blacks gradually evolved to reflect their changing status and came to affect their portrayal in areas of the South as well. Blacks were sometimes dignified in paintings with a clear individuality and their physical characteristics were not nearly as simian and demeaning as they had been in the middle to late nineteenth century. These images were more representative of their true status in the social order and were certainly more representative of the truth than the very nostalgic paintings composed during the period immediately post Civil War and early during Reconstruction.

The effect of the First World War and other foreign conflicts of the early decades of the twentieth century seemed to have little effect upon the artistic depiction of blacks. However, movements in the art world were to have significant effects, in particular the emergence of realism. The Eight, later enlarged as the Ashcan School, was a very influential artistic force through the first four decades of the twentieth century in American art. These Ashcan artists celebrated physical labor, which was the primary activity of blacks. In some ways the emphasis upon the human physicality in this genre elevated the status of the images of the black male body. The paintings of Robert Henri, George Luks, and especially George Wesley Bellows legitimized the unclad upper male torso. At the same time black athletes were gaining national and international recogni-

Rosie, *Agnes Richmond (1870 – 1964), 26" x 21½", oil on canvas, signed upper right, dated 1928. Courtesy of Knoke Galleries of Atlanta.*

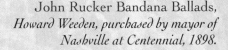

John Rucker Bandana Ballads, *Howard Weeden, purchased by mayor of Nashville at Centennial, 1898.*

tion and these became subjects for paintings by artists working in this genre.

The Ashcan School's influence was at first mainly in the Northern cities where these artists painted alleyways, trash cans, street urchins, and urban construction as well as city squalor. Their particular form of realism also had a profound effect upon the rest of American art inspiring the regionalists such as Grant Wood, Thomas Hart Benton, and Eugene Healan Thomason. This influence is seen in the characterization of blacks in art of the 1920s and 1930s by Southern artists. Christopher Murphy, an aristocratic Southerner, painted historical black churches as specific sites and not the formulaic depiction of a structure beside a moss-laden oak and a black graveyard as Alfred Heber Hutty often did. He dignified the black architectural legacy as well as the people.

While the Harlem Renaissance was in many ways a regional phenomenon, it did give rise in the South to a heightened awareness and appreciation of the inherent creativity and talent among blacks. These artists of the Harlem Renaissance ranged from the self-taught painters to those classically trained like Edwin Harleston of Charleston who studied at

Gentleman by Open Door,
Christopher Murphy (1902 – 1973),
24" x 20", oil on board, signed lower
right. Courtesy of Knoke
Galleries of Atlanta.

Lowland South Carolina Church, *Alfred Hutty, 25" x 30". Farmer/James collection.*

the Boston Museum of Fine Arts (BMFA) School. The images from the black artists characteristically portrayed blacks and their activities in a realistic manner and in some ways legitimized them as subjects for fine art expression. As the opportunities for training at schools such as the Art Students' League, the Pennsylvania Academy of Fine Arts (PAFA), the BMFA, and the National Academy of Design the acceptance in fine art circles of their work and in juried exhibitions broadened the scope of treatment of blacks as subjects.

The Works Progress Agency (WPA) had a particular subagency to create images through paintings. Some 3,000 "artists" were hired and they produced 10,000 works of art featuring a vast latitude of subjects. At the height of its activity and influence, the WPA allowed a great deal of artistic freedom for its painters. Thus, there was a spectrum of black images that came from that effort depending upon the artist's personal intent and were not as dictated by social influences as in previous times.

Certain blacks were gaining national recognition for their achievements outside the arts, entertainment, and sports; and black artists were gaining confidence in depicting fellow blacks in responsible and successful roles with little fear of rejection by the establishment based upon a bias for racial subject matter.

As black artists gained in national reputation, they became confident not only in portraying accomplished blacks but everyday workers as well. Their images gave the black figures dignity. At the same time, all artists found that the public was now

Geddes Cooper, *Christopher Murphy, Jr., Savannah, Georgia, 22" x 27¼", oil on canvas, circa 1930 – 1940. Farmer/James collection*

Negro Settlement (Biloxi, Mississippi), *Ethel Conney, 23¼" x 28".*

accepting of images celebrating successful and powerful blacks. While there exists some disparity in the depiction of successful blacks compared to whites, great progress has been made and in the character of American art, in general, has benefitted by this change.

One affirmation of the value of art depicting blacks in a positive manner has been the reaction of the large collecting public. The single icons of post-Civil War black life by William Aiken Walker now regularly fetch $15,000 to $20,000 and a large plantation scene recently brought several hundred thousand dollars. A representative work by Alfred Hutty or Elizabeth O'Neill Verner of black life in Charleston sells for $20,000 to $45,000. The works of black genre by Christopher Murphy, Jr. have a wide range from $5,000 to $15,000 and Maria Howard Weeden (the rare Huntsville, Alabama, artist) from $10,000 to $15,000. There is a great deal of present interest in Edwin White's documentation of black religion in the South in the 1930 – 1940s. Certain black artists like Robert Duncanson, Henry Ossawa Tanner, Will Henry Johnson, Edwin Harleston, and Romaire Beardon through efforts of the Harmon Foundation and public exhibitions have become appropriately recognized nationally. Works by Tanner and Bearden sell for over $100,000 and Harleston $15,000 to $20,000 but they are very rare.

Art texts with black imagery reflect the improved status of blacks in American life, but the traditional images of this earlier period discussed here remind us

Mammy in New Orleans Courtyard,
Wayman Adams, 24" x 20", oil on canvas.

Lady with a Basket of Flowers,
Alfred Hutty, watercolor. Hutty was originally from Woodstock, New York. Farmer/James collection.

of the complexity of this issue and a place which we do not wish to return. The evolution of black imagery in America has not been one of consistent progress but its impetus has been forward and a positive reflection of social changes and public attitudes. The value of painting visualizing images of African-Americans have increased markedly in value and because rarity is a fac-

tor should continue to do so.

Acknowledgement

I am appreciative of the thoughts of colleagues David Driskill, Kevin Grogan, Dave Knoke, the late Bob Coggins, Rob Hicklin, Jesse Poesch, John Shelton Reed, and Rick Powell in my development of this section.

Tenament Shacks, *Elizabeth O'Neill Verner,*
21" x 28", pastel.

Black Female, *Neola Harwood,*
16" x 12", pencil drawing.

Tent Revival, *Edwin White, 25" x 35", oil on board. White was an instructor in the Ringling School in Sarasota. In the 1920s – 1930s he painted images of black religion in the South. Farmer/James collection.*

Young Black Male, *Augusta Oelschig, 22" x 18", oil on canvas.*

Feeding the Chickens,
*Clarence Reeder, 22" x 16¼", oil
on canvas. Compassion and
humor. Note the attire of the child.
Farmer/James collection.*

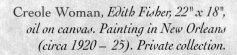

Creole Woman, *Edith Fisher, 22" x 18",
oil on canvas. Painting in New Orleans
(circa 1920 – 25). Private collection.*

Cotton Pickin, *Jesse Rhodes, 16" x 20", oil on board. Rhodes was from Alabama (circa 1930 – 1935). Farmer/James collection.*

The Cook, *Edwin Harelston, 22" x 16", oil on board. Harleston, from Charleston, South Carolina, was a graduate of the Boston Museum of Fine Arts School. He later embraced realism to produce compelling portraits. Farmer/James collection.*

Young Island Black, *circa 1899.*

The Concert Singer, *W.A. Cooper, 24½"
x 21¾", oil on board. Cooper, a theologian
who also read the law, was largely self-
taught. Cooper illustrated his text on negro
life in the South with a series of portraits.
Farmer/James collection.*

Crabbing in Blue (Salt)
Creek, *Rufus Zogbaum,
8" x 10¾", mixed media.
Farmer/James collection.*

Preaching Day, *Winona Bell,*
16½" x 18¾", watercolor.
Private colletion.

The Red Cabins,
Mabel Cabiness, 22¼"
x 19¾", oil on canvas.

Black Cabin Scene, *Elizabeth O'Neill Verner, 16⅛" x 20⅛", pastel/panel, signed lower right. Courtesy of Knoke Galleries of Atlanta.*

Black Cabin Scene, Palatka, *Anthony Thieme, 25" x 30", oil on canvas, signed lower left. Courtesy of Knoke Galleries of Atlanta.*

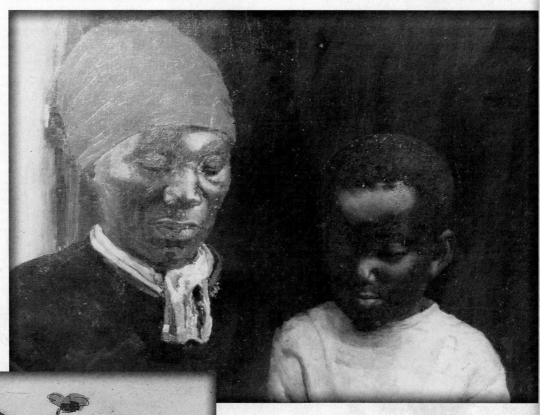

Grandmother with Child (The Reading Lesson), *A.C. Healon, 56" x 40", oil on canvas. Farmer/James collection.*

Negro Boy, *George Henry Clements, 13" x 10", watercolor on paper, circa 1890, signed lower right. Courtesy of Roger H. Ogden, New Orleans, LA.*

Church Social, Geor-
gia, *Nell Choate Jones
(1879 – 1981), 25" x
30", oil on canvas, signed
lower left. Courtesy of
Knoke Galleries of
Atlanta.*

Baptism, *Eugene
White, 26" x 28", oil on
canvas. Farmer/James
collection.*

The Old Solider, *Mayna T.
Avent, 20" x 16", watercolor.
Farmer/James collection.*

Cotton Fields, Coffey
County, Alabama,
*Jessie Rhodes, 16" x 20",
oil on board.*

Mammy's Prophecy,
*Harry Roseland (1868 –
1950), 20" x 30", oil on canvas, signed upper right.
Courtesy of Knoke Galleries
of Atlanta.*

Two Figures, *Robert Loftin
Newman, 8" x 10¼", oil on
canvas. Private collection.*

 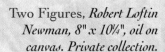

Landscape Painting in Tennessee

Today it is hard to imagine that slightly over a century ago there existed no formal schools of art in Tennessee, no proper museums, and little financial reward for painters unless they engaged in portraiture. Most of the aspiring artists did not have sufficient wealth to travel elsewhere for formal training.

Lloyd Branson, a Knoxville native, was one of the earliest painters to seek training outside the state, first at the National Academy of Design (NAD) in New York and later in Europe. Branson (1853 – 1925) was a student at the Academy in 1873 – 1874 which would have made him a contemporary of Frederich Church, one of America's leading artists of heroic landscapes and the Hudson River School previously discussed. Branson was probably taught by Lemuel Wilmarth and he won a traveling fellowship which allowed him to travel to France and be taught by Barbizon artists at Fountainbleau.

Upon his return in 1876, Branson began his mentorship of local artists and raised art standards in all East Tennessee by his influence. This group of disciples later formed the Nicholson Art League. His students included Catherine and Eleanor Wiley and Beauford Delaney. Although Branson's early work reflected both his academic training in his portraits and the Barbizon aesthetic in his landscapes, his later paintings reflect the influence of impressionism.

To a lesser extent Willie Betty Newman (1863 – 1935) of Nashville and Mary Magdalene Solari (1849 – 1929) of Memphis inspired artists in their regions. Newman studied at the Cincinnati Art Academy where Duveneck and DeCamp taught and several of the founders of the Taos School trained. She also studied in Paris at the Academie Julian for three years enabled by a scholarship she received. She remained in France for over a decade and exhibited at the Paris Salon in the 1890s. When she returned to Nashville around the turn of the century, she founded the Newman School of Art. The curriculum was based on her experience in Paris much as Tarbell and Benson at the Boston Museum of Fine Arts School had done.

In the early decades of the twentieth century, a number of artists were practicing in middle Ten-

Irises, *Eleanor McAdoo Wiley*, 25" x 30", oil on canvas, Knoxville, Tennessee.

nessee. Cornelius Hankins studied with Robert Henri in St. Louis but his inspiration for landscape painting came from his study under the great impressionist, William Merritt Chase. Hankins moved back to Nashville in 1904 and supported his family by commissioned portraits for the next 40 years. He rendered a number of landscapes and was especially noted for his cornfields following the harvest. He also painted the formal gardens of mansions in the Belle Meade area. Later artists such as Bertha Herbert Potter, Ella Hergenshiemer, Sue Joy, and Mayna Avent painted in Nashville and created a body of competent landscapes.

Ella Sophonisba Hergesheimer (1873 – 1943) was an accomplished artist when she came to Nashville due to a commission to paint the portrait of a founder of Vanderbilt University. She had studied two years at the Philadelphia School of Design and four years at the Pennsylvania Academy of Fine Arts (PAFA). She was exposed to Cecelia Beaux and William Merritt Chase at the PAFA. Hergesheimer became an accomplished lithographer and did produce landscapes but was noted for her examples of modified portraiture.

Bertha Herbert Potter (1895 – 1949) trained at the Ringling School in Sarasota, Florida. She exhibited in group shows at the National Academy of Design (NAD) in the 1930s as well as the PAFA and the American Women Painters Society (AWPS). She was best known for her depiction of African-Americans but her Barbizon landscapes and those outdoor gardens after she was in Taos, New Mexico, demonstrate her painterly abilities. Potter, from a prominent banking family, used her influence to promote the arts in Nashville. In 1925 she arranged for a Grand Central Galley exhibition at the Parthenon and was one of the representatives who accepted the important gift of the James Cowan Collection of major American paintings to the City of Nashville. Potter and others recognized the significance of this collection which included landscapes by such notables as Sanford Robinson Gifford, George Inness, Thomas Moran, and Elliott Daingerfield.

Mayna Treanor Avent (1868 – 1959) was born at Tulip Grove mansion across from Andrew Jackson's Hermitage. She studied in Cincinnati and later at the Academie Julian in Paris. She taught in Nashville but exhibited her still lifes and landscapes throughout America.

Landscape, *Bertha Herbert Potter, 25" x 30", oil on board.*

Sue Joy was born in Nashville in 1903 and studied first at Sophie Newcomb College and later at the Art Institute in Chicago. Following this she studied in Paris with Leger and Marchand. She was primarily a landscape artist depicting familiar local scenes.

While this group of artists was not sufficiently cohesive to constitute what might accurately be described as a colony or a school, they benefitted from their mutual interest. These painters increased the awareness and support of the arts in Nashville and in middle Tennessee. They along with Cornelius Hankins painted the portraits of wealthy Nashvillians and encouraged their support of the arts.

Chattanooga in East Tennessee did not have as many practicing artists as did Knoxville and Nashville, but there were a number in the surrounding areas capturing the beauty of the Appalachian region and the rivers and lakes of East Tennessee. Thomas Campbell had been a minister in Maryville, Tennessee, and after the death of his wife, left for Europe to study art. Upon his return his bright clear landscapes were composed with a distinct European bias and influenced a number of artists painting in East Tennessee such as Louis Jones.

William Posey Silva (1859 – 1948) was a successful businessman in a Chattanooga china and glassware concern. After painting with the colony along the New

England coastal towns of Glouchester and Ogunquit, at age 52 Silva sold his business interests and embarked upon a formal study to become an artist by profession. His clear, sparkling landscapes of southeastern Tennessee rendered in an impressionist manner are among the most compelling depictions of this area.

William Posey Silva and his wife became members of the Carmel Art Colony and moved to California where he lived until his death. Although Silva had received rudimentary training in china painting from his father, he became an artist when he was middle-aged and had a very successful career despite this late beginning.

William Brantly Smith was born in the village of Lacassas, near Murfreesboro, Tennessee. He studied at the William Merritt Chase School in New York. In World War I he worked for the YMCA in Paris and after remained in France painting at Aix-les-Bains. In the 1930s Smith had winter studios in Palm Beach and later taught at the Monteagle Assembly Ground in Tennessee. Much of his work there was burned in a fire. Smith's landscapes have a painterly fashion with elements of impressionism but mainly evidence of the controlled technique of the post-impressionists.

Charles F. Naegele (1857 – 1944) was born in Knoxville and studied with William Sartain and William Merritt Chase. He was a member of the Lotor Club and

Farm in East Tennessee, *Mayna Avent, 28" x 38", oil on canvas.*

exhibited at the NAD (1892 – 1900) and the Charleston Expo (1902). He was a champion of public collections and indexing paintings for archival purposes. Although primarily a portrait artist the rare landscapes of Naegele are quite competent and demonstrate his academic training reflecting also that he remained part of the Establishment by his chosen venues of exhibition.

Eleanor and Catherine Wiley, sisters, were from a prominent Knoxville family with extensive coal rights in East Tennessee. Catherine (1879 – 1958), the better known, studied at the Art Students' League where she was influenced by William Merritt Chase. Her compositions in broken color of females in light, bright settings and dappled sunlight represent triumphs of American impressionism. Catherine Wiley was influential in local art circles and taught at the University of Tennessee, a rather avant garde circumstance for that era. The last three decades of her life, due to poor health, she painted very little.

Eleanor (1876 – 1977), the oldest and lesser known of the two sisters, composed landscapes in an impressionistic manner and was also known for floral still lifes. She had a long career as a portrait artist and was active in local art circles and documented her career through extensive entries in her diary.

The landscape of Tennessee is varied in its topogra-phy and has been captured in the artistry of these native artists as well as by others such as Gilbert Gaul who moved to the state and painted there. In 1904 he was a teacher at Cumberland Female College and moved to Nashville in 1905. Certainly, Gaul created a body of work around the farm he inherited in Van Buren, Tennessee, that has been the subject of two recent exhibitions.

The mountain lakes and streams of East Tennessee rival the natural beauty of any area in America. This geography gives way to the plateau of Middle Tennessee and the rolling farmland depicted in views of wooden fences and rural buildings. The city of Nashville with its parks and stately residences provide the landscape artist interesting and beautiful subject matter. West Tennessee has the numerous streams and rivers emptying into the great Mississippi. Artists like Fred Green Carpenter, born in Nashville, captured life along the banks of that great body of water.

Thus, the state of Tennessee provided images and inspiration for its landscape artists. Certainly, the images created by these artists do not rival those of the Hudson River School in the mid-nineteenth century nor those capturing the heroic vistas of the American West, but they represent a true rendering of a beautiful state. These works also show the important legacy of the native artists.

Lake in East Tennessee, *Thomas Campbell, 20" x 24", oil on canvas.*

Landscape Painting in North Carolina (1850 – 1940)

The natural beauty of the Tar Heel State has inspired both native and visiting artists to compose images reflecting their appreciation of these resources. However, North Carolina has no major schools of art nor collection of artists that one could define as a colony. Despite this circumstance, the beauty of its terrain and its climate, especially in the western North Carolina mountains, attracted painters from many other areas throughout America.

Probably the most recognized landscape artist in North Carolina was W.C.A. Frerichs. Frerichs was born in Ghent, Belgium, and was an accomplished artist before he moved to the United States and settled in New York. He painted in upper New York State with the members of the Hudson River School. By the middle of the nineteenth century he was living in the Piedmont region of North Carolina, teaching at Greensboro College for Women. He made many trips to the North Carolina mountains and summer resort towns and captured these scenes on large canvases composed in the Hudson River manner. Unfortunately, much of his work was lost when the school burned, but the retained extensive notebooks and sketches. Frerichs used these to compose major works depicting North Carolina landscape vistas.

Lake Lure, *L. Griffiths, 22" x 28", oil on board. Griffiths, an Indiana artist, painted in western North Carolina.*

Lake Lure Western North Carolina, *L. Griffiths, 14" x 22", oil on board.*

A number of artists who were trained at the Art Institute of Chicago (AIC) summered in the area around Asheville and Hendersonville. Some lived in the small town of Tryon. One Chicago affiliated artist, Laurence Mazzanovich, was so taken with the pleasant climate and beautiful landscape in this area, that he became a permanent resident of Tryon. By the time Mazzanovich came to Tryon, he had lived in France and had become well known for his tonalist works and nocturnes. Using this technique he and others composed sensitive images of the great Smoky and Blue Ridge Mountains.

Rudolph Ingerle, born in Vienna in 1879, also trained at the AIC and was a resident of Chicago. He was an outstanding colorist and was particularly adept at capturing the vivid contrasts in the foliage that occur in the early fall in western North Carolina, known to tourists as

Tryon Woods, Tryon, North Carolina,
Lawrence Mazzanovich (1872 – 1959),
30" x 30", oil on canvas, c. 1925, signed
lower right. Courtesy of Knoke Galleries of
Atlanta.

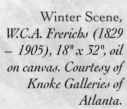

Winter Scene,
W.C.A. Frerichs (1829
– 1905), 18" x 32", oil
on canvas. Courtesy of
Knoke Galleries of
Atlanta.

the "leaf season." Ingerle used a technique of controlled impressionism to create light, often bright images of the beauty of western North Carolina during this specific time of year. He exhibited at the Mint Museum and influenced a number of other artists as did Mazzanovich.

Members from the faculty of the Ringling School in Sarasota held summer classes in Little Switzerland. Julian Lamar and Wilhelm Richter were among the instructors. They were joined by North Carolinians Winfred Conrow and Paul Whitner. Native Paul Bartlett and his

wife Pauline painted North Carolina landscapes around Valle Cruses, as did Eliot Clark. Paul Bartlett, best known as a sculptor, trained with Robert Henri and John Sloan of the "Immortal Eight" and the Ashcan School.

A true Ashcan artist painting in North Carolina was Eugene Healon Thomason. Thomason, a Charlotte

Cherokee County, W.C.A. Frerichs, 38" x 46", oil on canvas. On loan to U.S. Department of State. Frerichs painted the western North Carolina landscape in the Hudson River manner in the 1850s and 1860s until his return to Staten Island.

Near Tryon, *Lawrence Mazzanovich, 25" x 29", oil on canvs.*

205

native, who with the assistance of James B. Duke trained at the Art Students' League in New York City. Upon his return to North Carolina, after more than a decade, he lived in Charlotte but later settled in the village of Nebo near Lake James. Thomason was noted for his portrayal of the mountain people (who he collectively named "the Hankins") during the Great Depression but also composed landscapes in a realist manner. The importance of this artist is yet to be realized despite a retrospective and traveling exhibit after his death and the publication of a

Landscape (western North Carolina), *Lawrence Mazzonovich, 24" x 28", oil on canvas. Private collection.*

Landscape, *John C. Lutz, born in Hickory, North Carolina, 1908, 10" x 12". He studied at Cincinnati School.*

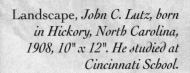

text placing him in the context of life in Appalachia in the 1930s and 1940s.

Despite the unique landscapes with long leaf pines and the barrier islands of the Outer Banks, this area of the state only became a popular subject after the mid-twentieth century. Traveling artists such as Truman Fassette and J. S. Brown did find the North Carolina coastal dunes interesting to paint. Francis Dobbs Speight from Bertie County left the state and enjoyed a long career at the Pennsylvania Academy of Fine Arts and lived outside Philadelphia. He captured some of his native eastern North Carolina when he returned late in his life to be artist in residence at East Carolina University.

While Hobson Pittman was born in the area of Epworth outside Tarboro in Edgecombe County, he is noted for his still life works and interiors rendered while living in Pennsylvania. Pittman painted few North Carolina landscapes. After his training at the Carnegie Institute, Pittman's career was mainly in the Philadelphia area and his return to the South was to visit the Luce family on their plantation outside Charleston and not especially to North Carolina.

Besides the migration of the instructors from the AIC and the Ringling School, other artists such as Robert Hodgell, Mark Dison Dodd, and A. Colby Hawkins traveled to western North Carolina. The evidence we have is their documented paintings that are owned mainly in private collections.

While he was best known for leading regional painters to modernism, Will Henry Stevens began his career producing painterly impressionist works. His subtle use of color and depiction of interspersed sunlight and shade are some of the most compelling intimate landscapes of the region. His work has become better known as his estate has been actively promoted.

The Minnow Seiners, *Eugene Healm Thomason, 30" x 36", oil on board, circa 1936.*

Tonalism employed as an artistic technique to capture the North Carolina landscape was different from what one would see in the works of Joseph Rusling Meeker and Knute Heldner in Louisiana or Martin Johnson Heade and Herman Herzog in Florida, but the works of Laurence Mazzanovich, Julian Lamar, and William Cooke of Pinehurst embraced this aesthetic.

Trailer Court, *James Wharton, oil on canvas. Farmer/James collection.*

A Man Hunting, *Walter Granville Smith, 16" x 20", oil on canvas. Private collection.*

The art sponsored by the Works Project Administration (WPA) in the mid-1930s provided opportunity for a number of North Carolina artists, mostly women. Ruth Lanier Ogden and Callie Braswell were the leaders of the active group in Greensboro and Mabel Pugh, a New York and European trained artist, was the major force in the Raleigh area. Most of the examples of their works are portraits and still lifes but Pugh painted landscapes, mainly in Europe.

Probably the most famous artist of the nineteenth/twentieth century with North Carolina ties is Elliott Daingerfield (1859 – 1932). Daingerfield came to North Carolina when his father assumed the administration of the Fayetteville Arsenal following the Civil War. He trained in New York and had a large group of artistic colleagues but was most influenced by George Inness Sr. when he had his studio near Inness in the Holbein Building.

Daingerfield also maintained an impressive residence, Westglow, in the affluent resort of Blowing Rock. He had several technical evolutions in his career, from realism to a modified rendering of Barbizon/tonalism to symbolism. Certain of his North Carolina landscapes are major works of this subject matter. The Mint Museum had an extensive exhibition of his paintings. Many were collected by the late Robert P. Coggins and these were purchased by the Morris Museum of Southern Art to form a major part of their permanent collection.

Augustus McClean of Lincolnton, North Carolina, trained at the Pennsylvania Academy of Fine Arts under Daniel Garber and was an instructor at North Carolina State University. He and Albert Kenneth Ness both trained at the AIC. Ness was on

Landscape, *Callie Braswell,
12" x 14", oil on canvas. WPA
Greensboro, North Carolina,
circa 1938.*

North Carolina
Mountain Land-
scape, *W.C.A. Frerichs,
31" x 40", oil on canvas.
Private collection.*

the faculty at University of North Carolina in Chapel Hill for 30 years (1941 – 1973). In their free moments they captured North Carolina scenes, McClean in a realistic Ashcan manner and Ness with modified impressionism.

Ida Crawley (1867 – 1946) of Asheville and Elizabeth Chant (1862 – 1947) of Wilmington were among the most celebrated of the North Carolina female artists. Crawley trained at the Corcoran School, the National Academy, and in Germany and France. Many of Crawley's landscapes did not depict a specific geographical location but were used as social statements. Chant's legacy of art continues as she was an outstanding teacher and her influence continued through such well-known North Carolina artists as Henry and Helen McMillan and Claude Howell. Chant visited Scotland and the English Lake District and some of her North Carolina landscapes reflect this exposure.

From the Blue Ridge and Smokey Mountains eastward through the red clay of the Peidmont and pine barrens of the Coastal Plain to the windswept barrier islands, the landscape terrain of North Carolina is varied and each presents to the artist its own beauty. The landscapes of native artists and those who have traveled here to capture this subject matter have given the Tar Heel State a legacy that is truly remarkable and is only now coming to be properly appreciated.

Catawba Valley, *Leitha Conoley, 32" x 24", oil on canvas.*

Carolina Woods (Near Blowing Rock), *Elliott Daingerfield, 20" x 24", oil on canvas. Farmer/James collection.*

Cabin in Western North Carolina, *Robert Hodgell, 28½" x 36¾", oil on canvas.*

North Carolina Cabin Scene, *Will Henry Stevens, 1881 – 1949, 18" x 22", pastel on paper. Courtesy of Knoke Galleries of Atlanta.*

Other Venues

While there are certainly other prominent regionalist groups, including the Rockport, Massachusetts, artists, the Ozark and Silvermine painters, several Western groups, and the California impressionists, those I have discussed are identifiable from a stylistic viewpoint and better known to me. Also examples of these artists may remain in the region of their origin and may be acquired privately. The quality of the examples is often high and a collection of regionalist works from different colonies can provide variety and visual appeal. Major examples can be acquired because they are available, adding to the overall importance of your collection from an aesthetic perspective. You can also have a bit of the sense of adventure and the satisfaction of engaging in an acquisition that is creative by collecting the art from a clearly identifiable region, chosen by you.

Rockport, *unsigned, 25" x 30", oil on canvas.*

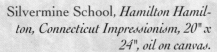

Silvermine School, *Hamilton Hamilton, Connecticut Impressionism, 20" x 24", oil on canvas.*

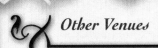

Lady in Green, *Lee Lufkin Kaula, 30" x 25", oil on canvas, BFMA School. Private collection.*

Woodland Interior, *Lilla Lowell Cabot Perry, 16" x 20". She is the signature artist for the National Museum for Women in the Arts. Private collection.*

Rockport in Fog, *Emile Gruppe, 25" x 30", oil on canvas, circa 1920s. The colony at Rockport, popularized by Theime, Mulhaupt, and Gruppe, is active today.*

Rockport, *Curry Bohem, 25" x 30". Private collection.*

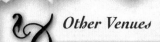

Indiana Landscape, *W.R. Eyden, 28" x 32", oil on canvas.*

Town Street Scene, *Jack Embry, 12" x 14", pastel, Spartanburg.*

Near Kent, Connecticut, *Eliot Clark, 25" x 30". Private collection.*

Cabin, Ozarks,
*unsigned, 20" x 24",
Ozark School.*

Coast Near Virginia Beach (circa 1940), *unsigned, 25" x 30".*

Ozark Landscape,
*Oscar Erickson, 23" x
28", oil on canvas.*

Along the Mississippi, *Henry Moser, 26" x 22", oil on canvas.*

An Old Time
Cabin at Howard
Gap, Tryon, North
Carolina, *Fred W.
Reich.*

Montreat Sunlight,
18" x 12", J.S. Couper.

"Shotgun" Hankins, *Eugene Healon Thomason, 25" x 23", oil on canvas. Thomason lived in Nebo, N.C., and he painted the Appalachian people during the Depression. He trained at the ASL and was an "Ashcan" artist. Private collection.*

The Red House, New England,
*Agnes Richmond (1870 – 1964), 12" x
16", oil on canvas. Courtesy of Knoke
Galleries of Atlanta.*

Young Boy Smoking a Pipe,
*Burr H. Nichols (1848 – 1915),
14" x 11", oil on canvas, signed
lower left, dated 1885. Courtesy
of Knoke Galleries of Atlanta.*

Delaware Watergap, *Cullen Yates (1866 – 1945), 30" x 40", oil on canvas, signed lower right, circa 1909. Courtesy of Knoke Galleries of Atlanta.*

The Harbor, *Haley Lever, 20" x 24", oil on canvas. Private collection.*

Winter Landscape, *Walter Schofield, 21½" x 24".*
New Hope Colony

In White River
Valley, Vermont,
Stephen Parrish,
12" x 17¼", oil.
Courtesy of Vose
Galleries of Boston.

Brook in Winter,
E.W. Redfield,
founder of the New
Hope Colony.
Private collection.

Shoeshine Boy, *J.G.*
Brown (1831 – 1913), 24"
x 16", oil on canvas, signed
lower left. Courtesy of
Knoke Galleries of Atlanta.

Indian Encampment, *A.R.M. Cooper (1856 – 1924), 20" x 28", oil on canvas, signed lower left, dated 1913. Courtesy of Knoke Galleries of Atlanta.*

Swamp Landscape, *Alice R.H. Smith, 8¾" x 12¼", watercolor on paper, circa 1930, signed lower right.*

Madonna and Child, *Elliott Daingerfield, 21¼" x 19¾", oil on canvas. This is an example of Daingerfield's symbolist oeuvre.*

Landscape, *William Merrit Post, 25" x 30". Very competent landscape artist whose works are reasonable. Private collection.*

Woodland Landscape,
*Robert Nisbet, 20" x 24", oil
on canvas. Private collection.*

Ogunquit Harbor,
*John J. Erneking,
24" x 32".*

East Tennessee
Landscape, *Bertha
Herbert, 16" x 20",
Farmer/James collection.*

Expatriate American Artists

American artists have traveled abroad to study since we were a virgin and not yet founded country. However, in the 1870s until the turn of the twentieth century this phenomenon became a true movement. Many of the expatriates lived in Paris but a good number were in England, Germany, Italy, and the Netherlands as well.

At the turn of the century many art critics viewed our native effort as a regional school subject to stylistic influences from abroad. Some felt we had not broken away to create a distinctly national expression. However, one could point to the Hudson River School (circa 1835 – 1875) as an independent development initiated and championed in America. Luminism was exported to Europe and the diffusion of light became the impetus for movements outside the United States. We could also lay claim to elements of tonalism as well.

In the 1880s luminism began to wane and a number of American artists tired of the often romanticized subject matter of the heroic American landscape. They entered the pure stream of European painting. Artists like Mary Cassatt, James Abbo McNeil Whistler,

and John Singer Sargent became accepted and acclaimed for their work abroad. American and European art from their brush became so interpenetrating that for them it was indistinguishable. The press lionized European art and patrons were influenced by this bias. At that time all of the renowned American collectors except for Thomas B. Clark favored European artists. Even American artists like William Merritt Chase would lead an entire school of students to

Landscape in Winter, *Walter E. Schofield, 20" x 24", oil on canvas. Private collection.*

Venice: The Grand Canal, *C. Myron Clark. Private collection.*

Europe. They would leave just after the National Academy Exhibition in March for the Royal Academy in London and thence to the Paris Salon, often summering in Italy.

An entire generation of artists during that period studied abroad for several years; and a few even longer. They would be totally immersed in European styles and artistic trends for that time. Munich and Paris were the favorite destinations, but vacation spots and sites of colonies were also important.

The intimate landscapes of the French were incompatible with the Hudson River style and subject matter; and the French prevailed primarily due to simple artistic tastes. The isolated Hudson River School aided by advances in technology and transportation had been brought abroad and this option grew pale beside the excitement of the Barbizon movement and the vibrancy of impressionism.

The turning away from the signature idiom of the Hudson River School was not due to disillusionment with American values and sensibilities or the fratricidal struggle of the Civil War, but the influence of international taste. French painting became the international ideal. Some artists felt that they needed to be in France

to produce the best they were capable of. This did not indicate a lack of patriotism by the expatriate Americans; in fact, they formed national groups in their adopted country and were ready to assist aspiring young Americans when they came to study. In fact, many American artists drifted into a defacto expatriate status.

The usual period of study of four or five years for the Americans also included painting in the countryside such as Pont-Aven in Brittany (1865 – 1890) and at Etaples and Entretat as well as Venice. Thus, they came to be familiar with not only the classroom but the country and people as well as facilitating their later resident status.

The first opportunity that the American collecting public had to respond to these changes was at the annual exhibition of the Society of American Artists in 1878. Many freshly returned American artists exhibited their work. It was visibly clear that the Hudson River School had acceded stylistic hegemony and that these artists lost no opportunity for American patronage by their European identification. This also demonstrated an existence, even success, of an artistic statement without the imprimatur of the conservative National Academy of Design. This was later confirmed by exhi-

A Fete Day, Venice, *Walter Lansil (1846 – 1925), 20" x 30", oil on canvas, signed lower left, dated 1892. Courtesy of Knoke Galleries of Atlanta.*

bition of the group of celebrated painters known collectively as "the Ten."

Many of the Americans were attracted to a diffused light technique rather than the true "glare aesthetic" of bright full sunlight. They also embraced the noble peasant subject matter so prominent in the French genre paintings of which there was no exact American equivalent, Winslow Homer's and Eastman Johnson's work notwithstanding.

Daniel Ridgeway Knight became a devotee of the work of Jules Bastien-Lepage and certain elements of this style were adopted by Charles Sprague Pearce, Elizabeth Nourse, and Frank Boggs. Alexander Harrison became a leader of the Pont-Aven group and later with his brother, Birge, the well-known tonalist, was a founder of the art colony in Woodstock, New York. Harrrison's work is relatively underpriced considering his importance in the history of American art.

The first true impressionist exhibition in 1874 inspired a number of expatriate Americans as well as those studying in Paris who would soon return home. Mary Cassatt and Theodore Robinson employed this style of painting which evolved into a number of plein air variants. By the mid 1800s, this movement had splintered into mannered individual variations. The limited palette of the Hague School also influenced a number of the Americans and some returned to the United States to practice "tonalism" and specialize in nocturnes. This poetic mood of intimism was practiced by a number of Americans who exhibited at the Society of American Landscape painting.

While Paris was the most popular setting of art matters in Europe during the late nineteenth century, some American expatriates were attracted to Italy, especially Florence and Rome because a large number of American neoclassical sculptors were there. Several of the "Duveneck Boys" along with others settled in Venice

producing many images of the Grand Canal and the Piazza San Marco. Some of the less distinguished artists painted images of these well-known scenes that can be acquired reasonably today.

The population of expatriated Americans in Europe peaked in the 1880s and by the 1890s a significant number had returned to the United States. The Columbian Exposition of 1893 rivaled the Exposition Universible in Paris (1889) and was a breakthrough event for American art. This event in Chicago proudly celebrated America's artistic coming of age. Impressionism was given emphasis and mural painting provided great opportunity and exposure for the Americans.

By 1900 American schools of art provided the equivalent training experience to that found in Europe. Frank Weston Benson and Edmund Tarbell attempted to duplicate their experience in France with the training and curriculum at the Boston Museum of Fine Arts

Afternoon Cambridge, Anna Richards Brewster (1820 – 1952), *16" x 12", oil on canvas, signed lower left. Courtesy of Knoke Galleries of Atlanta.*

(BMFA) School. The Art Students League in New York appealed to those who felt encumbered by the National Academy of Design. The Pennsylvania Academy of Fine Arts (PAFA) offered a similar experience and was headed by Thomas Eakins and Thomas Anshutz.

A number of art colonies were formed in America such as Old Lyme, Connecticut (1898); Woodstock, New York; Rockport, Massachusetts; Brown County, Indiana (1903); and others which provided the equivalent convivial relationship that was available only in Europe in the 1870s and 1880s. American social and industrial progress became a subject of national passion and was expressed in the paintings of the "Immortal Eight" (Brown) and the Ashcan School of realism. This was decidedly an American phenomenon; not requiring travel abroad or supportive of an expatriated status.

Certain artists such as Theodore Earl Butler, Henry Ossawa Tanner, Eugene Vail, Lilla Lowell Cabot Perry, Richard E. Miller, Frederick Frieseke, and others chose to be near the icon of impressionism, Claude Monet, and paint the French countryside near Giverny and other small French towns in that area.

With extended scholarship regarding these artists and an emphasis on the so-called "post-impressionists," they have become quite expensive and their works range from $25,000 to over $100,000. The impressionist works of F.V. Bridgeman, who was known for Egyptian and North African scenes, can be acquired. The text by R.H. Love on Theodore Earl Butler, Monet's son-in-law, raised collector and historian awareness of this work and his prices as well.

American impressionism had its ascendancy after the Chicago Exposition in 1893 and this "look" when applied to American scenes conveyed the experience of the outdoors as well as with European landscapes. Artists could apply this technique without the necessity of any particular teacher or mentor and in any locale of their choosing. There was a shift in taste and acceptable subject matter in America that no longer favored foreign residence and an avid national market came into being around the transition between the late nineteenth and early twentieth centuries.

Of the generation of American artists of the 1870s and 1880s some of our best painters were expatriates and they still represent a group about which much is to be learned and admired.

The Lieutenancy, Honfleur, 1906, *T.E. Butler (1861 – 1936), 26"x 32", oil on canvas, signed lower left. Courtesy of Knoke Galleries of Atlanta.*

Portraiture

The human face and torso represent among the most acceptable and interesting of visual images portrayed in paintings. Early in this nation's history, portraiture represented the most common attempt at representation through painting. Even rudimentary attempts at landscape often involved documentation but not in the same manner as portraiture. It was not until the advent of the Hudson River School and exploration of the American West that landscape painting for aesthetic reasons alone gained widespread popularity.

The austere portraits of the first half of the nineteenth century became less popular and were almost rendered unnecessary when the daguerreotype came into widespread use. This form of representation could much more faithfully depict the human anatomical features. Even "ancestor portraits" became relegated to impersonal settings unless they were displayed in the homes of relatives where these stiff images had a certain nostalgic value. These works would only be desired by collectors if the sitter were famous or a body of the artist's work had received some independent scholarship.

Lady in Floppy Hat, *Joseph R. DeCamp, 28" x 18", oil on canvas, America the Beautiful collection, "La Femme," Cheekwood. Private collection.*

Self Portrait, *Irwin Ramsey Wiles, 30" x 25", Chapellier Gallery.*

Even the Peales, Stuart, West, and others added elements to their portraits to make them more painterly and interesting and their success was already assured by the public.

Throughout the last half of the nineteenth century and early decades of the twentieth century, artists derived most of their incomes from commissioned portraits. Some of these artists in acceding to financial considerations produced so many portraits that their technique became formulaic and predictable. Today these paintings are considered by most collectors as dull and uninteresting.

For dealers, they represent inventory that is difficult to sell. A large segment of this market for these works is in institutions and they often do not have the funds necessary to acquire the most important paintings.

Artists have throughout history added certain embellishments to paintings to make them more interesting for the viewer. Thus, a rudimentary type of modified portraiture has historically been present for several centuries. This may have been the simple addition of a distant vista related to the much larger figure in the foreground.

Exercising a bit more creativity, the artist might have the sitter engaged in some activity. For observers, this will almost always increase interest from the activity especially if it has social merit. For a physician, they

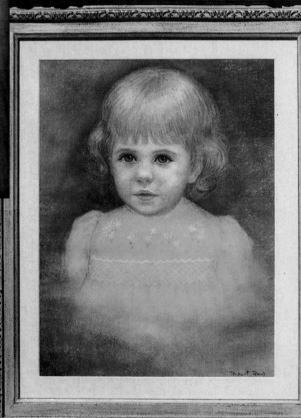

Beautiful Lady, Cornelius Hankings,
30" x 25", oil on canvas.

Portrait of Blond-Haired Child,
Robert L. Reid, 23¼" x 19½".

might be shown examining a child, the attorney before the bench or consulting a volume of legal opinions, or the planter out working in the field of harvest. The most popular images of modified portraiture were those of women caring for children, fetching water, and actively engaged in some leisurely activity. With the Barbizon artists, they might be working in the fields providing a modified portrait as well as a statement about the value of physical labor.

With the advent of impressionism in the mid-1870s, the modified portrait seemed to be much more consistent with the purpose of that aesthetic than in previous genre. Often the anatomical depiction of the subject was subordinated to either the activity or the ambiance of the environment in which the artist had placed the figure. The activity depicted was often that of leisure. The Boston Museum of Fine Art School, for example, has as its characteristic format women engaged in a leisure activity in an elegant interior. Often the sunlit room would have

original paintings on the walls, fine porcelain or crystal, and period furniture scattered about.

These impressionist images appealed to the public because they represented an ideal. The combination of beautiful figures, light-bright palette, and an elegant environment made the paintings compelling for the general public. They remain so today. In fact, impressionism is the most highly appreciated genre by the general public. Modified portraiture can take several forms. A figure might be placed in a flower-filled garden or the central figure might be seen in an elegant interior.

Modified Portraiture, *John J. Enneking,*
oil on canvas. Farmer/James collection.

Portrait of Evangline Walker, Artist,
Phillip Leslie Hale. Hale was a teacher at
Boston Museum of Fine Arts School and
Walker was a pupil. Phillip Leslie Hale
was a member of a distinguished Boston
family that included Ellen Day Hale and
Lillian Wescott Hale. James collection.

A modified portrait or an interior with a central figure by Sargent, Hassam, Tarbell, Chase, or an artist of comparable fame may well be over a million dollars in value. However, many of their students and colleagues have produced quality works of this imagery that are aesthetically appealing and quite collectible.

In the first decade of the twentieth century a group of artists known as "the Eight" by intention departed from the impressionist genre to espouse a form of realism that was a significant departure from impressionism. They rendered their images in colors of the lower register, grays and blacks as opposed to the whites, lavender, and other bright colors of impressionism. They celebrated the physical labor of the American worker, city streets, and alleyways. The brush strokes were bold and pigment was applied thickly producing an appearance of dimension through the use of this impasto technique.

The group who were later described as the "Ashcan School" had their first exhibit in 1908 and again in the famous Armory Show of 1913. The modified portraits often had figures in postures emphasizing their physical effort or with limbs curved and elongated to emphasize their physical labor. The public was at first shocked by these realistic images and in the second decades and beyond reacted by embracing certain non-representational artistic movements. However, the Ashcan School continued as a major artistic influence throughout the 1920s and 1930s, even during the WPA programs.

Elegant Lady, Southern Potratit, *30" x 25",*
on loan to Center for Study of the American
South, University of North Carolina.

Young Girl, *George Wesley Bellows, 28" x 23", oil on canvas.*
Original stretcher and frame inscribed. Private collection.

Whatever genre one is considering, the modified portrait represents a lasting type of work that can offer pleasure for its anatomical detail as well as the activity depicted for the viewer. They usually provide lasting satisfaction for the collector or museum and are inherently saleable for the art dealer. The admixture of the environment, activity depicted, and the inclusion of face and human form provided a format of great interest and an opportunity for the collector and dealer.

A Young Lady, Margaret Fitzhugh Browne, 30" x 25", oil on canvas. She studied under Joseph de Camp at the Boston Museum of Fine Arts School. She was one of the fine women painters at the BMFA School, along with Lee Lufkin Kaula and Gretchen Rogers. James collection. Gift to Martin County Courthouse.

Portrait of a Man, John Stuart Curry, 26" x 21", oil on canvas. Gift to North Carolina State University School of Veterinary Medicine.

Civil War Physician,
artist unknown, 16" oval.

Man with Glasses, *G.E. Cooke,*
25" x 30", oil on canvas. Cooke was
a Tennessee portrait artist.

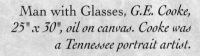

Mother and Child, *unknown Charleston artist, 30" x 36". On loan to Center for Study of the American South, University of North Carolina at Chapel Hill.*

Myself, *Bertha Lucy Derrick Swindell (1874 – 1951), student of Chase, Hawthorne Academie Juliene.*

Young Boy, *Roy Gamble,*
30" x 25", oil on canvas.
Private collection.

Robert E. Lee, *W.A. Cox,*
22" oval, painted from life after
Civil War in Richmond.
Farmer/James collection.

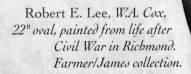

A Young Boy, *Myrtle Jones of Savannah, Georgia, 32" x 26", oil on canvas. Jones began as an Ashcan School artist and evolved into an Impressionist. James/Farmer collection.*

Young Girl,
*Thomas Whiteman,
26" oval, oil on canvas.*

Lady Next to a Vase,
Robert Ryland, 24" x 20",
oil on canvas. Ryland was a
Kentucky artist.

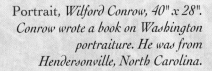

Portrait, *Wilford Conrow, 40" x 28".*
Conrow wrote a book on Washington
portraiture. He was from
Hendersonville, North Carolina.

Lady in Green Dress, *Edwin W.D. Hamilton, 62" x 38", oil on canvas, in period frame.*

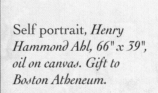

Self portrait, *Henry Hammond Ahl, 66" x 39", oil on canvas. Gift to Boston Atheneum.*

Young Female, *George Drury,* 24" oval,
oil on canvas. Private collection.

Portrait of a Woman in a Chair, *Anne Dehon Blake (active
circa 1897 – 1919), 32" x 35", oil on canvas, signed lower right:
"Anne D. Blake." Label on frame: "This picture/was exhibited/at
the/New Gallery. . . / Boston, November D..."*

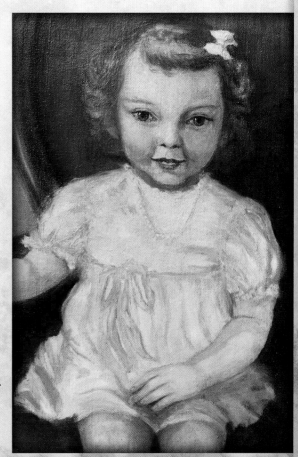

Young Female, *Ann Cadwaller
Coles,* 24" x 20", *oil on canvas.*

The Mink Stole, *Leopold Seyffert, 66" x 32". Note use of Oriental vase, sophisticated composition, elegant interior. Private collection.*

A Lady, *Anna Taylor Nash, 30" x 25", oil on canvas. Nash, a Savannah artist from Pittsboro, North Carolina, often dressed models to make a statement from their attire. Private collection.*

Elegant Lady, *W.B. Cooper, 30"
x 24½", circa 1870. Portrait
artists Washington Bogart or
William Beauregard Cooper, Central Tennessee (1840 – 1880).*

Mary Durand, *Gilbert Stuart (circa 1850 – 1860).
Mary Durand was the wife of
the Hudson River artist Asher
B. Durand. Farmer/James
collection.*

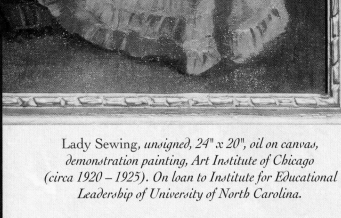

Lady Sewing, *unsigned, 24" x 20", oil on canvas, demonstration painting, Art Institute of Chicago (circa 1920 – 1925). On loan to Institute for Educational Leadership of University of North Carolina.*

Lady in a Hat, *attributed to William Churchill, Boston Museum of Fine Arts artist, 30" x 25", oil on canvas. Private collection.*

Mr. Douglas, *Bernice Fernow*, 12" x 10", oil on board. *Fernow was an art historian and teacher. The sartorial elegance of the sitter is the "message" of this modified portrait.*

Lady in a Kimono: Agnes Kellogg, *J. Alden Weir, 70" x 40", oil on canvas. Private colletion.*

In Repose, *Anita Ashley, 22" x 16", pastel.*
This artist's best works rival her mentor,
Mary Cassatt. Farmer/James collection.

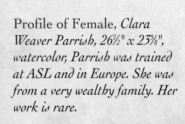

Profile of Female, *Clara*
Weaver Parrish, 26½" x 23⅞",
watercolor, Parrish was trained
at ASL and in Europe. She was
from a very wealthy family. Her
work is rare.

Mother and
Daughter, *Robert
Reid, 64" x 32", oil on
canvas. Reid was a
member of "The Ten."
Foothills Fine Art,
Tryon, N.C.*

Mr. Stearns, *William McGregor Paxton,
36" x 30", oil on canvas. Paxton was a
leader of the Boston Museum of Fine Arts
School. His landscapes and interior scnes
sell for over $100,000. He was an excellent
portrait painter. His portraits are
valuable if sitter was important.
Gift to Boston Atheneum.*

Stonewall Jackson, *W.A. Cox, a Richmond artist, 21" oval, oil on canvas, circa 1870.*

Mrs. McClean, *Charles Bird King, 30" x 25", oil on canvas. Johnston Center for Excellence, University of North Carolina at Chapel Hill.*

A Young Girl, *Hattie Saussey, 20"
x 16", oil on canvas.*

My Wife, *Joshua Hayward,
30" x 25". Johnston Center for
Excellence, University of North
Carolina at Chapel Hill.*

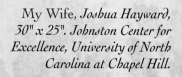

Still Life

One genre that the collector will often fail to properly appreciate and to acquire examples of are still life works. Because the appeal is in the inherent beauty of the composition we often apply criteria in judging still life paintings that are more appropriate for landscapes. Still life historically came to be a subject matter in the sixteenth and seventeenth centuries. One of the reasons was the urge toward describing objects in an accurate manner.

Still life paintings can be appreciated from the aspect of verisimilitude. They can demonstrate the resonance of pure formed relationships. Do they appropriately represent the object they are to portray? Often the compelling attraction may be the portrayal itself; flowers, a fish, dead game, or an imported ceramic object. In this assessment our criteria may have less tolerance than a sunlit landscape or a moonlit nocturne. The object, because of it familiarity, may be judged with a historical bias; we feel we know exactly how the object should appear. However, the artist can make the surface of the painting the subject of the work.

Still life works are alternatives to other genres in a collection and offer both structural and emotional balance to your acquisitions. We have collected a number

Still Life, *E.K. Skinner,*
student of Mabel Pugh.

Flowers, *Daisey Erb,*
28" x 22", oil on canvas.

of botanical still life works because they appeal to the viewer for their exquisite anatomical precision. At the same time, these paintings serve as details charged with symbolism and with symbolic meaning.

Some collectors view the paintings of dead game as an unwelcome visual endpoint, but they represent true reality and the exotic appearance of a richly feathered duck or a carp on a string is appealing in a way far different from an impressionist landscape. The still life may be submerged in formal and emblematic symbolism.

Floral still life paintings evoke the outside in an interior and will seem to brighten a dimly lit room and appear to bring sunlight into dark. Thus, the still life not only creates an aesthetic message but can have a more decorative/utilitarian function as well.

Many women composed floral still life paintings because the form of expression reflected their daily life. Women were often indoors in their homes where they could fashion a flower arrangement and paint it while attending their daily tasks. Male artists might be more attracted to still life subjects of fish. Examples like William Merritt Chase or William Aiken Walker come to mind. Women with knowledge of ceramics would present these objects not only with structural clarity but with compassion as well.

Lillies, *Alice Rubenstein, 24" x 20",*
oil on canvas.

Botanical Study, *Emma Coulan, New Orleans.*

Most of us do not acquire still life works with the avidity we do certain other styles. In the hierarchy of genre, still life rates below many others. Often cited as a reason is lack of activity in the image layer and their consideration as devoid of spontaneity that can be more easily presented with genre works or landscapes with figures. However, we as collectors intellectually appreciate that it is difficult to structure the elements in a still life as it is in a pleasing landscape. Hence, in our acquisition posture we should accord the financial commitment of an arrangement of glads to the same quality as a sunlit field with figures. I trust that the illustrations in this text will provide us with examples that will allow still life paintings to achieve a proper distribution in your collection.

The discussion has probably not added to the desire to pay a great deal of money for a good tromp l'oel and a basket of roses. However, in the order of things technically they represent the same degree. The post-impressionist created many icons of still life works

Still Life, *Callie Braswell, 14" x 19½", oil on canvas, WPA artist active 1930s – 1940, Greensnsboro, North Carolina.*

Flowers in a Blue Ginger Jar, *Edmund C. Tarbell, 25" x 30". Courtesy of Vose Galleries of Boston.*

and while we may not be able to afford a Cezame or a Monet or a Severin Rosen we can have a wonderful Edith Flischer, Laura Coombs Hill, or a Catherine Wiley for a balance in our collection.

The writings of Bill Gerdts, Buck Pennington, Jesse Poesch, Ella Prince Knox, and Martha Severans were helpful in preparing this chapter.

Still Life (Glads), *Eleanor McAdoo Wiley, 31" x 24", oil on canvas.*

Still Life with Peaches, *Hal Morrison, 20" x 24", oil on canvas, signed lower left. Courtesy of Knoke Galleries of Atlanta.*

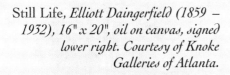
Still Life, *Elliott Daingerfield (1859 – 1932), 16" x 20", oil on canvas, signed lower right. Courtesy of Knoke Galleries of Atlanta.*

Peregrine Falcon, *Athos Menaboni (1895 – 1990), 32" x 24", oil on board, signed lower right. Courtesy of Knoke Galleries of Atlanta.*

255

Roses, *Caroline Carson,*
Charleston, South Carolina,
12¼" x 9", watercolor.

Still Life with Figure, *Edith*
Flischer, Chase student.

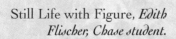

Oranges, *Emma Bell Miles, 14¼" x 10½", pastel, Chattanooga, Tennessee, circa 1910.*

Basket of Grapes, *Catherine Wiley, 22" x 28", oil on canvas.*

Still Life, *Lucy Derrick Swindell, 38" x 32", oil on canvas. Lucy Derrick was from Baltimore and painted both portraits and still lifes in a large and bold format.*

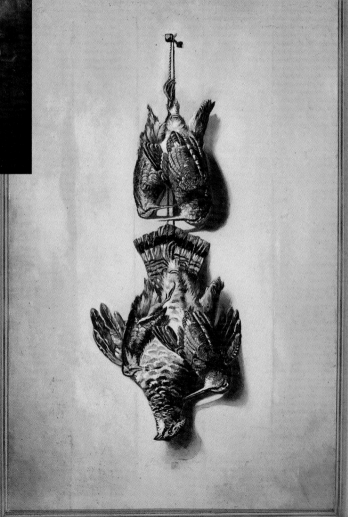

Nature Mort — Birds, *Louis Winterhalder, 28" x 18", oil on canvas.*

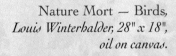

Still Life, *Hobson Pittman, oil on canvas. Pittman, from Tarboro, North Carolina, studied at the PAFA with Anshutz and Eakins. He remained and taught for two decades. He is well known for his interiors. Farmer/James collection.*

Still Life, *Susan Ritman, 20" x 16", oil on board, Baltimore artist.*

Enhancing Value

Collect paintings for the pleasure derived from the process and subsequently the proprietary implications. As aesthetically pleasing objects, paintings have value but they have financial implications as well. Aesthetic appeal and technical virtuosity do correlate with the commercial value and worth of a painting but other factors are also significant. One of these is the "importance" of the work. This ascribed value may appear complicated and sometimes arbitrary but can be quite significant. One can enhance the value of a painting in many ways that address both the aesthetics and the perceived importance.

Probably the single most important determination of commercial value of a painting is the documentation of the creator of the work — who painted it? One may uncover a signature through removal of varnish or overpaint, through black light inspection, or simply removing a liner or the work from the frame.

A number of years ago I bought a lovely impressionist painting of a young female at a famous northeastern auction house. Since it was unsigned it was inexpensive but technically excellent and in a wonderful vibrant style. The composition was reminiscent of the work of John J. Enneking which it was, but more importantly, it was a modified portrait of his daughter, Grace, from a photograph, and was later confirmed by the Enneking expert. Good paintings are usually executed by well-trained, good artists, so do not overlook the opportunity to uncover a signature if you have a work that is technically excellent.

Church on Hill, *Kathleen Bartlett, 24" x 20", watercolor.*
Wife of Paul Bartlett.

A signature is not the only means in determining the authorship of a particular painting. Provenance may provide just as compelling documentation as a signature and can be of superior evidentiary nature. As discussed, we have a Childe Hassam watercolor that has a watermark through the artist's signature and was deemed a fake on the basis of subject matter. However, we uncovered documentation that it was painted in Havana, Cuba, in 1895, matted in New York City, and sold in St. Louis in 1897. It remained in the same family of ownership since the 1930s. Establishment with a relative degree of certainty the artist's identification will definitely enhance the value of your painting — not always 100-fold as in this instance but significant. This fact is illustrated by the importance of history's identification texts like *Who Was Who*, Benezit, Young's, Davenport's...and the plethora of books demonstrating artists' signatures.

The importance of a painting can be enhanced by documenting that it was shown publicly especially in a juried exhibition. There are extensive exhibition records of institutions such as the National Academy of Design or the Pennsylvania Academy of Fine Arts. Exhibition labels may be plainly visible or hiding beneath some well intended framer's covering. The data may have been inscribed on the stretcher or the back of the canvas.

Removal of a previous relining may uncover the exhibition label, the canvas stencil, or you may have identified the date of the painting, the artist's name, and can match this with the description of the work in the exhibition records. We once matched an Ernest L. Major painting with a damaged undecipherable signature with the data and description in NAD records.

Girl with Flowers, *Lynn Simpson, The Onslow Impressionist, bought at house sale.*

The painting is an important addition to the art collection of the Cosmos Club of Washington.

Certainly, documentation that a painting represents a historic event, a famous place, a noted person, reason for it to be of special interest to the artist, or previous ownership by a famous collector will enhance its value. Here, we are not speaking about Marilyn Monroe's one performance dress; more like Washington crossing the Delaware, the Hassam flag series, and in our collection Gilbert Stuart's rendering of Mrs. Asher B. Durand, wife of the celebrated Hudson River artist or Henry Ward Ranger's painting of his studio on the Long Island Sound. The documentation may require some research, but there is pleasure in the intellectual process and the rewards in financial terms can be astronomical.

Museums for many reasons deaccess paintings that may well become significant additions to your collection. Many times these museum deaccessions will be well researched and have attendant documentation, but do not fit the goals of the institution. They simply may have too many examples of a particular artist and by deaccession are creating funds for acquisition of other artists for their collection. Thus, they may deaccess works of historical significance. Labels and museum records will "enhance" the importance of any painting. Additionally, this may provide the primary information upon which subsequent data may be acquired to further enhance the value of the work.

I once acquired a museum deaccession of a landscape with building by J. Frances Murphy which was entitled "Arkville, New York." Further investigation uncovered that it was the painting of Murphy's home and studio enhancing its exhibition interest and commercial value of the painting. This painting, because of the documented subject matter, has been illustrated in several art texts.

Public exposure of the appropriate setting can greatly enhance the value of a painting, especially if it has inherent and visual appeal. Curators of exhibits are usually delighted to

Charles Rienere, *published in* Southern Cultures, *New Orleans artist.*

exhibit a painting from a private collection because it represents "new" material. The same can be said of authors and editors of art texts. We have had most of our permanent collection published in a public document and many have been exhibited publicly. The primary motivation is sharing one's acquisitions but the secondary benefit of enhancing the value is not without merit as well. To have the work of an artist described in the context of or comparison with a painting you own is very rewarding.

Walter Clark's oeuvre has been described in the context of "Noank" illustrated in Bill Gerdt's monumental text *American Impressionism* and as the cover of the *Journal of the American Medical Association*. Inclusion in the news media, monographs, a catalog, a magazine, and newspaper articles as well as texts will enhance the value of a painting.

Most collectors take pleasure in affirmation of their choices, sharing their experiences and in the preparatory activities and fellowship surrounding openings and exhibitions, but all collectors enjoy the enhancement in value of their paintings and these are some of the methods that may well do so.

Lady with Bonnet, *Raymond Rogers Perry Neilsen, 70" x 40", oil on canvas.*

Boothbay Harbor, *Edward Willies Redfield, 30" x 40", oil on canvas.*

Decorative Value

Collectors decry the consideration of painting as decorative objects because of the overstated fear that artistic merit will not be appreciated or the aesthetic significance of the work will be lost in the mundane considerations of color, texture, uniformity, and balance. However, the sheer beauty of paintings does have great decorative value. We should accommodate both biases with emphasis upon the artistic consideration but awareness of their decorative appeal as well.

To many collectors, an ideal room should be filled with nineteenth and early twentieth century paintings, Sheraton, Hepplewhite, or Victorian furniture, and vintage oriental rugs; possibly complemented by important pieces of crystal, silver, and examples of art pottery. We have attempted to combine our collection interests in Southern "high style" furniture, Caucasian rugs, and North Carolina art pottery. However, our most important considerations revolve around the choices we make in displaying our painting collection.

While we bow to certain conventions as to horizontal paintings over sideboards or large sofas and vertical ones over card tables, cellarettes, narrow chests, or bedside tables, the subject matter is often our chief determinant of what hangs where. While life-sized portraits may be spectacular in a gallery or museum, one should have a special place to accommodate such a large painting in their private dwelling. This does not mean that the dimensions fit but the image of the painting should be appropriate for the intended space.

At some fundamental level without being formulaic certain subjects appear more appropriate for certain

Use of easel in decorating with paintings.

Note mixture of Tonalism, Barbizon, and Impressionism.

spaces depending upon their use. Sitting areas are most often decorated with landscapes and still lifes for the most part and the formal areas portraits and genre works. No rule is sacrosanct and as a collector you should hang paintings to reflect your personal taste.

Tonalist works of a dominant theme can set the mood of a room as a tranquil, subdued level whereas light, bright vibrant impressionist paintings should elevate the palettes of a room and create a more lively atmosphere.

Barbizon works are in the lower register of the color scale and often depict quiet pastoral scenes. They work well with impressionist and some post-impressionist pieces but hung with a preponderance of moody tonalist works will sometimes create an evocative atmosphere that only the sophisticated collector can appreciate. We have our swamp and bayou works hung with impressionist scenes for variety of mood.

Genre works range from the quaint to provocative. They often provide scholarly substance to a room.

They are most effective in intimate settings where the viewer has the opportunity to visualize and understand the message they convey.

Should the predominant hue in your favorite tonalist masterpiece "match" the predominant color in your nineteenth century Oushak or the geometry of a still life complement the form of your large chrome red early twentieth century porch vase? Those are the considerations that sometimes are "off putting" for the serious collector but these are personal considerations for which you have the right to a valid and strong opinion.

Do you need to acquire a work because it fits over the sofa or will be an impressive "mantle hanging"?

While there is legitimacy to this approach and it fulfills certain realistic considerations, most collectors would prefer to acquire a large horizontal landscape by a painter that they admire and discover that it complements the space over the couch. We have never acquired a painting to fit a space but have resisted acquiring works the dimension of which might not be accommodated in our house. We have also used a vertical painting to dominate a large wall over a sofa in a great room as we could flank the painting by complementary works.

Guest or "public" rooms in one's house are most often decorated with techniques and subjects that are not controversial. They often reflect a more generic statement than the private rooms that you enjoy and that "company" (in the vernacular) does not spend a great deal of time in. Our guest bedrooms, for example, contain many pleasant impressionist landscapes mixed with still life works.

This might be analogous to instrumental classic or Baroque music compared with romantic opera featuring the many voices of the characters. Leave the dialogue for your public space where conversation is a natural phenomenon of enjoying interchange.

If your dining room is formal, then you might logically wish to have the paintings there be formal. While we have a Gilbert Stuart and an elegant genre work by Anita Ashley in our formal dining room, we have a tonalist George Inness and a luminist John J. Enneking with a modified portrait by Cornelius Hankins and a genre work by Gilbert Gaul as well. The sideboards, corner cupboard, and southern cellarette provide a formal ambiance, the paintings offer such a variety that the room is not "stiff and foreboding." The paintings are more about content than considerations of color and texture.

Academic student drawings and nudes are sometimes problematic for your guests whose knowledge and appreciation of art are rudimentary. For this reason, we do not display this genre in our public space but we have exam-

ples of African/American imagery in Southern paintings from before the War Between the States and the WPA hung throughout our house. This specific interest of ours is well known and most guests are aware making these subjects more acceptable than they might otherwise be. Of course, if I were Dr. Barnes I could hang my post-impressionist works in any space utilizing any arrangement and they would be enjoyed by guests at any level. With such a plethora of impressive Cezanne's, Manet's, and their colleagues, you probably would adopt a "salon style" hanging arrangement to share the bounty of your holdings.

Frames make a difference in the arrangement of paintings. For example, one could put a simple aluminum framed work alongside a Newcomb Macklin period frame but I suggest a Carrig-Rohan would be preferable. As noted elsewhere in this text, I make every attempt to conserve or restore important original frames; but if choosing a reproduction one, I order a style that will reflect the period and style of the painting.

While I never allow frames to dominate a work or the decorative value of a painting to a space, I feel a frame does offer significant data to a visual composite. To examine the validity of this, consider your positive reaction and attraction to certain well-framed works on your dealer's wall. Those paintings "stand out" and they will in your home as well. Frames will significantly contribute to this reaction by you and most other viewers of the object or objects so their decorative quality is determinant.

Obviously, this has been a personal discourse and as a collector you can acquire and display your paintings any way you choose; after all, it is your personal statement. However, I hope that certain considerations I have shared will be useful in your choices. We all have biases. We often react to those that are subconscious but based upon data stored in our frontal cortex. I hope I have provided useful and effective frontal cortical information that will be reflected by your good choices.

Series of paintings, great room.

Sharing and Managing

Collectors can be best characterized as avid acquirers. They most enjoy and devote their greatest effort to the process of accumulation of the genre and the example they are attracted to. This continued acquisition is a pleasurable process that cannot persist unabated, however, for there are realities of space and funds. At some juncture adding additional paintings and paying for them will be difficult for the collector; more thoughtful and sometimes painful choices in this process will need to be made. The collector can consider this as much connoisseurship as is the accumulation phase. The collector is not without resources; however, the previous acquisitions have present value and they now occupy the potential space for other alternatives.

If a superior example of an artist's work becomes available, the collector may "trade-up" by substitution of this new example for a comparable one already in their collection. Deaccession of one painting to exchange space and funds for another may be achieved at auction or through a dealer. Auction is considered to be more expedient, but if your collection is specialized, a dealer might be able to place the painting in a short period of time.

I once needed to gather funds to acquire a major Southern watercolor and decided to part with a painting that did not fit my Southern collection. The potential deaccession was a wonderful painting of blacks by a renowned woman artist from Philadelphia. After almost a decade of ownership, I came to realize that this painting had been executed in Philadelphia and did not fulfill my own criteria for a Southern painting. I discussed the deaccession with a

Savannah Fountain, *Christopher Murphy, 16" x 20",
watercolor, "lost" from exhibit.*

*Transporting Daniel Ridgeway
Knight to U.S. Department of
State for exhibit in Art in
Embassies Program.*

major auction house. They gave me a presale estimate of several times my purchase price but just to explore other alternatives, I offered the work to two well-known Southern dealers.

I thought the subject matter alone might be appealing to collectors in the region. One dealer said the auction estimate was about what he could sell the painting for while the other said he had a collector who would acquire it at a large multiple of my acquisition cost. The amount of funds realized and the fact the painting was not what I had acquired it for, made deaccession a satisfying process. Acquiring its replacement was a pleasure.

Sometimes "trading up" may involve just this process type of seeking a "fit" and it can add validity to your often painful decision to deaccess a painting. Sometimes a dealer or fellow collector can use a less important example of an artist than the one you want to acquire. I once made this type of decision for a wonderful George Inness Sr. painted in Tarpon Springs, Florida, near the end of his life in 1893. I had owned a genuine but undistinguished example of Inness's work titled, as were many of his works, "After the Shower." Receiving credit for that as a trade, I acquired the better painting for a differential that

fit comfortably within my acquisition resources. Every day I can look at the better Inness and reaffirm the wisdom of that deaccession.

One of the more exhausting deaccession processes may result from a major change in your collecting direction. This will obviously involve a number of paintings. If you sell 10 – 15 paintings, the most efficient method is by auction. Consigning them to a half dozen dealers might be complicated and inefficient. Auction often times means instant funds to begin the acquisition process for the new direction as well.

If the impending deaccession process is simply about display space for the collector and due to this limitation the inability for you to acquire more paintings, there are a number of viable alternatives. One is to donate a collection intact. Institutions are very receptive to the gifting of collections that have an identifiable theme and make a statement. In fact, they may also receive these as long term loans so you free space but retain ownership. For example, we have loaned the

Hanging salon style. Note one grouping of landscapes (top), another of portraits. George Watts Hill Alumni Center, Alumni Hall, University of North Carolina at Chapel Hill. Both gifts and loans in exhibit.

historical and documentary paintings from our collection, "The South 1840 – 1940," to the Center for Study of the American South at the University of North Carolina at Chapel Hill. The theme of these paintings was determinative of their acceptance by the Center. They could not be in a more appropriate space and this allows us to share them with the public.

After we had acquired over 50 paintings of the Indiana impressionists, we toured that collection to a dozen venues in the South and around the state of Indiana. It was then deaccessed to an insurance company in Indianapolis where it remains on public display. While I miss certain paintings such as the T. C. Steele of his home, "Tinker Place" or the tonalist works of Adolph Shulz, I feel closure realizing the touring exhibit, our presentations at the various openings, and the publication of a catalog had accomplished our desired aims. Knowing now that the exhibit is on public display to provide an ongoing testament to our efforts provides us continued satisfaction. Is this collection valued at a large multiple of it what was when we deaccessed it? Most certainly, but we were more interested in its being

kept intact than its commercial value when we chose to deaccess it.

Some deaccessions, although logical, are painful. Early in my collecting experience I acquired a large R. A. Blakelock that had been over-restored. My conservator removed the excessive restoration to bring the work closer to the original and my research revealed that it was a Category I in authenticity and owned by the well-known family of painters, the Gruppes. The wife of the patriarch, Charles Gruppe, had purchased the painting from Blakelock before the artist was incarcerated as a result of his mental problems.

I had 20 years of satisfaction for "discovering" a Category I example of one of American's more important artists, but the painting did not fit any of my present collections nor the direction I had been heading for the past several years. I consigned it to a well-known New York dealer and hoped I would be resigned to its sale. I asked a very strong price probably in an attempt to preempt my guilt when the sale was made. We had several offers but never the full asking price and I never reduced my valuation. Finally I realized that I did not really wish to sell the painting. Several years later our alma mater (where were also live) renovated the most beautiful building on campus as the Center for Honors and Academic Excellence and we donated the work to that effort. We can enjoy the painting whenever we like and, because of the tax implications, we received financial benefit as well.

Another method of deaccession is trading paintings to dealers or fellow collectors. I once traded the late Robert Coggins several important Southern paintings for a work by the female artist of the Boston Museum of Fine Arts School (BMFA), Mary Brewster Hazelton. The legendary collector was having an exhibit by women artists and had several examples of Alfred Hutty, Alice Smith, and Elliot Daingerfield that he traded me for. This fit well with his acquisition plans and were important acquisitions for our Southern Collection. At the time the Hazelton had increased in value more than the three Southern works but over the last decade the Hutty, Smith, and Daingerfield individually became considerably more valuable than the BMFA example. It is rare that a trade will so clearly meet both participants' needs, but it does represent a unique means of serving one's collecting interests.

Hanging exhibition.

Thus, there are a number of viable avenues of both acquisition and deaccession of paintings. There is no impediment to the collector pursuing any of them to meet their needs. The acquisition of paintings has been likened to the institution of marriage; entered into with the expectation and hope of permanency but with the tacit understanding that dissolution of the partnership is a possibility.

Southern Scene (Moss Laden Tree), William Lester Stevens (1888 – 1969), 12¾" x 16¼", watercolor. Exhibited Mint Museum 1940s. On loan to Center for School Leadership Development, University of North Carolina.

La Femme Exhibit, organized by the late Robert Preato. Portrait by Edward Wilbur Dean Hamilton (left).

Funding and Financing

The appropriate resource allocation to your collections depends upon a number of variables and a few imponderables. Collection is often such an all-consuming passion that many collectors philosophy is "commit whatever it takes." My advice is "whatever you can afford."

Remember American art is not necessarily an "investment" or at least one from which one should expect liquidity or a short term profit. Thus, you should consider the acquisition cost in relation to your alternatives of resource allocation rather than in simple investment terms. For example, it would be more productive to judge the possible acquisition of a Thomas Moran, Winslow Homer, Child Hassam, or Jackson Pollock as a percent of your net worth or a certain fraction of your available funds than to anticipate that the percent value will increase from your allocation over a specified number of years.

"Affordability" of a particular painting depends as much upon your collection philosophy as it does the actual number of dollars you have available. Paintings are not as perishable as racehorses, but their value can sometimes drop almost as precipitously. Remember, it is a very rare incident when deaccessing a painting happens as rapidly as "unloading" a thousand shares of the XYZ corporation. Painting acquisition is a complex series of decisions and deliberation, a usual strategy which requires time — in money terms it is illiquid.

The majority of the time acquiring a painting is an intellectual exercise, using by definition, your discretionary funds. Sometimes, it becomes an activity driven almost entirely by emotion and, thus, is difficult to put in financial perspective. Every true collector at some time in their career will be faced with the circumstance that they believe they simply must have a particular painting. In this situation, collectors are predisposed to throw caution to the winds and to overextend themselves financially. For this, they may later become very defensive if challenged and promise themselves "never again will I engage in this behavior."

Do not overfeast or you will lose some of the pleasure of the process. This is not always a rational exercise and it may well be your passion. Never accept that it is your "vice"; vice is overeating, smoking, substance abuse for which you never receive a pretty achievement.

From purely a business viewpoint, you should not have more than 10 – 15% of your assets in art. The knowledgeable and experienced collector may choose to have more because they are presumably better able to identify a prudent acquisition and to negotiate a more favorable acquisition price. However, anything over 25 – 30% and you have, whether unwittingly or purposefully, now become an investor/dealer. This level of commitment usually means that at some future time, you will need to divest some of your art either to create exhibition space or to raise funds.

If you read the comments of collectors in the introduction to exhibition catalogs, there usually will be personal stories relating how various dealers may have allowed the collector to pay for the work over time. By the most generous of accounts, this represents an interest-free loan. One should understand that this is a special arrangement between a trusting and appreciative seller and faithful client. This represents a particular type of relationship based upon a long-standing history between the two individuals. Sometimes for a major purchase, a dealer will allow terms, but that is because they are realizing a great deal of profit from what represents for them an important transaction. Private parties in selling major works may wish to have you divide payments so that their income will span multiple tax years or some anticipated activity that they have a reasonable idea about the cost; like the future acquisition of the estate of an artist. One of my collector friends sold a single major work to finance an art museum he had promised to give his hometown.

You can discuss these payment considerations with your dealer in a candid fashion. One cardinal principle that applies to all human endeavor — the longer it takes a transaction to consummate will increase the risk that one of the parties will become dissatisfied during this period. Art payment schedules for you should be considered an alternative, not a necessity and an accommodation that may well alter your behavior and acquisition patterns.

On a personal note on this subject, in completing my "Southern Paintings 1840 – 1940" collection, a major example of a rare but important artist became available through a well-known dealer who is a colleague and, I feel, a close friend. The asking price was "substantial" (that means more than you have available). Sufficient funds from my resources for the purchase were not immediately apparent and a museum was "waiting in the wings" (isn't that always the case) for me to exhibit the piece. This opportunity would enhance the value several fold. Every effort was expended and every possibility considered to reduce or at least accommodate the debt burden for me. Exchanges and trades became too convoluted to offer much hope for mutual satisfaction. Thus, an outright purchase seemed to be the only reasonable alternative.

Learning of the museum's interest, the dealer became more flexible and we agreed upon a lower price, payment schedule, and discussed any contingencies or circumstances that might compromise the financial arrangement in the future. Afterwards, the painting became and remains one of the cornerstones of my collection.

The agreement was successful because both parties appreciated the circumstances and the significance of the acquisition from my side of the troublesome equation. We agreed to terms we believed would eventually work out and well it has. The point to emphasize here is that dealers will many times accommodate a client with a mutually satisfactory relationship if you are candid about the true nature of the circumstance.

At first blush you would not think of going to a lending institution to borrow money to purchase a painting. Imagine your average conservative banker, already having been burned by loans on real estate and start-up companies for genetic manipulation, now listening to the wisdom of lending to a client who admits they will be putting a half million dollars in a perishable object about which neither he nor his advisor has any experience or knowledge. That same lender is also not likely to be impressed with your "collateral" of other paintings. However, circumstances are changing. Certain banks and other agencies are even offering a con-

sultative investment service that includes advice to clients about the acquisition of art. You might presume that this service would include the arrangement by this same lending institution of loans to acquire art. Does this facilitation extend to those acquisitions that you select without consultation from the potential lending institution? Possibly, but a great deal will depend upon your collateral; as in size and nature. If these paintings represent a very small part of your overall assets and the success of the arrangement does not depend upon your disposal of some personal essential like your house, car, yacht, or favorite retriever, then the lender is more likely to view the transaction in terms of your ability to repay the loan rather than in terms of the wisdom of the acquisition. If the painting turns out to be a "dog," they can always repossess your Maserati or your 80-foot Bertram.

Unfortunately, for some collectors, acquisitions become so compelling that they lose perspective. You can always live without any painting and the pain of deprivation will gradually subside. Although you may think that the present opportunity for a particular acquisition is unique, this is rarely the circumstance. For even the mildly aggressive, there will be another chance for you to make "the most important acquisition."

You can adopt the posture that by "passing" you have saved your funds to make an even better choice at some future date. When you are out of balance with your acquisitions in relation to your resources, you can become so involved in paying for your art you will not have time to enjoy yourself and that is a violation of the first principle. Collecting art should be pleasurable, not painful, so do not overextend yourself physically or fiscally.

From Collector to Patron

Most collectors of paintings begin their experience as acquirers with emphasis about the process of gathering the works they want to own. At some time in the continuum of this activity most collectors will come to the realization that they have a resource that has implications beyond their original intent.

As I have noted throughout this text, my own experiences have been with nineteenth and early twentieth century American paintings. My intent in every collecting endeavor was to have groups of paintings with a clearly identifiable theme. This facilitated my scholarship in each activity and the opportunity to later share my collections through publications and exhibitions. It has allowed me to group paintings with sufficient identity to have these acquisitions judged by others for external validation or helpful criticism. This strategy also facilitated receiving specific and helpful advice from art historians, dealers, and fellow collectors.

Landscape, *Ben Austrian, 22" x 28", oil on canvas. North Carolina Wesleyan College.*

Snow Scene, *Walter Launt Palmer, 16" x 20", oil on canvas. Palmer is especially noted for his treatment of snow. George Watts Hill Alumni Center, University of North Carolina at Chapel Hill.*

In general, this organized, studied approach before acquisition resulted in a collection that could be recognized by others for whatever merits or shortcomings it might possess. While your activities, individual penchants, and choices might not be universally admired, if you follow this approach you will have a high likelihood of being respected for your efforts.

You will, as a matter of course, be asked to loan paintings to exhibits, and serve on museum boards and in leadership roles in art organizations; responsibilities that can be interesting, informative, and rewarding. These opportunities come to you from an appreciation of your achievements as a collector, recognition of your independent scholarship; the tacit hope that you might make a contribution to the museum or organization (possibly as a gift " in kind") and that your presence as a member of the representative body will add expertise.

Unwittingly or by intent, you have now evolved from a collector to a patron (a contributor). You should understand the implications of this, properly assess your resources, and enter into those activities where you feel you can make a contribution and would enjoy doing so. The pleasure of having your name listed among some nonfunctioning board of a famous museum is hollow and short-lived. To be a member of

a "figure head" or "advisory" board in which all major decisions are made by the museum staff or higher deliberative body such as a city council, political appointees, or the legislature will probably be frustrating or boring or both.

Western North Carolina Mountain, *Francis Crain (Farthing), 21" x 15½", watercolor, Durham, North Carolina, circa 1940s – 1950s, Rocky Mount Museum.*

Florida Sunset, *J.A. Wilcox, 9½" x 18¾", watercolor. Given to University of Florida Medical School.*

Any of these opportunities may have an unwritten but understood "quid pro quo" and while your expertise may have secured your position, eventually there will be an expectation of a contribution of a more tangible nature. If you have chosen the appropriate board or boards properly this obligation might become a singular opportunity for you to use both your painting collection and expertise. We have had the pleasure of donating many paintings individually, as groups or as entire collections.

Possessing what hopefully is perceived as a valuable art collection, you can donate a painting that will significantly add to an organization's holdings as a "gift in kind." This may assist the museum to obtain a painting they would have difficulty otherwise acquiring because of rarity or acquisition cost. The propensity of the museum to accept your offerings can be enhanced by selecting a charitable institution in which their permanent collection is of the same or similar genre and period as yours. Thus, it will then be likely that among your collection you will have a painting that will be a significant asset to the museum. A particularly rewarding circumstance is to donate a painting that has increased in value many fold since you acquired it. You should receive an appraised fair market value at the time of

New England Farm Scene, *Carl Runguis, 24" x 28", oil on canvas. Johnston Center for Undergraduate Excellence, University of North Carolina at Chapel Hill.*

Girl with Doll, *Robert Brackman, 20" x 24", oil on canvas. Given to Women Studies, Duke University.*

transfer to the receiving institution and your record for the Internal Revenue Service.

As mentioned earlier, in the 1970s I began selectively collecting works by women artists of the Boston Museum of Fine Arts School as a theme. These were well-trained and talented but relatively unappreciated painters selling at that time generally for $1,500 – $5,000 for good examples. I collected major examples because they were affordable. These included such now acclaimed artists as Lilla Lowell Cabot Perry, Lillian Wescott Hale, Lee Lufkin Kaula, Gretchen Rogers, Jane Peterson, and Ellen Day Hale.

Since that time a number of publications individually about these

artists have appeared, many exhibitions featuring women artists (including my own and colleagues such as the late Robert C. Coggins and the late Allan Sellars) have been prepared and the National Museum for Women in the Arts has become a reality. The value of these individual paintings by women have increased some 5 to 25 fold resulting in the acquiring of a valuable asset for the receiving organization and substantial tax benefit for you.

Family Farm, *Aaron Henry Gorson, 20" x 24", oil on canvas, Johnston Center for Undergraduate Excellence, University of North Carolina at Chapel Hill.*

Barnstable, Massachusetts, *William Southgate, 28" x 24", oil on canvas. Martin County Courthouse.*

There are certain practical guidelines regarding loans and donations I have learned from experience. Portraits add interest to any collection and provide an outstanding resource for donations to public institutions. One reason, of course, is their documentary nature and the transient environment in which they are viewed by the public. Among our portrait collection are a quite representative Gilbert Stuart (of Mrs. Asher B. Durand) which we loan but intend to always retain as

most museums have examples of this accomplished but attainable artist.

Besides exhibiting, publishing, contributing individual works, and serving on museum boards, there are other means by which a collector can act as a patron. One of the most rewarding is to donate a representative body of paintings to an organization, museum, or institution in honor of some individual or group. We have donated entire collections, often with monographs or brochures, to institutions and to honor or in memory of individuals. Often no intact collection of works existed in the museum before the time of our gift extending our patronage to the role of curator as well as donor. Charity auctions provide the collector an opportunity to contribute to some organization that they have a special interest. Choose works that are aesthetically attractive, have uncomplicated subject matter, and of subjects that appeal to the general public.

Having participated in the Art in Embassies Program of the U.S. Department of State for a number of years, it occurred to me that large dramatic paintings

Profile of Horse, *artist unknown. Gift to North Carolina State University School of Veterinary Medicine.*

Pond and Houses, *attributed to Chauncey Rider. Gift to Robersonville Public Library.*

were very well received and those with any diplomatic implications were particularly appropriate. I had the opportunity to acquire a large (70" x 40") oil by the well-known artist, J. Alden Weir. The subject was a young female member of the Kellogg diplomatic family and its provenance suggested it was painted by Weir in London, possibly at the Court of St. James. I placed it on loan to the U.S. Department of State.

An often overlooked form of patronage is mentorship of other collectors. While, in fact, this may represent a contradiction in terms, your knowledge and the resource of your collection can influence other collectors. No doubt, the philosophy, writings and the private collection of Duncan Phillips greatly influenced collectors of his and later generations. The presence of this private Phillips collection in Washington open to the pub-

lic today continues to offer inspiration and guidelines to collectors in many forms. Museums can be influenced by the donations given to them by a patron. A patron should not unduly restrict or encumber the museum, but they may request reasonable conditions of a loan or gift.

We gave parts of the Southern collection and our

Coastal Scene, *T. Lindenmurth. School of Education, University of North Carolina at Chapel Hill.*

Provenancetown Massachusettes, *Stephen Parrish. George Watts Hill Alumni Center, University of North Carolina at Chapel Hill.*

contemporary folk art or "outsider" collections to several small museums hoping to create an interest in these particular genres. From time to time we have given them other examples hoping to continue this influence but we can only inspire and influence as no strict condition was part of our agreement.

As a collector, you have a number of valuable resources; your knowledge and experience, and the most tangible, your art collection itself. In your role as patron, this asset has a multitude of functions and uses. Properly employed, you can become an effective contributor. Patronage is a very rewarding activity and should be considered the responsibility of any accomplished collector.

Sand Dunes, *Truman Fassette, originally from Indiana, 25" x 30", oil on canvas. Fassette painted along the East Coast. Given to Univeristy of North Carolina at Chapel Hill.*

Landscape with Figures, *Maurice Gerberg, 16" x 20", oil on board. Gift to Pfeiffer University.*

Landscape in New England, *Vladimir Jacik, 25" x 30". Gift to University of North Carolina at Chapel Hill.*

The Covered Bridge, *Faye Brown, 16" x 20", oil on board. Pfeiffer University.*

Lady in Flower Garden, *Lawton Parker, 26" x 21", oil on canvas, circa 1910. Gift to Bellmonte House, Wesleyan College.*

Farm, *Frank K.M. Rhen, 20" x 24", oil on canvas. Royster collection, Granville County Museum.*

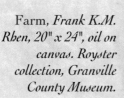

Cows in Stream, *Joseph Greenwood, 20" x 24", oil on canvas. The Royster collection, Granville County Hospital.*

Coast Near Newport, *Dey de Ribkowski, 30" x 36", oil on canvas, circa 1890s. Gift to U.S. Department of State, Art in Embassies Program. In memory of Geneva J. Weaver.*

Breten Women at Seashore, *Walter Saterlec, cover Pi Kappa Alpha Catalogue, 28" x 32", oil on canvas. Pi Kappa Alpha, Memphis, Tennessee.*

Autumn Landscape, *Henri Marchand, 30" x 25", oil on canvas. Memory of Charles Putnam. Gift to Duke University.*

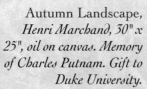

Lake in Georgia, *T. Addison Richards, 25" x 30", oil on canvas. Given to Johnston Center for Undergraduate Excellence, University of North Carolina at Chapel Hill.*

Street in Philadelphia, *Arthur Metzler, 12" x 16". Given to American Roentsen Ray Society.*

Hudson River with Falls, *18" x 21", oil on board. Donated to Wesleyan College.*

Iced Harbor, Symphony in Grey, *T. Scott Dabo, 18" x 24", oil on board. Given to American Roentgen Ray Society (ARRS).*

Landscape with Houses, *Karl Oberteuffer, 23" x 29",* oil on canvas. Painting won bronze medal, AIC. Gift to University of North Carolina at Chapel Hill.

Landscape with Birch Trees, *H.V. Murray, 25" x 30", oil on canvas. Given to Johns Hopkins Bloomberg School of Public Health.*

Farm Scene (Landscape with Buildings), *Maurice Gerberg, 20½" x 23¼", oil on board. Given to American Roentgen Ray Society.*

Still Life, *H.H. (Harold) Betts, 24" x 20", watercolor. AIC artist, brother of Louis Betts. Donated to Vanderbilt University.*

Hudson River Landscape, *24" x 30", oil on canvas. U.S. Post Office.*
Robersonville in memory of Postmaster Geneva James Weaver.

Asheville, North Carolina,
Lawrence Mazzanovich, 21" x
24", oil on canvas. Trained Art
Institute of Chicago, painted
North Carolina mountains
with Ingerle, Lamar, Griffiths,
Hockings, and others. James
collection at George Watts
Hill Alumni Center,
University of North
Carolina at Chapel Hill.

289

Landscape, *Thomas Patten, 16" x 20", oil on canvas. Given to Pfeiffer University.*

In the Ozarks, unsigned, attributed to Robert Neudescher, 20" x 24", oil on canvas. Given to John Hope Franklin Center, Duke University.

Albermarle County (Virginia), *Eliot Clark, 25" x 30"*. Clark was a member of the National Academy, and wrote this history. This work was composed late in his career and lacks his characteristic painting composition. Johns Hopkins Bloomberg School of Public Health.

Lake in Minnesota, *Armin Burkhart, 24" x 27", oil on canvas.* AIC artist. Given to Pfieffer University.

Mistakes and Mishaps

After you have been collecting American art for a period of time, it is useful to look at the errors you have made and what lessons you might have gleaned from the experience. Other chapters in this text have been involved with the prevention of mistakes but the lessons derived can be emphasized as well.

Early in my collecting career, I tried to depend upon my memory to avoid errors. I felt that lugging reference books with me was a great effort and that if the artist was accomplished or important, I would remember enough facts to render an informed opinion and make the correct choice. The three-volume *Who Was Who* did not fit properly in my carrying bag, so I left it home for awhile.

I encountered at Brimfield ("the greatest outdoor show on earth") a landscape painting by "Howe" who I assumed was the landscape artist W.H. Howe. I assumed this was an Old Lyme inspired landscape and purchased it for an "Old Lyme" price as that art colony had already been celebrated among the collecting public.

When I got home, I discovered the painting was done by an obscure member of the Ozark School and was not an Old Lyme landscape. This was not a painting that would fit my particular collecting criteria and I would have avoided acquisition had I had the reference books with me. They now are always in the trunk of my car even when going to a local flea market or antique mall. After all, I found a major Aaron Henry Gorson and Eliot Clark last year for an outlay of less than $500.

There are over 30,000 "listed" American painters in the standard reference books; so to rely upon one's personal recall to uncover a single artist at random is not a reasonable expectation.

Mistakes are often made when perspective is lost. I remember once purchasing a small J. Alden Weir landscape at auction because I had a very strong desire to own an example of that artist. Weir was a leader in many important American art groups and was a prominent member of "the Ten."

Despite my knowledge of the artist I failed to appreciate the fact that my auction "bargain" was only a poor example of his work. Fortunately, when I realized this, I was able to rather painlessly deaccess the painting by auction — P.T. Barnum was correct.

From this I learned to avail myself to the spectrum of the work of any artist I intended to acquire; you simply must have sufficient knowledge that you can distinguish a good, or at least representative, example from a poor one of the artist's work.

Once at an auction, I left a bid on a painting with the correct bid from the standpoint of the description, but in haste I left an incorrect item number. I bought the work of an artist I had never heard of nor intended to ever collect. Now, I not only check but verbally confirm the auction catalog number with one of the auction house staff.

Another "mistake" was not to exhaust every avenue of authentication including sending at least a photo or transparency if not the entire work to the expert on identification of a particular artist. If someone has done a catalogue raisonne or a complete text regarding a particular painter, they receive, by public acceptance, the mantle of "the authority on... ." Norman Geske on R. A. Blakelock or Ted Stebbins on Martin John Heade are examples. I might be on Eugene Healon Thomason or Henry Hammond Ahl.

I once bought a wonderful floral still life, unsigned but assured verbally by a Connecticut auction house that they could obtain a letter saying from the consignor that this painting was the work of the celebrated female artist Jane Peterson.

I acquired the painting at a fraction of the acquisition cost of a well documented work by Peterson. However, months later and a number of entreaties, the letter never came and the auction house was not particularly helpful. I was offered a trade for the piece allowing me a small multiple of my acquisition cost and I took it. Later the private dealer told me he sent the painting to the Peterson authority after a heated discussion with the auction house. The "expert" not only authenticated the work but also sent him an exhibition catalog that revealed Peterson had shown the work. He subsequently sold the painting for more than $10,000 over our trade price and to another dealer at that.

From this experience I learned several lessons. On valuable or potentially valuable works, never stop short in your quest for authentication if you know the appropriate avenue. Also, get any promise in assistance in identification from a seller in writing whether the offer is authentication by letter, provenance, or expert opinion. Otherwise, in reality, you have no recourse when authentication is not forthcoming. Sometimes, however, seeking an expert opinion when all you plan to do is own a painting forever can be a mistake. I have a very late George Inness (1891 – 1893, a year before his death in 1894). It was composed while he was staying in Tarpon Springs, Florida, and is one of several tonalist/impressionist versions of *The Picnic*. The provenance is impeccable and I enjoy the painting each day.

However, I once wanted to exhibit the work and asked one of the two declared and accepted experts on the work of George Inness, Sr. He said that it might be an Inness but opined that it was by Elliott Daingerfield and the signature had been changed early in the twentieth century.

I was disappointed, but since Daingerfield was a favorite of mine, I was not entirely crushed. I went to my dealer who said the Inness was as "right as the Holy writ" (or "rain" for that matter) and sent the painting to the other Inness authority who declared it to be a genuine late George Inness.

From this I relearned a lesson I knew from my experience as an "expert" in medical malpractice trials — experts can differ in fundamental ways and never take the word of one authority as the final answer. An expert opinion is just that, an opinion. Also recognize that experts have a bias in that it is less memorable to declare a painting uncertain or problematic than to subsequently discover a painting they assured was authentic to be a fake. Later, my first expert offered the revelation that the Daingerfield designation was a "hedge" and he could have substituted Robert C. Minor or George Inness, Jr. as well. Having owned a number of Daingerfields and studied all of Bob Coggins's vast collection, I had always been uncomfortable with that concession from the time it was offered. *The Picnic* version was recently in a traveling exhibit where its intrinsic Inness qualities were widely appreciated in a public forum.

Consignment is another area that needs to be clearly defined. For example, you should know what the asking price will be. If not, the dealer may offer the work at such a high price it is not sold, and the painting, after being shipped back to you, becomes tainted goods. The analog is pricing a house too high with a "for sale" sign. After a passage of some period of time the house is considered a "did not sell" and may require taking it off the market and leaving it off for a period of time. With paintings, I tell the dealer what I expect to realize and then reach an agreement for the asking price. Whatever negotiation then occurs is between the dealer and the acquirer only. This removes me from the actual selling process and is not unlike placing a painting at auction with a reserve, except you have no control over the bidding process. With the dealer, you, in theory, have a personal advocate.

I once consigned a painting to a dealer and after a reasonable time it did not sell and at the time I could not understand why. I retrieved the work and took it to a local auction. The auctioneer told me to hold the painting for awhile because it had been widely shopped around and everyone in the trade had had an opportunity to buy it from the dealer. Then he informed me of the dealer's asking price. I was shocked as it was a multiple of what I had asked to be realized by me. To me it seemed to be an unreasonable figure and I could now easily understand why it did not sell. I followed the advice of the auctioneer and kept the painting off the market for over a year and then consigned it to auction at a venue several thousand miles away. It sold for more than my reserve but well below the dealer's asking price. After this experience, I always agree upon what the dealer will ask as well as what I expect to realize.

Today one of the most difficult assessments is what the extent of a restoration will be required and what it will cost before you acquire a painting. I recently had the opportunity to deaccess a major painting at a favorable price. However, I wanted to have it in pristine condition, as it had been mounted on masonite almost two decades ago. Thinking that the conservator would be able to remove the painting without difficulty from the rigid support, I estimated the cost to be $1,200 – $1,500, but asked the potential acquirer to wait for a professional estimate before we progressed further with the sale.

The adhesive material used previously to fix the canvas to the masonite was very difficult to remove. In fact, our conservator was fairly certain that some of the masonite would adhere to the back of the canvas and would have to painstakingly be shaved off by a scalpel. His estimate was "at least $3,000 and three months." Now I get the opinion of the conservator before I enter into any negotiation in which I am anticipating that significant conservation or restoration might be necessary.

Some of my most profound memories as a collector have come with mistakes, mishaps, and misadventures. These each contained a message, and some, a lesson. Hopefully, they improved my competence as a collector and the learning experience became a part of my realized history — not to repeat itself.

Donating

Very few activities are more pleasurable than sharing our tastes and collections with others. This may take many forms with paintings such as loans or exhibitions, but the most significant and potentially rewarding are "gifts of kind" by donations. However, as with any important endeavor, there are certain methods in which the donor can maximize the enjoyment and give meaning to the process for both themselves and the recipients.

The emphasis of collectors initially, as we have noted elsewhere in this text, is the acquisition process whereby they will add to their holdings and most of, if not all, of their energy will be devoted to this endeavor. Usually this accumulation process cannot remain unabated as there is almost always a finite limitation of exhibition space and acquisition funds.

Collectors eventually come to realize that they possess a rather unique and valuable resource in their art collection. Most collectors will come to view their collection as not only a unique asset, but feel some responsibility to share with others as well. From this point forward, a collector's enjoyment of their art will be significantly impacted by the creative manner in which they deal with these perceived responsibilities.

Properly structured, donations should be very rewarding activities. For an astute collector to be transformed into a successful donor, certain changes, however, will be required. Just as the signature of your collection will reflect your individual tastes and proclivities, the recipient's acceptance requirements and wishes should be similarly reflective and these need to be recognized and accommodated.

If your major emphasis has been upon a particular genre and period, such as American impressionism, then offering an example from your collection to a museum of modern art may be inappropriate if you intended to add to their permanent collection. If, however, the painting is a wonderful example by an accomplished and valuable artist, the museum may indeed accept your offer hoping to later trade or sell the work to benefit the museum endowment.

This may be entirely acceptable to you but this is important to reach some understanding about this disposition of your gift prior to transfer. The worst fate of all for any donation is that it will be relegated to the museum's archives and never again see the light of day. This is embarrassing for the museum and disappointing

for the donor. This circumstance can be avoided by a candid discussion initiated by the collector with the director or curator of the museums or their committee on acquisitions at the time the painting is offered.

If the gift is to an organization or institution and not a museum, then the response guidelines are not as well delineated. Museums have guidelines of conduct and a tradition of housing art which affects, if it does not dictate, their responses to donations.

We have had a great deal of personal experience in this institutional area because many of our donations were given to honor the memory of particular individuals who made significant contributions to particular organizations during their lifetime. Prudent behavior for a potential donor would include a discussion with the administration as to their opinion of the preferences of the institution's membership.

Anytime you can involve the recipients in the donation process, you increase the likelihood of acceptance and long-term success. Once we wanted to honor a colleague who before his death had been a very effective senior vice-president at one of America's great private universities. Working with the development office we met with the deans of the college where he had made his greatest contribution. We offered them a series of paintings from which they made their choices on the basis of their assessment of aesthetic appeal and appropriateness of subject matter. This process had a high likelihood of success because of the involvement of the recipients.

We once made a donation of a collection and presented it as a fait accompli to an organization. A brochure describing the collection outlining the reasons for the gift and profiles of the individual honorees of the gift was published by us a short time later (monograph). There was almost no response from the recipients and it was then we realized they had not been made part of the process. This demonstrates the need for dialogue between the donor and the receiving institution in the process; they must be vested or the importance of the gift and pleasure from it will not be fully realized. The organization later wanted to sell the collection at auction but chose not to because of the dedication to former members of the organization.

Because they feel it is a delicate subject, most donors find it difficult to be specific about their expectations regarding the intended gift prior to the donation process. If the gift is offered for a specific purpose, this should be clearly stated and documented. Any restrictions should be discussed with he recipients and then committed to a written document or they may not be legally binding. The issues of exhibition and deaccession should be part of the discussions and expectations and constraints made part of the agreement.

One of the most common disappointments of donors is that museums seldom exhibit their gifts. This may simply be a manifestation of the amount of exhibition space of the museum related to the number of paintings they have in their archival storage. It is not unusual for a museum to have space to exhibit only several hundred paintings and yet have thousands of paintings in storage. Thus, it would be unrealistic to require that your gift be exhibited frequently unless it is a monumental painting or collection.

One particular strategy to obviate this to donated paintings to public institutions such as universities, government buildings, and organizational headquarters where the art is considered a permanent part of the general ambiance of the space. We have done this often in recent years.

If you do not specifically prohibit deaccession, a museum can assume that they have every right to do so. Recognize that there was no legal impediment to a sale unless specifically stated in the gift agreement. Regarding deaccession there are avenues for museums and institutions but so that the transaction by the recipient must appear to have been done "at arm's length" in a public forum; auction is the most common avenue. As a donor, you can request that you be informed of the deaccession and reacquire the work at auction if you wish.

Besides the transfer agreement, the most important step in the process is a fair market appraisal as discussed previously. This should be done by an expert in the specific genre and with documented experience and expertise. You can bring whatever information available to the appraisal process such as cost, exhibition records of the artist or provenance, but your appraiser must act free of your influence.

I would not like to emphasize the negative aspects of donating because the vast majority of these experiences will be positive and some even singularly rewarding. To consider that you can derive a great deal of satisfaction from the gift and its purpose while concomitantly achieving a significant tax benefit is certainly a compelling prospect. The fact that your pleasure might be ongoing only adds to the potential of a proper donation.

Disposition

If you plan to donate all your paintings during your lifetime or take them with you into the hereafter, do not read this chapter but have your CPA, your legal guru, or your personal banker do so. We get so involved in the acquisition process that we simply do not devote a great deal of effort to the mechanics of deaccession or disposition of our paintings in the form of an outright gift, permanent loan, or transfer by a trust instrument.

There are proper methods for disposition of a painting or paintings at the time of death. You should be aware of the necessary documentation as well as the legalities involved in order to assure that your wishes are subsequently met. Your paintings mean a great deal to you and if you consider their possible fates you realize how much you care about them.

A painting will usually be conveyed as a specific bequest. If a painting is specifically bequeathed, your will or legal instrument should expressly address how the expenses and taxes are to be paid. In some states, title will invest in the legatee at your death and the bequeathed painting will generally not be applied to pay creditors until the residue and general legacies have been exhausted. You should be certain that your appraisals are reasonably current and they represent fair market value for your paintings. Liens and litigations involving your paintings will become the responsibility of the legatee unless your will directs that such costs and expenses are paid out of the residuary estate. Should you wish to leave paintings to your spouse, funding through the marital deduction will allow a painting or paintings to escape taxation in the estate of the first spouse.

There are several new entities that will allow the postponement, if not the escape, of taxes. If you wish to have a painting in a qualified terminable interest property (QTIP) trust, the painting can also be used to fund the trust. Although a painting will not generate income, it can be a substantial part of a trust. Treasury regulations note that "a power to retain trust assets which consist substantially of non-income property will not disqualify the interest if the trust requires that the trustee convert the property to income or liquid assets within a reasonable time."

The reason for this qualification is that sale of paintings is often a prolonged process, and to dispose of a painting under duress often means that it may well be sold below its market value. Thus, you are given time to ascertain fair market value.

In order to qualify for a QTIP trust, your spouse must have the use of the painting and can fully direct its sale. Often, if your surviving spouse wishes, they can, under the terms of your will, hold, exhibit, and enjoy a painting while it hopefully increases in value with time rather than be required to have the painting sold soon after your death.

Because of the speculative nature of the art market and the downside risk, an appointed trustee should be expressly authorized to retain a painting or a collection, but subject to the surviving spouse's right to request the deaccession of the work or collection. The trustee should be exonerated from any loss incurred as a result of this retention. A provision in a will exonerating an executor or testamentary trustee for failure to exercise reasonable care, diligence, and prudence is void and could jeopardize the marital deduction benefit.

Because of art's lack of productivity in generating income and cash flow, when a painting is held for more than a year in an estate or trust and then sold, the proceeds may be treated for tax purposes as not only principal but also as delayed income.

The Uniform Principal and Income Act, adopted in most areas, states that: "the sum allocated as delayed income is the difference between the net proceeds and the amount which, had it been invested at simple interest at 4% per year while the property was underproductive, would have produced the net proceeds less any carrying charges and expenses previously charged against income, such as restoration and insurance."

The tax allocation provision of your will should be given particular attention by your tax or estate attorney if your estate has valuable paintings. If a valuable (or potentially valuable) painting or collection will be specifically bequeathed (and if there will be no offsetting marital or charitable deduction), a tax clause or statute that directs the payment of all estate and other death taxes out of the residue could eliminate a substantial portion of the residuary disposition.

If the painting is held in a revocable trust or if an irrevocable grantor retained interest trust that is included in the grantor's gross estate, the same result may obtain. This could give you a significant problem with the allocation of your painting assets.

This tax apportionment problem could be exacerbated if there is a great increase in the value of your collection between the time your will is drawn in relation to your date of death. This has certainly happened in the last 15 years with American paintings of the nineteenth and early twentieth centuries and you may unwittingly leave your heirs a problem if you do not take this into account. For example, you bequeath a painting to your son or daughter and direct that all estate taxes on property passing under your will be paid from the residue. You leave the residuary estate in a QTIP trust to your spouse, but by the time of your death, the painting has quadrupled in value. The estate taxes would then substantially reduce your marital residuary gift in this particular circumstance.

Your spouse may realize very little or even nothing from the painting — unless they exercise their right of election. Your spouse may exercise their right of election and thereafter disinherit the children — not a result foreseen by you or your children. In many cases, estate taxes should be apportioned against a painting or the trust holding the painting. What you need to do is tell your attorney what you wish to achieve and have them prepare the documents that will accomplish this goal.

You should ask your attorney these questions. How might the taxes resulting from your bequest be paid without the necessity of deaccessing a certain painting or a group of your treasured acquisitions? Might there be made available resources from insurance that can be used for this purpose? Is the beneficiary of the insurance policy also the person or trust that will receive the painting or bear the responsibility for the taxes? Should the estate taxes on the insurance be allocated against the proceeds from the insurance? Does the beneficiary of the trust have other resources or borrowing power, so that the beneficiary or trust has the option of borrowing funds to pay the estate taxes? These alternatives can only be considered if a carefully orchestrated disposition plan has been previously thought out by you.

If there are few or no liquid assets in an estate and, in order to preserve the art collection, administrative expenses are paid out of income and deductions taken on the fiduciary return, the value of the residuary bequest to the charity or spouse will nevertheless be reduced by these expenses. If the expenses are chargeable to principal under local law and the decedent did not otherwise provide an alternative method, this is especially applicable. This says if you do not provide funds for expenses, some of your paintings may be sold under duress to raise capital for the retention of others.

Your collection can be incorporated like a business so that the payment of estate taxes can be deferred under estate law. Deferral in this circumstance would enable your family to choose to retain the paintings for possible appreciation of their value in a rising market. The consents of the beneficiaries obtained as to the retention of the art could be speculative, if the art market should decline, and leave your fiduciary at risk of a surcharge claim.

Whether the possession and use of the paintings by the shareholder constitute a dividend and/or generates income to the corporation is an interpretive risk by the IRS that must also be considered a potential problem by you.

The location of your paintings at the time of death may indeed have tax consequences. State death taxes are usually imposed on paintings by the state in which the works are physically located at the date of death. This could present planning opportunities for you to minimize state death taxes on a valuable work or collection by locating the paintings in a state with only a "pick-up" estate tax equal to the amount of the federal credit. If a painting is on exhibit in a not-for-profit museum in a state other than your domicile, the work may be exempt from the death tax of the state where the object is being exhibited as in the estate of a non-resident.

If your estate involves a sizeable art collection and the executor has no expertise in that regard, you may provide for the appointment of an art advisor. This advisor can make decisions concerning the sale or retention and conservation of your collection. The exercise of authority by advisors appointed by your will to direct the co-executors if there is a disagreement can be upheld over the objections of one of the co-executors, as in the case of *Matter of Rubin*. Your advisor should be then considered a fiduciary of the estate and the co-executors will not be personally liable for losses if they follow the directions of the advisor.

Rubin also held that the directions of the advisors are not subject to the court's review in the absence of improper motive. The question of compensation for the advisor should be addressed in your will or settled by an inter vivos agreement between you and the art advisor.

The nominated executor of your estate should ascertain whether the works of art are secure in their location and should expedite the issuance of letters of the testamentary. An itemized appraisal should be arranged as soon as reasonable following your death. Obtaining an accurate and timely appraisal of the works is of great importance and should be done by an expert in that specific area of art. The provenance and exhibition record should be documented, as these data can often enhance the value of a painting. If the federal estate tax return is audited, the IRS will probably, as a matter of course, submit works valued in excess of $20,000 to the IRS Art Advisory Panel for valuation. The Art Advisory Panel is not told whether the work of art is being valued for income, gift, or estate tax purposes. Your executor should also evaluate the adequacy of the insurance coverage and obtain a rider to the insurance policy, covering the interest of the estate and the beneficiaries. At the time of death, art collections are often underinsured and appraisals are often outdated. You should make certain yours is not.

The executor should ascertain whether anyone other than the decedent has a fractional or remainder interest in the art, a security interest or any other interest in any of the paintings.

Collectors sometimes purchase major examples jointly. If a painting has not be properly characterized, the family may not be aware that earlier a museum had been given a remainder interest in the work and that at the time of your death the painting or paintings should be properly delivered to the museum. Whether a painting represented a loan or a gift has often been confused and can be the subject of somewhat lengthy and hostile litigation tried in the newspapers. Remember the clamor over the sale of the Wyeths by the owner when a museum did not appreciate the meaning of a "long term loan." The legal language of the transfer clearly (to a legal authority) made the transfer a long term loan and not a gift. Many administrators and board members may not understand the difference but they should and you should assume the responsibility that they do in your case.

If your entire collection or a single painting is to be sold by the estate, it is important that the manner of disposition be arranged to achieve the fair market value of the objects and that any conflicts of interest be avoided. In the Matter of Rothko, contracts for the sale of the 798 paintings made by the executors of the estate of the famous colorist Mark Rothko through Marlborough A.G. were voided because of conflicts of interest. One of the three executors was an officer and director of the Marlborough Galleries, were surcharged for appreciation damages of more than $7 million based on the value of the paintings at the time of the decision. A third executor was surcharged for the loss incurred at the time of the sale because of a failure to exercise "prudence" (avoid errors of the p's — prudence, parsimony, and propriety). Certainly, this case is extraordinary in the fame of the decedent and the financial implications involved, but the circumstance of conflict of interest is not that unusual.

If your paintings are to be auctioned, depending on their quality, the executor often can negotiate certain terms of the sale with the auction house. The auction house can waive the seller's 10% fee, the advertisement publication costs, and guarantee your executor a minimum price. For valuable, prestigious works, such terms are almost always possible. While this is not the regular business practice of most auction firms, this is done as an exception to secure the inclusion of important works to enhance the specific auction as well as the image and standing of the auction house. If a single painting is particularly valuable, your executor can arrange for the auction house to have it placed as a color illustration in several publications, thereby greatly increasing public awareness and presumably interest in purchasing it. If you believe that the cover illustration of the advertisement of the sale in *Antiques* or *Art in America* are chosen at random — I have a bridge I want to sell you.

If your paintings are on loan to a museum, your executor should request their return at your death or confirm the loan status and notify the museum of the estate's intent to preserve its interest in the property. If the painting is to remain on loan, your executor should notify the museum of changes of address or changes in ownership. Timeliness in discharge of this responsibility is of the essence. In Redmond v. New Jersey Historical Society, the court held that the statute of limitation did not start until there had been a demand and refusal to return the loaned object. The issue in this case was a portrait by Gilbert Stuart on loan to the New Jersey Historical Society for more than 50 years. An "old loan" statute in one of approximately 20 states can pass title in the loaned object to the museum on a deemed gift, abandonment, or statute of limitations theory. These statutes generally apply to an indefinite loan (or a loan for a definite period which has expired) to a museum, where the lender is unknown, cannot be contacted, or where there has been no written contact with the lender for a stated period. Notice to the institution is usually required, and the lender is given a reasonable period of time to retrieve the loaned object from the museum. If the piece is not retrieved during that period, title of the object will generally pass to the museum.

If a work was stolen or is lost for unknown reasons before your death or is discovered missing in the course of the administration of the estate, the theft should be reported to the proper authorities, the Art Dealer's Association or other appropriate bodies, and a stolen art archive such as the International Foundation for Art Research (IFAR). Efforts to locate the art should be continuous, so that the cause of action to recover the work when it is located will not be time-barred or barred by states applying a discovery or demand and refusal rule.

A claim by you or your heirs for the recovery of an allegedly stolen work may not be brought for decades. The statute of limitations in a replevin action (often three or four years) may start to run at the time of the good faith purchase, because the purchaser is treated as a "converter." The New Jersey Supreme Court in O'Keefe v. Snyder applied the discovery rule, holding that the cause of action does not accrue until the owner, exercising due diligence, discovers the whereabouts of the stolen work or should have discovered it. Once the limitation period expires, O'Keefe held that title to the good faith purchaser.

If an estate has a claim for the breach of warranty of authenticity — because the "Monet" is a fake — the executors should investigate initiating legal action immediately. Actions for breach of warranty of authenticity normally accrue at the time of sale. In Wilson v. Hammer Holding, Inc., an action for breach of warranty that a painting was a "Vuillard" was instituted more than 25 years after the purchase was ruled to be time-barred. In Rosen v. Spanierman, the court held that a cause of action for breach of an express warranty of authenticity that a painting was a "John Singer Sargent" accrued at the time of sale (in 1968) was barred by the four-year statute of limitations. Obviously, there are no specific guidelines with regard to the timeliness

of reporting, due notice, or for the initiation of causes of action. However, the temporal proximity greatly enhances a positive outcome. Sometimes collectors will never really investigate the authenticity of a painting but this can become an issue during valuation at the time of death. So know what you have.

Planning for the testamentary disposition and administration of art necessitates that you obtain documentary information and records of the artworks, and that you provide for the security and preservation of the collection. The rights of all co-owners holding the remainder or undivided interest in the paintings should be documented. Special attention should be given to your estate, gift and income tax by generation delaying legal instruments, treatments of the transfer, and the payment and allocation of such taxes at your death.

Testamentary disposition of paintings requires professional legal advice but also your involvement to assure that your desires are respected. While general legal principles of ownership transfer and inheritance statutes will serve as benchmarks, there are nuances that may have to do with unique relationships of you and art institutions, you and appraisers and dealers, and your advisors that often require the special and specific expertise of persons outside the legal profession. Collaboration in which you combine expertise and wisdom from several disciplines I believe is the most appropriate manner to assure the proper testamentary deposition. You have a responsibility to yourself as a collector to make certain your acquisitions achieve your purpose even after you have passed to that larger museum in the sky.

Epilogue

This portion of my text should serve to emphasize the key points made in the various chapters. Therefore, I will repeat, for emphasis a number of "messages." The acquisition of objects of value has many compelling features, which range from the satisfaction you gain from the ownership of your collection to enabling your entry into valued circles. Curators, art historians, and fellow collectors often extol the benefits of collecting paintings in their public pronouncements and their contributions to the literature. The downside risks of this activity are not as often or completely described as I hope they have been in the body of this text.

The acquisition endeavor itself can be very stimulating and the entire process rewarding, as I have expressed. Appreciating and sharing your collection can certainly be a very pleasurable experience. Many people will assume that because of this activity that you are affluent as well as having good taste. Both assumptions have attendant responsibilities.

Various art and financial publications have emphasized the vast sums of money that have been realized on the sale of individual American paintings and the general increase in value for certain groups of artists. The public often ascribes this phenomenon to paintings in general (or all paintings) and not to selected artists of specific works that are deemed newsworthy.

A profit of about $42 million in less than a decade for a single Picasso in the 1980s or the prices fetched by Van Gogh's (try $87 million plus buyer's premium at public auction) and Cezanne's works are more than simply newsworthy. These numbers affected the traditional standards for desirable art objects in general as well as the canons and codes of conduct for the entire art world. They undoubtedly changed public perception about art, art collecting, and art collectors as well. The more recent price fixing by the highest echelons of Sotheby's and Christie's have tarnished the reputation of both houses.

In considering this phenomenon, one should realize that market forces in the art world have their own unique creations to supply and demand. These are not the same as commodities; even pork bellies or the more exotic small economic markets. The art market represents ascribed value by very arbitrary criteria.

Because paintings are treasured rather than utilitarian consumable objects, the demand can be more easily artificially manipulated and to a much greater extent than in the usual commercial environment of responding to the traditional market forces. As noted earlier, the perception of rarity can be manufactured, especially with artists that are deceased.

The value of a painting depends upon a number of variables but to a large extent upon the artist, documentation of authenticity, the condition of the work, and whether the painting demonstrates the genius of that particular painter or the desirability of the school that it represents. These are the most determinative criteria but may rightly have biases.

I trust by now in this text you understand that this is an emotion laden environment in which you may be acquiring objects whose authenticity, condition, and typicality are based largely upon opinions and not upon the usual laws of evidence or strict reliance upon burden of proof. In the art world, there is very little scientific data attendant at times, to decisions and considerations involving very large sums of money. Although the art world is not unique in this regard, it involves large and fragile egos, except for possibly the world of entertainment or, in my own experience, academic medicine.

A milieu composed of emotional volatility, a paucity of objective data, significant sums of money, and sometimes contentious participants may prove to be a combination that might be hazardous to your financial and physical well being if you are not circumspect in your actions. Can you practice prevention to diminish the emotional and financial stress? Can you avoid some of the more obvious pitfalls, and can you accurately balance the risks against the expected benefits before any significant art undertaking?

Knowledge in this instance is definitely power. Experience is one way to gain knowledge, but the pathway is long and arduous, and the tuition can be expensive.

As noted in my chapter on "Authenticity," purchasing a fake painting is a traumatic and costly method to learn about fakes. Instead you should acquire enough knowledge beforehand so that you can identify a representative example of that particular artist's work and, at least, identify an obvious misrepresentation.

As I have recommended earlier, you should be able to do this initially deciding on the genre of painting you want to collect and then studying as many examples of this style or artists practicing that technique as you can.

This learning experience will occur in museums, commercial galleries, and viewing other collections. Read everything about American paintings; devour what has been written on the subject within your reasoned allocation of time for this endeavor.

Fortified with this data, you can also make another very important informed choice, that of choosing a mentor. Mentors can be the art equivalent of the legal expert witness; they can assist in your search for artistic "truth." The truth being the appropriate examples of the paintings you are seeking and at a reasonable price.

Mentors can be fellow collectors, art historians, dealers, or "consultants" (although I am not certain what this contemporary term means). Your mentors can change as your own tastes become more refined, your resources vary, and as your collection matures. I have had two determinative mentors, the legendary Southern collector, the late Bob Coggins, and the late Bob Vose who had the oldest gallery of American art paintings.

I was able to first interact with the Vose Gallery for my early acquisitions and having a mentor like the late Robert C. Vose Jr. was a very fortunate circumstance for me. Due to financial limitations, I was not in the market for a major or even representative Fitz Hugh Lane or a Martin Johnson Heade. In fact, the artists I was first attracted to, Edmund Tarbell, Frank Weston Benson, Joseph DeCamp, and William M. Paxton, were also beyond my financial means.

I know collectors who are made to feel inadequate if they do not exercise "courage" and financially "reach" to acquire museum examples by these major artists or, more important, minor examples by these famous names by certain dealers.

This attitude by your mentor can be very hazardous to both your physical and fiscal well-being. Bob Vose guided me to consider major paintings by lesser-known artists of the Boston Museum of Fine Arts (BMFA) School which were of museum quality both in size and technical competence. I acquired excellent examples representing the best of the graduates of the BMFA that had been former students of Tarbell, Benson, DeCamp, and Paxton. These included such painters as Gretchen Rodgers, Phillip Little, Marguerite Pearson, Lee Lufkin, William J. Kaula, Phillip Leslie Hale, and Marion Howard to cite a few.

The acquisition of these paintings allowed me to achieve several things simultaneously: first, to obtain the best works of these artists, acquire enough examples to have a true collection of substantive works that made an artistic statement, and to stay within a financial commitment I could accommodate. This avoided the before mentioned symptoms of tachycardia, night sweats, and even delusions of grandeur.

This collection strategy also lessened the probability of my inadvertently acquiring a fake or a deliberate misrepresentation. The profit potential of the transaction at that time would not make it worth the perpetrator's risk. There was simply not enough money involved to make this type of perfidy, cum malfeasance, worthwhile.

Take, for example, the controversy over "faked" Edmund Tarbells, the leader of the BMFA School. This received little public notice initially but those avid collectors of that group of painters and interested scholars knew about the dispute. Certainly, a visit to your home by the FBI to investigate your Tarbell could produce a touch of angina, if not a myocardial infarction.

This controversy was fueled by the rapid escalation in the value of Tarbell's work following publication of a text in which he was the featured artist (*Tarbell and His School*, Patricia Pierce, Rumsford Press). Despite claims and counter charges, no litigation ever occurred but some collectors were momentarily anguished and behavior patterns in that art world were altered.

From this litany of events, one might develop a strategy for practicing a bit of stress prevention. Choose a dealer who is known to the trade, who has been in the business or in the art world in some capacity for a number of years. Your dealer should have a defined approval and return policy for paintings and a willingness to listen to your assessment of your resources and not just follow their own instincts as to your collecting activities and resource allocation.

As I have noted, you must stay within your financial limits remembering that these purchases should involve only discretionary money. Following these practices you will minimize the chance of buying a painting that turns out not what it was thought to be, paying too much for a painting and if this proves to be so, you will have the opportunity to return the work you have decided was a mistake.

As noted in the chapter on funding, your purchase should not place you in Chapter 7 or even Chapter 11. After all, wasn't this supposed to be a pleasurable activity and enhance the creativity in your life? If your desire was to get rich from your art purchases, you could have tried futures, genetic manipulation, or something like a venture capital effort. Of course, we all hope for good value in our paintings acquisitions, but we should not imprudently try to make them "too good."

As I have noted, many collectors feel that an inexpensive manner of acquiring paintings is at auction and there is validity in this belief under the correct circumstances. This may not always be the case, and the risks at auction are substantial. I have personally acquired a number of paintings in this fashion, but not without substantial preparation on my part as I have indicated. I have also acquired during the process, wittingly or unwittingly, the good and helpful advice from the competition — dealers and other collectors. My steps for acquisitions in this manner as previously stated are reasoned and deliberate. More importantly, my discipline is resolute.

My own personal assessment of my desire translated into a realistic consideration of my resources is recorded in my auction catalog. If I have any doubt about my self-control, I will leave an absentee bid and avoid the adrenaline surge that can overcome reason during the excitement of the auction proceedings. I can bid over the phone but I always wonder in this process who I am bidding against.

A great deal of energy is often expended at auction, feigning concern or pretending as a bidder that you are not emotionally involved. This is all posturing and not necessary for success in this activity. Your preparation for auction is designed to minimize this stress by preventing panic and irrational behavior because of your acquired knowledge and anticipation of the process.

Dismiss the idea that when you bid against a major gallery you are riding along with their expertise and are financially safe because, if they are the successful buyer, they will necessarily mark the price of the painting up at least 100% when they offer the work for sale. This may not be the true circumstance. The gallery may well be acting as the agent for a collector or an institution that does not possess your knowledge or judgement. The principal may have told the agent "buy it," so you might very well see the biding reach the ozone layer. If you allow yourself to follow this bidding ascent to the stratosphere and then happen to purchase the painting at this lofty sum, your fall into reality may be very painful.

If you have significant doubts about whether the auction house warrants the authenticity or condition of a painting, read the disclaimers in the front of the catalog. In general, the painting you successfully bid on is what you have acquired; warts and all. That is not to say that the major houses don't have experts to evaluate paintings (because they do) and they also exercise quality control as to what paintings are vetted and which paintings make the auction catalog. A certain amount of comfort can be taken in this process; but once the hammer falls, you, for all intents and purposes, own the piece that you bid on successfully.

If you feel but do not have a prima facie evidence that you have been misled by the auction house or the consignor, do not "compound your felony" by considering legal redress. Save your time, funds, and psyche by swallowing the mistake. It will protect your health and may conserve your wealth. Only if the mistake is obvious should you do more than inform the auction house of your concerns and express your disappointment. This is an area that litigation is usually unsuccessful for true legal redress.

Life is a series of gains and losses; success can be measured by how effectively we minimize our losses — not just by the recognition of our triumphs. The most important aspect of this is you must simply accept what has happened and move to a rapid conclusion. Rumination about mistakes is a great method of depleting one's creative energy and can significantly compromise the pleasure of your collecting American paintings. There are other areas where one should exercise caution in your art activity.

Despite even a studied avoidance of publicity, if you have been collecting art for a number of years, "pickers" will seek you out. This is a breed representing a cross between a gypsy and a patent medicine salesman. While they are important for the artistic "food chain," be assured that in some pickers there is the potential for perfidy befitting a flimflam man. They sometimes know the characteristics of their finds but you may never be informed about the paintings. In the Old West, these characters would have stood on the tailgate of a wagon and extolled the virtues of some elixir of cactus extract or condensation of bitterroot oil. In the art world, the potion purloined is the painting; laced with turpentine and varnish.

As I have noted, pickers will often regale you with tales that they supply the leading galleries with their most important paintings that are then marked up 100 – 2,000% by the time they are offered to you. They claim to be able to save you substantial amounts of money. You must resist being impressed with these vignettes and should be mindful that, even if these are not fabrications, as opposed to you, a gallery represents repeat business and an ongoing placement of paintings for the picker. Thus, the picker, for the long term survival must maintain a good relationship with a gallery. The owner of the gallery can pass negative information to others in the trade and the picker will find himself an unwelcome guest in other areas of the art world. For these reasons you may not be offered the same acquisition opportunities the picker presents to a gallery. As a collector, you have none of the safeguards a gallery has when dealing with a picker. Your leverage is simply not as great.

The condition of the painting according to the picker is always good; though it "may need a little cleaning" — and provenance is that "it came out of a house." (How could a painting not come out of a house?) This implies that it is pristine, not a trade worn piece — sort of virginal. With the picker you are protected largely by your knowledge and your faith, however misguided, in this individual. Pickers come in all types or stripes but they have certain common characteristics.

Pickers usually have no gallery because they simply cannot conform to a schedule, they sometimes fail to keep appointments, often ship your purchases whenever it suits them, and are in financial circumstances where they are constantly shifting resources.

Experienced galley owners treat these people with a great deal of skepticism, and this is despite the inherent safeguards the galleries have that you do not. As an individual who is engaged in this activity for pleasure and not for profit, deal with pickers only in those areas where you feel you know more than the picker does and as much as any dealer or gallery.

Standards and credentials exist in the world of art, but they are much less codified and structured than in many other areas of commerce where goods are exchanged for large sums of money. Value of an object is what someone can be induced to pay and the criteria are very subjective.

Art dealers, as I have previously stated, tend to be a critical lot and very litigious with each other and, at times, with collectors. As a collector, you can usually avoid this peril by certain measures such as remaining on a straightforward, simple payment basis for goods received. Also, require the assurances of authenticity, provenance, and condition be in document form. If you become involved in trades in kind, payment schedules or the intradealer business of art, you may become unwittingly involved in litigation as well.

If you exchange paintings in kind, make certain what you warrant in the exchange. Document the value of the credit you have been accorded by your dealer for your painting or paintings. Dealers have been known to trade paintings with collectors and, when the trades they acquired did not sell, or they received less than anticipated profit, declared that these works were misrepresented by the collector at the time of trade. The damages they may request initially may even be in excess of that you were allowed in trade but represented the dealer's anticipated profit.

Another claim by dealers in requesting compensation is to cite damage to the reputation of the gallery because of the transaction. This is sometimes accompanied by a fabricated tale of offering the exchanged goods to a valued client and then having to rescind the offer. Although obviously self serving, this ploy can be effective in settlement proceeding or with a jury.

The criterion initially evaluated in accessing the authenticity of a painting is most commonly the signature of the artist. This has been discussed previously but is so important in this determination that there are texts devoted to the appearance, signature, inscription, or symbols artists might have used to indicate that they are, indeed, the creator of the painting. Variations of the artists' known signatures are included in texts because many artists, as one might expect from creative people, changed their signature over time or even used a variety of signatures throughout their careers. Some artists even changed their names or altered the composition of their inscription.

Edmund Tarbell, the leader of the Boston Museum School, signed his paintings by a variety of signatures which are, by now, quite well known to the collecting public, as there has been the aforementioned and well-publicized controversy regarding the authenticity of examples of his paintings.

J. Alden Weir was at one time Julian A. Weir and James Abbott McNeill Whistler, about whom all things were extraordinary, used a monogram suggesting on Oriental inspiration for his tonalist paintings. The Dabo brothers, who also wanted to emulate the other characteristics or Whistler's tonalist aesthetic, copied this practice. The Boston artist, Louis Kronberg often, but not always, affixed the Star of David with his signature which was probably a very bold statement at the time. This did not dissuade the influential Isabella Stewart Gardner ("Mrs. Jack") from collecting his work. Experiences involving threatened litigation over authenticity may be a matter of conducting business in the art world but not for the collector and can be very hazardous to your happiness and well-being.

You will eventually reach the point you have a "collection" which presumably you enjoyed acquiring and are satisfied with the results. These paintings embellish your home and office. They give you pleasure when you view them as well as recall the manner and moment of your acquisition. For reasons of your personal tranquility alone you might cease and desist activity in the art world at this juncture, but many collectors will not do so. They want to feel the "rush" that occurs when they see their name on the identifying museum plaque stating "on loan from the collection of …" or "gift of… ."

Even more permanently rewarding is to be mentioned and recognized in the exhibition catalog. This represents public exposure to you, which is not without risks. Another order of magnitude of personal exposure and hopefully reward is to loan not just an individual painting but all or a number from your collection for an exhibition in which you are the single exhibitor.

You cannot always correctly anticipate the public response to your artistic judgement. First, the museum staff and curator are going to accept for exhibit only what they feel appropriate, arrange the exhibit to their standards and preferences, and probably describe your works according to their assessment of the important data and artistic merit.

Then there is the risk of damage and theft of your paintings during exhibition. When you loan paintings, if the exhibit travels, how will it be packaged and shipped and when will it return? How is the exhibit insured and is it for the replacement or "real" value of the paintings? Will the temperature and humidity be regulated properly during the exhibition? Sharing one's collection with the general public can be taxing but very rewarding.

I know collector friends who cannot attend museum openings involving their paintings for fear of public criticism of the works as well as their tastes and artistic judgement. With my very first painting exhibition, the "consultant" hired by the institution to mount the exhibit punctured a major painting. This was the first time I had thought about who insured the works, and if there was adequate insurance or just whose insurance applied. Should you or the institution have replacement insurance or only enough to cover your acquisition cost or just for the cost of the restoration? Almost any damaged painting is probably devalued even after competent restoration. Thus, much more important for me, and I suspect for most collectors, was whether or not the damage to the painting would decrease its value no matter how competent the restoration.

After several "expert" opinions about what should be done with the painting, I realized that if you believe that you are going to be fully compensated for significant damage to, and the subsequent devaluation of, a painting, you predictably will be disappointed. Assessing devaluation due to damage accurately is too imprecise and is not usually covered adequately by insurance.

It is human nature to invest a great deal of emotion in personal tastes which go on trial when you loan paintings for public exhibition. Having one of your paintings rejected by the curator of an exhibit as a "fake" could place you in shock, but to be told that your painting represents a social faux pas will predictably put you into a state of indignation. This, in your gestalt, is a personal insult. We have had this experience.

A nude by George Luks that for years was part of our permanent collection was also typical of both the artist and his artistic circle; the "Immortal Eight" and Ashcan School. Additionally, it was a moderately important painting because of the reputation and influence of Luks. In going through the exhibit at the opening with some colleagues, we noticed that my Luks was missing. My theories as to the cause of its absence ranged from damage at the hanging to unreported theft. When I finally located the curator, he apologetically told us that "certain patrons" had found the painting offensive and had demanded its removal. After our respective heads came together, I demanded to speak with these self-appointed "arbiters of taste" so that I could inform them about the Ashcan School of Artists, nudes in general, George Luks' typical nudes, realism, etc.

Fortunately, the curator did not comply with my demands for an audience and my anger soon passed, but I learned a truth. If you exhibit paintings outside the confines of your private space, you are subject to the whims and vagaries of the public. If your emotional composition cannot accommodate their response, decline to exhibit publicly.

I do not wish to discourage you from being or becoming a collector in the full sense of the activity and the broadest context of the meaning. However, you should have a realistic appraisal of the risks involved and behave in a prudent manner to ensure a long and healthy art collecting career which may or may not include exhibition. You can identify your patron/collector concept of well-being by periodically assessing the reality of your activities and expectations. Perform a risk/benefit analysis for the entirety but the issue of authenticity regarding paintings is of such fundamental importance it should be treated again.

The principal determinant of a painting's value is the stature and reputation of the artist who composed the work. Despite aesthetic considerations, this single characteristic remains the most significant factor in assessing the relative worth of a painting. Thus as I have discussed, the importance of authenticity is almost unparalleled in the appraisal of any particular work.

The reasonableness of this notwithstanding, the fact is that this represents conventional wisdom in the art world, and the traditional methods to determine authenticity are rigidly and steadfastly held, despite sometimes flawed reasoning and problematic logic.

Some artists worked their signatures into the painting in such a fashion that they are almost undetectable by simple visual inspection. Certain landscape artists of the mid to late nineteenth century, often so intricately wove their signature into the brushwork of paintings that one can search unsuccessfully by simple visual inspection. "Soft" (low kilo voltage) radiographs may also uncover signatures. Signatures can be hidden beneath the frame liner or mat of a painting and can be uncovered when the painting is taken to be cleaned or restored.

The quest of a signature can sometimes achieve the character of a journey in search of the Holy Grail, and one's thinking can be so distorted that the faulty logic then becomes: if a signature is uncovered, then the painting is deemed genuine; and if one is not identified, the painting is not considered authentic. The signature, rather than a means to an end (authenticity), becomes inappropriately the end itself. Unfortunately, this circumstance all too often obtains even though the flawed logic should be apparent. As noted earlier, signature is merely evidence for authenticity not equivalent to authenticity itself.

Collectors, dealers, and conservators have experienced all of the above-noted revelations enough to pursue each of these avenues if there is some chance it will lead to the discovery of a signature. However extrapolating from the autograph and document collecting world, the fashioning of a signature or a symbolic inscription to perpetuate a deceit is not extremely difficult or that uncommon. Given the temptation of significant profit, little chance of detection, and minimal legal risks, misrepresentations will predictably occur. Not only is this perfidy difficult to uncover, but determining exactly when the deed was performed during the chain of ownership may be virtually impossible. Thus, for you to discover specific culpability is problematic and makes restitution difficult.

Another widely held belief in the art world is that by the considered analysis of the brushstroke and composition pattern, an "expert" can almost always determine the artist who painted the work with great accuracy. While this is a time-honored evaluation and has validity and inherent merit, the manner in which it is accepted defies standard concepts in science, well-validated positions in the canons of human logic, and takes great license with the legal concept of evidence.

Brushstroke analysis by art experts has been likened by many in the art world to fingerprint or DNA analysis, genetic matching, and possibly magnetic resonance (MRI) spectroscopy. These scientific techniques, however, are objective measures that are so accurate that they can even lend themselves to quantification, while brushstroke analysis is inherently subjective and not in a format that the degree of certainty can be measured.

Their legacy can be seen in the emergence of the regionalists such as Thomas Hart Benton and Grant Wood and to some extent among the most accomplished of the WPA artists whose realistic works reflect this artistic influence. Many of the more popular instructors of the Art Students League taught for several decades after the Armory Show, the realist style espoused by the Ashcan School. Thus, their aesthetic's life was greatly extended.

The importance of "The Eight" and the Ashcan School in American art cannot be underestimated, as they were largely responsible for establishing the legitimacy of everyday American life as an appropriate subject for visual art. Whether or not you are attracted to the bold images with their direct social statements, to collect them is quite another determination. Several are monumentally expensive, while others the primary determinant is the subject matter.

An appropriate analogy might be identifying the perpetrator from a police lineup in which the chronological age of the subject is unknown and recognizing that the physical characteristics of human suspects can vary significantly over time as can the visual appearance of a painting.

Subject matter of the painting under question is another parameter which experts often use to lend credence to their identifications. However, anyone who has seen the intact estate of an artist, participated in the gathering of examples for a retrospective of someone's oeuvre, or accumulated a catalogue raisonne has discovered that what is considered to be the characteristic subject matter for an artist or the number of subjects an artist might have painted over a career varies a great deal. Therefore, what is deemed "typical" for an artist may well change with time.

In the formative stages of their careers, artists might have attempted a variety of subjects, styles, and painting media that they may have later abandoned. The requirements of passage for aspiring artists during their academic training may well have dictated that they compose images of certain subjects fulfilling the desires and requirements of the school and not necessarily their own. These paintings later may come to be judged as atypical and nonrepresentative, but they are authentic. For an expert to declare that an artist "would never have painted..." is at best conceptually flawed.

Compositional materials are subject to scientific analysis and can often document when a painting was executed but will not identify the specific artist. This type of dating can eliminate an artist who was deceased at the time that material or support device was introduced. Scientific analysis and not expert opinion in this instance can often tell you who did not paint a specific painting.

Paper, support, and pigment analysis have not been as widely applied in the art world as their value and objectivity would suggest that they would. This may be because the methodology is expensive and, thus, only appropiate when the painting at issue is above a baseline value. You simply would not apply this technique to a painting valued in the low hundreds or even thousands for that matter.

The art world has certain beliefs that are so steadfastly held that they become "absolutes." However, experts often revise these "absolutes," that are based on opinion and not objective data. An example of changing of conventional wisdom was the evaluation of the pastels of the BMFA artist, Frank Weston Benson. Conventional wisdom for years held that Benson "did not do pastels." This was later revised when pastels by Benson came on the market from well-established sources and with impeccable provenance. Advertisments later stated "rare Benson pastels." Today it is well accepted the Benson did pastels. If these pastels were offered for sale today, they would probably be described as "by the noted artist Frank W. Benson," casting aside the previous "absolute."

To espouse the concept that a particular artist never produced an image using such a common medium as pastel represents a departure from common deductive reasoning. However, "old saws" die slowly and the pronouncements of experts have extraordinary meaning in the art world.

This leads me to the subject of provenance in the quest for authentication. The history of a painting can provide crucial evidence to its genuineness. Evidence legally is usually defined as "that data or fact that will assist in the search for the truth" — in this instance, the truth is the correct identity of the artist who is responsible for the painting in question.

Knowing the circumstance under which a painting was executed as well as the subsequent ownership and exhibition records will provide significant evidence of the painting's authenticity. A well-documented provenance is, I believe, more difficult to fabricate than a signature and easier to evaluate then someone's opinion — no matter how expert. Documentation by verbal testimony, written description, or photograph that a specific painting was executed, exhibited, and an image published by a particular artist may not be prima facie but

it can represent almost irrefutable evidence.

I can, however, recall some questioning by several prominent dealers of the authenticity of a major painting by the visionary artist, Ralph A. Blakelock, that I have had for several decades in my collection. This is somewhat understandable as Blakelock is one of the most commonly faked American artists.

Since I wanted to use this painting in an exhibit years after I acquired it, I documented the provenance of this "questionable" painting by sending it to the Blakelock expert. It had been purchased from the artist and owned by the wife of the Barbizon painter, Charles Gruppe. Later, his son Emile, the well-known Rockport impressionist owned the painting and, even later, it was the property of his daughter Virginia Gruppe Quirk, a well-known artist in her own right. The Blakelock scholar, Norman Geske, "authenticated" it as a Geske Category I (the highest mark) which was readily accepted by all.

If one examines this litany under the best evidence rule, the provenance would be very difficult to fabricate and, with all due respect to Professor Geske, his testimony is but an informed opinion. My point is that you may be able to uncover what may be the very best evidence — the well-documented provenance.

As I have noted in a previous discussion, the application of scientific tests to the authentication process has merit but is not without significant limitations. Radiographic (x-ray) images cannot authenticate paintings nor can computer analysis of stroke and pigment application patterns, but they can provide evidence. An expert's opinion is also evidence but a different type and less subject to evaluation.

Why may an exhibition record be important in evaluating the authenticity of a painting? It documents public exposure and the opportunity for the painting to have been seen and appraised for its aesthetic value and authenticity by many people. The curator of the exhibit also is presumed to have had a certain level of expertise and, in agreeing to include the painting in the exhibition, has at least tacitly accepted its authenticity. Publication of the work as an illustration in a catalog, text, or monograph provided additional evidence that there may have been public acceptance of the work's authenticity. Again, the selection of the painting by an art historian or curator for publication communicates their acceptance that it is generally what it is purported to be.

For these reasons, you should insist upon knowing and having documentation of the provenance and the exhibition record of any painting you are considering for purchase, if this is available.

Despite this discussion, can you as a collector feel totally assured that the authenticity of a painting will be unequivocally accepted if the evidence is overwhelming according to common logic? I will offer several personal examples which I hope will be informative and entertaining.

The authenticity of one of "The Ten" in my collection was challenged (declared a fake) by an expert despite the fact that the sitter was known, the circumstances of execution and the provenance were documented, a signature had been present and documented prior to restoration, and the painting had been in three exhibitions and published in a catalog and two texts. This painting had been on semi-permanent loan in a major public collection for several years. Upon subsequent "review" the painting was later declared genuine.

The "expert" had judged it from a photograph and was not aware and did not request the provenance — the courtroom equivalent of an attorney appearing without a brief or possibly Andre Agassi without racquet or Michael and no Air Jordans. Much to my dismay, I later found out that this was the methodology used by the dealer to void a contract.

Another painting of mine by a leader of "The Eight" was included in a museum exhibition of the late artist's work. At preview night, a relative of the artist told the curator "I have never seen this work."

Despite the fact that the sitter of the work was known, the painting was signed and inscribed, and the painting had been published as an illustration in a monograph and a cover for a magazine, the curator felt that was "questionable" from a relative of the artist. They asked permission to remove it from their local exhibition but it would be included in the traveling collection. I deemed this truncated logic at best. I agreed to the process rather than having a confrontation and the fact that this "questionable" painting would still be seen at eight museums during the traveling exhibition. Authenticity is sometimes an ethereal concept and not always on the one hand or challenged on the other by deductive reasoning or a logical process. Later we found the artist's inventory number on the obverse of the canvas but I felt this affirmation was unnecessary because, I believe, the challenge of its authenticity was without merit by any standard.

Again, you might learn several "truths" from our experiences. First, in the art world, the concept of evidence or evidence itself is not always treated in the same manner as it is in law, logic, and science. Also, the fact that an expert has written a text on the artist does not make them infallible in judging the authenticity of

works by that painter. I have written over a dozen texts on medical imaging techniques, but I could not correctly identify or authenticate every image I used as an illustration, even in these texts, and certainly not in all related ones. Writing a text certainly does convey expertise but does not convey absolute knowledge or infallibility. The art world seems to often fall prey to the type of logic which reasons that authorship connotes omnipotence in a specified area.

In considering authenticity in the second vignette, a statement by a relative of the artist would have validity only if one presumed that the "expert" had seen all of the paintings ever executed by the artist — a blatant impossibility.

These events demonstrate that in a relative desert of scientific principles, emotion rather than data often drives conclusions. The substantiation of authenticity by well-documented evidence is often lacking because the research and due diligence have simply not been done.

In this circumstance, the fate of a genuine work can rest soley upon the opinion of someone who may be both informed and expert but not infallible. As the collector you should gain all the data about your painting that is available before and subsequent to acquisition. You can feel you have addressed the issue of authenticity as best you can. Afterwards, enjoy your "real" paintings and never accept anyone's "logic" unless its validity seems in concert to standard principles to you.

Avoiding litigation in the art world requires a certain behavioral pattern that some of us have learned through personal experience. I hope my discussion will allow you to avoid this circumstance altogether. Avoiding litigation is a bit like eluding an IRS audit which can be obviated by having no income and claiming no deductions. If the IRS calls, provide data and be circumspect.

However, with regard to the IRS, all one in practicality needs to do is escape being found guilty of fraud. However, the downside risk of litigation in the art world can be more hazardous. The art world is a litigious environment as I have noted. You might expect this since much of its evaluation and validation is based upon opinion and emotion, and often guided by feelings rather than data.

Judgements can be centered on calculations of human value in financial terms with very little credentialing of the participants or standardization of practices. Every area of human endeavor has an emotional aspect and ego content, but the art world seems to contain some of the most fragile egos and more single-minded people than that of any field or endeavor.

Pride is often worn as an epaulet and, when wounded (even superficially), the response can be incredibly dramatic. In a microsecond, what could be viewed as a disagreement can escalate into the threat of litigation. The scenarios I have chosen from my own experience often defy logic and, many times, grow completely out of proportion to the subject at issue.

A prudent collector should objectively evaluate and calculate the legal risk of their activities to minimize the chance of litigation, for in this process the "winners," if there are any, are the lawyers. Prudent behavior in the form of risk management will decrease one's exposure to litigation in any interaction. Candor and honesty in relationships are obviously qualities that lessen one's chance of risking a courtroom experience. Documentation of every element of any transaction is not only preventative but often it is curative.

There is also that bit of traditional wisdom alluding to the canine world about "lying down with mongrels and coming up with vermin." If an art dealer has a spotty reputation, do not buy paintings from that individual hoping to obtain a bargain. If a painting is not signed, make certain that it can be authenticated through research into the provenance or some other form of conclusive evidence. Dealers will often verbally "guarantee" the painter of a work or the authenticity of a painting. Only accept this if they are authorities on that artist and the price reflects this circumstance.

If you are prepared to accept this level of documentation and intend to keep the painting for your own use, then you might acquire it. If you think you might subsequently sell or trade the painting, then pass. You should avoid future difficulties with authentication at all costs. Despite the fact that an unsigned painting can be reasonably "authenticated," this remains a controversial area in the art world. Rather than fly in the face of conventional wisdom, however flawed, you might avoid this arena, but recognize it when you acquire an unsigned painting.

If a painting is priced by a dealer much below the market, then you can proceed with several theories as to why it is underpriced. The dealer may not know how much the artist commands; he may be aware that it is a very nonrepresentative example of the author's work; the painting may be in poor condition; or worst of all, it may not be authentic. In polite circles, these are given the appellation of "not right' or in the real world "fakes." As a sophisticated collector, you may know more about any one painting than a dealer. However, this is a dangerous assumption, and remember that it is only your ego involved in this activity but it is the deal-er's livelihood. You *want* to be right; the dealer *has* to be right.

Collecting paintings has its educational process and its credentialing bodies. However, one may enter the commercial arena of art with no formal training whatsoever and, after exercising reasonable behavior for a short period of time, receive enough credentialing to keep the public from questioning that person's ability to offer paintings for sale.

Since this is not a standardized process, you must depend upon the opinions of other collectors and dealers to evaluate whether you should enter into an agreement to purchase, trade, or sell with a specific purveyor of art. If physicians engage in a "conspiracy of silence," art dealers engage in a "conspiracy of tales." Many dealers have a myriad of stories about the competition involving every possible shortcoming, perfidy, misrepresentation, double dealing, scam, etc. that the human imagination could produce.

There are certain dealers who have a reputation for character and honesty. If you will be patient, these dealers will become apparent and known to you. The fact is that they are never mentioned in the litany of evil doing by other dealers and they are not purveyors of this lore themselves; it should make them the type you are seeking to be your dealer. They have character and pride in their reputation. Most truly successful dealers fall into this category. They are successful because they have integrity and care about what they are and have been doing for decades.

Why do we, as collectors, not identify these dealers and have all of our acquisitions come through them? The major reason we don't is pure and simple greed; these dealers appear expensive, and we often want and attempt to acquire art at a "bargain."

You may sometimes forget everything you have learned about condition, provenance, and authenticity in order to acquire a painting at a cost much below what you convince yourself is its true value. If a dealer, in order to convince you to acquire a work, tells you that they could get much more for the painting from another dealer or if they sold it at auction, ask yourself why you are so fortunate to be the recipient of such extraordinary opportunity. This is simply the dealer's ploy to enhance your urge to acquire a "bargain."

There are dealers who do not have an elegant gallery and sell genuinely good paintings out of a station wagon, van, or the back of a truck. The problem when acquiring a painting from an unknown purveyor without a permanent place of business is that they may not have unencumbered ownership and often warrant nothing. They are much less accountable than your trusted dealer. Can one receive a genuine painting in this manner at a favorable price from such a dealer (picker)? Certainly, but it is risky just as is auction, but these safeguards for these activities have been previously discussed.

As a collector, when you complicate the transaction with a dealer such as trading a painting for value in kind, impose a performance contingency to make the contract valid, or have an extended payment scheme, you increase your chances of litigation from the encounter several fold. This is presented again for obvious reasons of emphasis.

The lawsuit or threatened litigation may often involve issues that are inherently those of the art world and in which you have little knowledge. You are at a great disadvantage. For example, if you trade a painting to a dealer in partial payment for an acquisition, that dealer will have an expectation for the amount they intend to realize from your painting. You really have no way of knowing what these expectations are. If the dealer's expectations are not met, you could well be in for threat of or actual litigation as a method of voiding the transaction. There are a number of areas in human interaction in which litigation is a strong possibility, but there seems to have an increased likelihood in art.

The personalities of the participants in the contract are such, the potential financial gain can be so enormous, the criteria not standardized, and quality control so unregulated that the chance of litigation is an increased consideration.

An example of an "art world condition" I find unparalleled is anticipated dealer profit. I know that some dealers have sued a client for the unrealized profit they had projected on a painting from the trade with the client. After the transaction with the collector, the dealer offered the painting at a large multiple of the trade evaluation which had been agreed upon by the dealer and collector. I unwittingly entered into a transaction that fulfilled these criteria.

The dealer had chosen my painting, believing that, due to ignorance, I had agreed to an allowed value in trade which represented only a small fraction of the true worth of the painting by their estimation. The dealer combined arrogance as well as greed in this transaction. Failing to achieve the expected profit, the dealer claimed that the painting had been misrepresented by me. I felt betrayed by the dealer. The dealer had enlisted an "expert" fellow dealer from whom I bought paintings to declare the painting as "questionable," "a fake," or "not by the artist." I later questioned this "expert" why they offered an opinion and was not given a candid answer.

You are at a distinct disadvantage in this situation because you are in an unfamiliar arena and probably unprepared to handle this type of challenge. Some self-protection among dealers is not unexpected and is often involved; usually, the expert is another dealer who has done and will often continue to do business with the plaintiff and probably not you as an individual client. Quid pro quo, while unstated, can be operative from dealer to dealer.

Painting dealers seem to use the threat of litigation to acquire the desired performance from one another much more often than competitiors or associates in other businesses. Almost monthly, a major art magazine will detail the wrongdoings of a dealer in relation to a collector, museum, or another dealer. While this may make interesting reading, it should alert you as to the risks of litigation in the environment of the art world.

What measures can prudent collectors take to protect themselves? Resist bargains, they probably are not what they seem. Insist upon written documented provenance, a certificate of authentication, and a statement of condition of the acquisition. Seek a "second (third) opinion" if you have the least bit of uncertainty. Discuss the dealer's return policy and what deaccession assistance you can subsequently expect after purchase. This does vary a great deal. Avoid payment schedules whenever possible.

Refrain from trading for value in kind, except with a dealer you know quite well. Deaccess most of your paintings at auction; the caveats of the auction house in the conditions of sale will practically absolve you of most of the downside risks of litigation. Take the proceeds from auction and purchase your desired painting as a monetary transaction only. Cash is "good" but certified checks are better.

Avoid selling paintings or trading them to dealers unless both parties have a large measure of trust and there is a candid discussion of the dealer's expectations. Ask dealers for their credentials. Only acquire paintings from dealers whom you can reliably locate and who have a reputation among other dealers and among your fellow collectors for honesty, candor, and fair dealing. Fellow collectors are an excellent data source in this regard.

Insist upon documentation of every transaction (a paper trail). Never pay in currency but only by some money instrument, usually a check — for your records and theirs. Study the bill of sale: "by artist x" is different from "signed artist x" and quite different from "attributed to artist x." The seller should warrant that the painting is by a certain artist or if not, then your price should reflect this difference or uncertainty of origin.

These practices are only safeguards; they will merely lessen the opportunity for litigation. If the threat of litigation is raised, attempt every effort of dispute resolution by settlement, compromise, or arbitration. Avoid the involvement of the legal profession and enter the courtroom with the full realization that the issues will probably not be resolved to anyone's satisfaction, and the emotion and monetary costs could very well be unreasonable, given the value of the paintings at issue.

In summary, collecting paintings can provide you with many pleasures, but litigation is not among them. Litigation is highly probable in certain circumstances, and you must recognize and avoid those.

What if I make an error or a mistake in any of my art related activities? Mistakes are a part of the collecting process as I have noted throughout this text and devoted a chapter to. An acquisition that seemed appropriate at the time may upon reflection have been an error. As a collector, you should not ruminate, second guess, or punish yourself. Merely develop a strategy to deaccess an unwanted painting. There are a number of alternatives and you should consider each to select the most appropriate for you.

Your choice of method to deaccess a painting may be largely determined by your manner of acquisition. If you acquired the painting from a reputable dealer, especially one you have had a long-term relationship with, they will probably take the work on consignment. This is part of your "insurance policy" that you paid for earlier by the acquisition price.

One thing you must accept in a consignment is that it may be a lengthy process. To some extent, this may be determined by the asking price. If you want a "retail" price, then you should be prepared to wait. The best is to decide what you would like to realize and then ask the dealer how much more they plan to offer the painting for. If the total seems unrealistic, discuss that with your dealer. Remember, you are invested with the asset you have placed at their disposal.

Another method of deaccession we have noted is to use the painting in trade to the dealer as partial payment for a work that you find currently appropriate. Will you receive credit for the entire purchase price, less, more? Also, should you discuss this method of deaccession versus consignment? Certainly, if your proposed acquisition is a very expensive one, the dealer may offer you a generous trade. If the value of the two works is approximately the same — the credit will be less because your dealer has many expenses to be met requiring cash flow. Your expectations should be realistic and take into account the dealer's overhead.

Auction houses in some ways offer you the least traumatic method to deaccess paintings. You must remember that there are major and minor auctions and auction houses. To initiate this process have someone from the auction house evaluate the painting. Be prepared for this to sometimes be brutally frank — your hope is that it will be accurate. Authenticity, condition, and desirability will be considered in commercial terms.

The stature of an auction house as I have stated is based upin public trust. Therefore, you should not be offended by what they think should be illustrated, described, and even an estimated price range for sale of your painting. This should be included in your agreement and fee to them. This estimate is the best prediction by an informed staff of the auction house and communicated to the consignor as to the range of reasonable expectation for that particular painting. Do not hope for better at auction; if you cannot handle the reality of achieving only the low estimate, withdraw the painting.

A question that the collector must have is the risk of auction and how do you safeguard against unrealized expectations. First, you and the staff person should decide upon a reserve. This represents the minimum you will accept for the painting; bids below the figure will be unsuccessful. The reserve is your opinion of the lowest estimate of value of the painting to you. It also should represent that figure you can accept.

However, the staff of auction houses are usually aware of the real value of the painting in the free market environment. They may have seen similar works under nearly the same circumstances, so their database should well be larger and more accurate than yours. Will this be less than your purchase price if acquired from a dealer? It will in most circumstances. Remember, the dealer sells at retail and auction houses; in theory, sell somewhere between wholesale and retail.

Might you realize a "super retail" deaccession price at auction? This is always a possibility as in the competative marketplace, bidders may drive the price beyond the auction houses and your expectations. This may happen, but do not ever anticipate this. Decide upon your reserve and be satisfied if you achieve that figure.

A method of deaccession that is somewhat complex is to trade or barter with another collector. If you are changing your collecting interests, find a collector with an inventory of the paintings you want. They may have so many paintings that good examples are available or the collectors may want to deaccess much in the same manner because their proclivities have changed.

Obviously, to expect a "perfect fit" to this exchange is naive, but with some flexibility, both collectors may partially achieve the goal of deaccession of a work thay no longer need and an acquisition of a painting they want to add to their collection.

There is a method of "win/win" deaccession that you may consider because of earlier discussions and that is donation of paintings to a charitable organization. Obviously, donations of paintings to museums are the most common method, but collectors often forget charity auctions, public buildings, and certain other not-for-profit organizations. The work is deaccessed and you receive the emotional benefits that one has from a worthwhile contribution. One of our great pleasures in life is to contribute American paintings to appropriate museums, public and private institutions, hospitals, selected universities, small art groups, and in memorial collections. You must enjoy the process or be committed to the result because it requires accurate documentation for every step of the transaction and these cannot be avoided.

In summary, you must recognize that as your tastes become more refined, or your interests shift, or you may have a simple change of mind about a specific painting, you should respond to this by appropriate deaccession. It may have been a good acquisition at the time, but now it should be a good deaccession using the appropriate methodological choice.

Thus, collecting American paintings has some degree of risk, but so does every human endeavor — just minimize those you can control and accept those that you cannot.

This epilogue may have seemed to address only litigation and deaccession; but collecting paintings is about pleasure, the thrill of discovery, the satisfaction of sharing, and the memorialization by a gift. Orderliness is laced with spontaneity. Fiscal pain can be relieved by aesthetic pleasure, feelings of loss can be obviated by a contemporaneous sharing, and affirmation can be enhanced by a public exhibition of publication. Collecting has many facets and should be a lifelong dynamic process. Hopefully, this text will guide you along this journey.

Bibliography

Adelman, E. *The Farmer/James Collection of Southern Women Artists*. Wesleyan College, 2000.

Alexandre, Arsene. *Frank Boggs*. Paris, 1929.

Arnheim, R. *Art and Visual Perception*. Berkeley, CA: University of California Press, 1974.

Bloomer, C. M. *Principles of Visual Perception*. New York: Van Nostrand Reinhold, 1976.

Bridgeman, C., and Keck, S. *The Radiography of Paintings*. Rochester, New York: Eastman Kodak Co., 1961.

Brigstroke, Hugh. *Oxford Companion to Western Art*. Oxford Press, 2001.

Brinton, Selwyn. "Modern Mural Decoration in America." *Int. Studio*: January, 1911.

Britt, David. *Modern Art*. Little, Brown and Co., 1989.

Boyle, R. J. *American Impressionism*. New York: New York Graphic Society, 1974.

Brody, W. R., Macowski, A., and Lehamann, L., et al. "Intravenous angiography using scanned projection radiograph: Preliminary investigation of a new Method." *Invest Radiol.*, vol. 15; 220-223, 1980.

Brooks, R. A., DiChiro, G. "Theory of Image Reconstruction in Computed Tomography." *Radiology*, 117: 561-572, 1975.

Brown, M. *American Art to 1900*. Abrams, 1977.

Brown, Milton, W. *American Painting from the Armory Show to the Great Depresssion*. Princeton, NJ, 1955.

Brunk, Robert. *Remember When, I and II*. Brunk Auction: Asheville, N.C., 2000.

Chambers, Bruce. *Art and Artists of the South: The Robert Coggins Collection*. South Carolina Press, 1984.

Chiarmonte, P. *Women Artists of the United States*. G. K. Hall, 1990.

Child, Theodore. "American Artists at the Paris Exhibition." *Harper's New Monthly Magazine*, September, 1889.

Chilvers, Ian and Osborne, H. *The Oxford Dictionary of Art*. Oxford Press, 1988.

Clark, Kenneth. *Landscapes into Art*. Boston Beacon Press, 1961.

Cook, Clarence. *Art and Artists of Our Time*. New York, 1888.

Corn, W. M. *The Color of Mood: American Tonalism* (exhibition catalog). M. H. DeYoung Museum, San Francisco, 1972.

Cornsweet, T. N. *Visual Perception*. New York: Academic Press, 1970.

Coulam, C.C., Erickson, J. J., Rollo, F. D., James, A. E. *The Physical Basis of Medical Imaging*. New York: Appleton-Century-Crofts, 1981.

Davidoff, J. B. *Differences in Visual Perception*. New York: Academic Press, 1975.

Diamond, David. *Art Terms*. Little Brown and Co., 1995.

Encyclopedia Britannica of American Art. Simon and Schuster, 1973.

Ericikson, J. J., Price, R. R., Rollo, R. D., et al. "A Digital Radiographic Analysis System." *Radiographics*, 1:49-60, 1981.

Foreshee, I. M. *Painting in North Carolina*. Chapel Hill, 1972.

Gerdts, W. *American Impressionism*. New York: Abbeville Press, 1984.

——. *Art Across America*. Abbeville Press, 1990.

Gibson, J. J. *The Ecological Approach to Visual Perception*. Boston: Houghton-Mifflin, 1979.

Hicklin, R. *The South on Paper*. Saraland Press, 1990.

Hobbs, Robert. *Elliott Daingerfield*. Retrospective, Mint Museum, Charlotte, 1971.

Hoobler, J. and Gaul, Gilbert. Exhibition Catalogue. Tennessee State Museum, 1998.

Hoopes, D. F. *The American Impressionists*. New York: Watson-Guptill, 1978.

Hounsfield, G. "Computerized Transverse Axial Scanning (Tomography). I. Description of System. *Br J Radiol*, 46:1016-1022, 1973.

Igoe, L. and J. *Two Hundred Years of Afro-American Art*. R. R. Bowker, 1981.

Isham, Samuel. *The History of American Painting*. New York, 1915.

James, A. E. "A Collection of Portraiture" (monograph). Vandy Press, 1992.

——. *A Collection of Tonalism and Nocturnes* (catalog). Vanderbilt Press, 1992.

——. "Acquiring at Auction." *Carolina Antiques*, 1999.

——. *American Art: Thoughts of a Collector*. Warren H. Green, 1994.

——. American Impressionism (monograph). Vandy Press, 1980.

——. American Impressionism. IJAM 1: 1993.

——. American Impressionism. NEAnt J, Mrch 2001.

——. "Collecting the Ashcan School." *Art and Frame*, 2000.

——. "Collecting Regionalism." *New England Journal of Art*, 2002.

——. "Collections in Hospitals." *Int. Journal Art Med.*, 1994.

——. "Collection in Hospitals: Humanity in Medicine." *Roy. Soc. Med. Journal*, 1995.

——. "Condition of Paintings." *Southern Antiques*, 2002.

——. "From Collector to Patron." *Southern Antiques*, 1998.

——. Impressionism in the South. *Carolina Centique*, 2001.

——. *James Collection at Cosmos Club* (catalog). Cosmos Club, 1993.

——. "James McLean North Carolina Painter." *Carolina Antiques*, 2004.

——. "Judging a Painting." S. E. Framer, 2001.

——. "Landscape Painting in North Carolina." *Southern Antiques*, 2004.

——. "Legacy of Southern Women." *Veranda*, 1990.

——. *N.C. Painters: Farmer/James Collections*. (Exhibition) Chapel Hill Museum Brochure, 1999.

——. North Carolina Artists. *Middle Atlantic Antiques*, 2000.

——. "North Carolina Painters." *Art and Frame*, 2002.

——. "North Carolina Painters (1850 – 1950)." *Southern Antiques*, 2001.

——. "Painting in North Carolina." *Carolina Antiques*, 1999.

——. *Radiographic Analysis of Paintings*. Kodak Monograph 63:1-28, 1987.

——. "Regionalism: Southern Art." *New England Journal of Antiques*, 2002.

——. "Selected Promising Radiological Imaging Techniques." *Radiology*, 17:144-148, 1977.

——. "Sharing Your Paintings: A Resource." *Southern Antiques*, 2002.

——. "Southern Tonalism." *Southern Antiques*, 1999.

——. "Southern Impressionism." *Southern Antiques*, 1999, 2000, 2001.

——. *Southern Paintings (1840 – 1940)*. (Exhibition). Knoxville Museum, 1991.

——. "Southern Women Artists (1840 – 1950)." *Middle Atlantic Antiques*, 1997.

——. "The Ashcan Artists." *Southern Antiques*. 1999.

——. "The Ashcan School." *Southern Antiques*, 2002.

——. "The Barbizon Aesthetic." *Antiques Journal*, 1998.

——. "The Regionalists." *New England Journal of Antiques*, 2001.

——. "The Visual Physiology of Tonalism." *Journal of Art in Medicine*, 1991.

——. *Thoughts of a Collector*. W. H. Green, 1998.

——. "Tonalism" (monograph). Vandy Press, 1991.

——. "Tonalism in the South." *Southern Antiques*, 1999.

——. "Tonalist Painting in the South." *Carolina Antiques*, 1999.

——. "Quality in Paintings." S. E. Framer, 2002.

James, A. E. and Framer, N. J. *A Collection of Southern Women Artists* (exhibition). Meredith College, 2001.

James, A. E. and James, A. E. III. *Indiana Impressionisms* (catalog). Vandy Press, 1992.

James, A. E., Rao G. U., Gray, C., Heller, R. M., Bush, M. R. "Magnification in Veterinary Radiology." *J Am Vet Radiol Soc.*, 16:52 – 64, 1975.

James, A. E., Ritts, E., James, A. E. III. *Eugene Healan Thomason*. Vantage Press, 1986.

James, A. E. Jr., S. J. Gibbs. Radiographic analysis of paintings. *Medical Radiography and Photography*. 63(1), 1987.

James, et al. *Radiographic Analysis of Paintings*. Eastman Kodak, 1989.

James, et al. *Radiographic Evaluation of Paintings by Radiography*. Eastman Kodak Co., 1989.

James, et al. X-Rays of Paintings, *Southern Antiques*, 2001.

James, Henry. "Our Artists in Europe." *Harper's New Monthly Magazine*. June, 1889.

Jonson, H. *History of Art*. Abrams, 1990.

Keck, C., *The Care of Paintings*. New York: Watson-Guptill, 1967.

Kelly, James. "Landscape and Genre Painting in Tennessee." *Tennessee State Historical Quarterly*, 44 Summer, 1985.

——. "Painting in Tennessee." *Tennessee Historical Quarterly*, Winter 1985.

——. *The South on Paper*. Robert C. Hicklin, Spartanburg, 1985.

Keyes, Donald. *Southern Impressionism*. Greenville Museum of Art, 1988.

Kruger, R. A., Mistretta, C. A., Lancaster, J., et al. "A digital video image processor for real-time x-ray subtraction imaging," *Optical Eng.* 17;652-654, 1978.

Love, R. H. *Willliam Chadwick: An American Impressionist*. Chicago: R. H. Love Galleries, 1978.

Mayer, R. *A Dictionary of Art Terms and Techniques*. Harper Collins, 1981.

Mistretta C. A., Crummy A. B., Struther C. M. "Digital Angiography: A Perspective." *Radiology*, 139:273-276, 1981.

Murray, Chris. *Dictionary of the Arts*. Gramercy Books, 1999.

Nudelman, S., Capp, M. P., and Fisher, H. D. et al. "Photoelectronic imaging for diagnostic radiology and the digital computer." *Proc SPIE*, 164, 138, 1978.

Osterman F. A., James, A. E., Heshiki A., et al. "Xeroradiography in Veterinary Radiography: A Preliminary Study." *J Am Vet Radiol Soc.*, 16:143-150, 1975.

Perlman, Bernard. *The Immortal Eight*. North Light Publishers, 1979.

Pennington, E. *A Southern Collection: The Morris Museum*. Augusta, Georgia: Morris Publications, 1992.

Pennington, E. *Look Away*. Saraland Press, 1988.

Pierce, Pat. *"The Ten."* Rumsford Press, 1981.

Poesch, J. *Art of the South*. New York: Alfred A. Knopf, 1983.

Poesch, Jessie, Stevens, Will Henry. Greenville County Museum of Art, Greenville, SC, 1987.

Preato, Roberto. *Tonalism: An Exhibit*. Grand Central Galleries, New York, 1984.

Price, Ronald R., Rollo, F. David, Monahan, W. Gordon, and James, A. Everette, eds. *Digital Radiography: A Focus on Clinical Utility*. New York, New York: Grune & Stratton, Inc. 1982.

Quick, M. *American Expatriate Painters of the late Nineteenth Century*. Dayton, Ohio: Dayton Art Institute, 1976.

Rathbone, Eliza. *Impressionist Still Life*. Abrams, New York.

Rewald, J. *The History of Impressionism*. MOMA, 1973.

——. *Post-Impressionism*. MOMA, 1978.

Roehig, H., Nudelman, S., Fisher, H. D., Frost, M. M., Capp, M. P., "Photoelectronic Imaging for Radiology." *IEEE Trans Nucl Sci.*, NS-28: 190-204, 1981.

Ruhemann, H., Kemp, EM. *The Artist at Work*. Baltimore: Penguin, 1952.

Safford, Hildegarde and Williams, Ben. *WCA Frerichs*. (catalog). N.C. Museum of Art, 1974.

Severens, Martha. *The Charleston Renaissance*. Saraland Press. Spartanburg. 1998.

Stewart, Patrick. *Painting in the South (1864 – 1980)* (exhibition and text). Richmond, 1983.

Tateno, Y., and Tanaka, H., "Low dosage x-ray imaging system employing flying spot x-ray microbeam (Dyanmic Scanner). *Radiology*, vol. 161; 189 – 195, 1976.

Thompson, Vance. "American Painters in Paris." *Cosmopolitan*, May, 1900.

Van Rensselaer. *American Art and American Art Collections*. Boston, 1889.

Virginia Museum Art. *Painting in the South*. 1564 – 1984. 1983.

Walker, Celia. "Twentieth Century Painting in Tennessee." *Tennessee Historical Quarterly*, Spring 2002.

Wilmerding, J. *What Style is It*. Preservation Press, 1976.

——. *American Light, The Luminist Movement 1850 – 1875*. The National Academy of Art. 1980.

Values

Adams, Wayman	$7,500 – 45,000
Ahl, H.C.	$1,500 – 8,500
Ahl, Henry Hammond	$2,500 – 22,500
Albert, Ernest	$6,500 – 24,000
Albright, Adam Emory	$6,500 – 45,000
Anshutz, Thomas	$25,000 – 675,000
Ashley, Anita	$1,500 – 12,500
Austrian, Ben	$2,500 – 6,500
Avent, Mayna	$4,500 – 8,500
Bailey, T.	$1,500 – 4,500
Baker, George Herbert	$5,500 – 7,500
Barkley, William	$15,000 – 20,000
Bartlett, Kathleen	$750 – 3,500
Bartlett, Paul	$3,500 – 18,000
Beaumont, Arthur	$4,500 – 6,500
Bell, Winona	$3,500 – 6,500
Bellows, George W.	$15,000 – 27,000,000
Berkhart, Armin	$1,500 – 3,500
Betts, H.H.	$1,500 – 6,500
Blake, Anne Dehon	$2,500 – 7,500
Blakelock, Ralph A.	$35,000 – 75,000
Boehm, Curry	$2,500 – 12,500
Bohrod, Aaron	$3,500 – 7,500
Brackman, Robert	$2,500 – 7,500
Branson, Lloyd	$4,500 – 9,500
Braswell, Callie	$500 – 2,500
Brown, Faye	$1,500 – 3,500
Brown, George Elmer	$4,500 – 22,500
Brown, John G.	$25,000 – 65,000
Browne, Margaret Fitzhugh	$2,500 – 8,500
Buman, Sydney	$1,500 – 6,500
Bunker, Dennis Miller	$25,000 – 75,000
Burpee, William P.	$20,000 – 60,000
Cabiness, Mabel	$4,500 – 7,500
Campbell, Jack	$2,500 – 7,500
Campbell, Thomas	$3,500 – 4,500
Cariani, V.J.	$2,500 – 8,500
Carles, Arthur	$2,500 – 5,000
Carlson, John F.	$6,500 – 27,500
Chadwick, William	$12,500 – 75,000
Chant, Elizabeth	$2,000 – 4,500
Chisholm, Virginia	$1,500 – 9,500

Clark, C. Myron	$1,000 – 3,500
Clark, Eliot C.	$20,000 – 50,000
Clark, Walter	$8,500 – 55,000
Coffin, W.H.	$3,500 – 14,500
Cohen, Isabel	$1,500 – 7,500
Coles, Ann Cadwaller	$1,500 – 4,500
Conglin, Sybil	$1,500 – 3,500
Conney, Ethel	$1,000 – 2,500
Conoley, Leitha	$500 – 1,500
Conrow, Wilfred	$1,500 – 18,500
Cook, George	$1,500 – 4,500
Cook, Isabel Vernon	N/A
Cooke, G.E.	$1,500 – 3,500
Cooper, J.S.	$1,000 – 2,500
Cooper, W.A.	$3,500 – 14,500
Cooper, W.B.	$2,500 – 4,500
Coulan, Emma	$1,500 – 4,500
Cox, C.W.	$4,500 – 17,500
Crain, Frances	$1,500 – 3,500
Crane, Bruce	$15,000 – 45,000
Crawley, Ida	$2,500 – 6,500
Curry, John Stuart	$3,500 – 7,500
Dabo, T. Scott	$1,000 – 7,500
Daingerfield, Elliott	$35,000 – 95,000
Davies, Arthur B.	$2,500 – 35,000
Davis, Charles H.	$35,000 – 65,000
de Ribkowski, Dey	$2,500 – 27,500
Derrick, Bertha (Swindell)	$1,000 – 3,500
Drury, George	$3,500 – 6,500
Embry, Jack	$500 – 2,500
Enneking, John J.	$3,500 – 32,500
Erb, Daisey	$1,500 – 3,500
Erickson, Oscar	$2,500 – 7,500
Eyden, William A.	$3,500 – 12,500
Faucette, Truman	$3,500 – 18,750
Fernow, Bernice	$2,500 – 3,500
Fisher, Edith	$1,500 – 4,500
Forsythe, William	$3,500 – 35,000
Frerichs, W.C.A.	$25,000 – 125,000
Gamble, Roy	$3,500 – 5,500
Gaul, Gilbert	$25,000 – 125,000
Gerberg, Maurice	$1,500 – 6,500

Gifford, Robert Swain	$15,000 – 35,000
Gilchrist, Emma	$5,000 – 25,000
Girrard, Washington	$1,500 – 4,500
Glackens, William	$75,000 – 1,000,000
Goldthwaite, Ann	$2,500 – 27,500
Gorson, Aaron H.	$15,000 – 95,000
Grabach, John	$7,500 – 12,500
Grafton, Robert	$7,500 – 45,000
Graves, Abbott Fuller	$35,000 – 225,000
Greenwood, Joseph	$1,500 – 12,750
Griffith, L.O.	$3,500 – 23,000
Griggs, S.W.	$2,500 – 4,500
Gruppe, Charles	$6,500 – 25,000
Gruppe, Emile	$3,500 – 30,000
Hale, Ellen Day	$45,000 – 65,000
Hale, Phillip Leslie	$3,500 – 25,000
Hamilton, Edwin W.D.	$2,500 – 18,500
Hamilton, Hamilton	$3,500 – 6,500
Hankins, Cornelius	$1,500 – 6,500
Harleston, Edwin	$5,500 – 20,000
Hartley, Rachael	$3,560 – 22,500
Harwood, Neola	$500 – 2,500
Hassam, Childe	$55,000 – 2,500,000
Hasselman, Anna	$2,500 – 17,500
Hawthorne, Charles W.	$12,500 – 125,000
Healon, A.C.	$15,000 – 25,000
Heldner, Knute	$25,000 – 65,000
Hergeshiemer, Ella	$2,500 – 14,750
Higgins, George	$3,500 – 5,000
Hodgell, Robet	$2,500 – 6,500
Holsclaw, B.R.	$2,500 – 3,500
Howard, B.K.	$3,500 – 16,500
Howard, Marion	$4,500 – 22,000
Howell, Claude	$3,500 – 27,500
Howland, A.C.	$2,500 – 4,500
Hunt, William Morris	$25,000 – 65,000
Hutty, Alfred	$12,000 – 60,000
Inness, George Jr.	$25,000 – 75,000
Inness, George, Sr.	$45,000 – 350,000
Jacek, Vladimir	$2,500 – 5,500
Jones, Myrtle	$1,000 – 3,500
Jones, Nell Choate	$10,000 – 45,000
Kaula, Lee Lufkin	$4,500 – 65,000
King, Fannie Mahon	$3,500 – 5,500
Kurtz, Wilbur	$3,500 – 6,500
La Chance, George	$1,500 – 8,500
Lane, Fitz Hugh	$125,000 – 750,000
Lane, Marian	$2,500 – 12,500
Lawson, Ernest	$25,000 – 125,000
Ledford, Freda	$1,500 – 3,500
Lever, Haley	$4,500 – 60,000
Lindenmuth, Todd	$2,500 – 5,500
Little, Phillip	$7,500 – 24,000
Lovejoy, Rupert Scott	$3,500 – 7,500
Lundberg, August	$25,000 – 75,000
Lutz, John C.	$2,500 – 4,500
Major, Ernest L.	$35,000 – 85,000
Marchand, Henri	$2,500 – 9,500
Mazzonovich, Lawrence	$7,500 – 45,000
McClean, James Augustus	$1,500 – 7,500
McCrea, E. Harkness	$2,500 – 12,500
Metzler, Arthur	$1,500 – 8,500
Miles, Emma Bell	$1,500 – 3,500
Moran, Thomas	$10,000 – 2,000,000
Morrison, Muriel	$3,500 – 4,500
Morrow, Nena	$500 – 4,500
Moser, Henry	$3,500 – 12,500
Moss, George	$2,500 – 3,500
Murphy, Christopher	$4,500 – 8,500
Murphy, J.F.	$7,500 – 25,000
Murray, H.V.	$1,500 – 7,500
Nash, Ann Taylor	$2,500 – 7,500
Neilsen, Raymond R.P.	$3,500 – 40,000
Neudecker, Robert	$3,500 – 12,500
Newman, Robert Loftin	$15,000 – 35,000
Ney, Edgar	$1,500 – 6,500
Nisbet, Robert	$2,500 – 17,500
Nordell, Carol	$45,000 – 80,000
Oberteuffer, Karl	$2,500 – 12,500
Ochtman, Leonard	$7,500 – 22,500
Oelschig, Augusta	$3,500 – 7,500
Owen, Robert Emmett	$5,500 – 47,500
Owsley, Will	$2,500 – 6,500
Palmer, Walter Launt	$25,000 – 75,000
Parker, Lawton	$5,500 – 35,000
Parrish, Clara Weaver	$2,500 – 25,000
Patton, Thomas	$1,000 – 1,500
Paxton, William M.	$35,000 – 275,000
Payne, Edgar	$25,000 – 125,000
Payne, Mae	$1,500 – 4,500
Pearson, Marguerite S.	$30,000 – 90,000
Perry, Lilla Cabot	$35,000 – 95,000

Phillips, Marjorie	$2,500 – 4,500
Pierce, Waldo	$3,500 – 25,000
Pittman, Hobson	$3,500 – 24,500
Porter, Mary	$500 – 1,500
Post, William Merritt	$2,500 – 12,000
Potter, Bertha Herbert	$3,500 – 9,500
Pritchett, Eunice C.	$250 – 1,000
Pugh, Mabel	$3,500 – 8,500
Ranger, Henry Ward	$25,000 – 75,000
Redfield, Edward W.	$30,000 – 475,000
Reeder, Clarence	$2,500 – 5,500
Reich, Fred	$1,500 – 2,000
Reid, Robert L.	$15,000 – 125,000
Rhen, Frank K.M.	$2,500 – 7,500
Rhodes, Jesse	$2,500 – 7,500
Richards, T. Addison	$2,500 – 22,500
Richter, W.S.	$1,500 – 5,500
Ritman, Louis	$60,000 – 450,000
Ritman, Susan	$2,500 – 8,500
Roseland, Harry	$25,000 – 75,000
Rubenstein, Alice	$500 – 2,000
Runguis, Carl	$3,500 – 5,500
Ryder, Albert P.	N/A
Ryder, Chauncey	$35,000 – 60,000
Ryland, Robert	$2,500 – 8,500
Saterlee, Walter	$3,500 – 15,000
Sausey, Hattie	$2,500 – 20,000
Schofield, Walter	$15,000 – 65,000
Seyffert, Leopold	$3,500 – 6,500
Shirlaw, Walter	$1,500 – 12,500
Shulz, Adolph R.	$5,500 – 35,000
Shulz, Alberta	$1,500 – 25,000
Silva, Francis A.	$125,000 – 225,000
Silva, William Posey	$5,500 – 45,000
Skinner, E.K.	$500 – 1,500
Smith, Alice R.H.	$35,000 – 125,000
Smith, Brantley	$15,000 – 55,000
Smith, K.A.	$500 – 1,500

Smith, Walter Granville	$3,500 – 7,500
Southgate, William	$1,500 – 6,500
Speight, Francis Dobb	$8,000 – 45,000
Spencer, Lilly Martin	$225,000 – 275,000
Stark, Otto	$4,500 – 25,000
Starkweather, William	$2,500 – 24,500
Steele, T.C.	$8,500 – 65,000
Stevens, Will Henry	$7,500 – 65,000
Stevens, William Lester	$4,500 – 14,500
Tarbell, Edmund	$75,000 – 450,000
Taylor, Anna Heyward	$3,500 – 6,500
Thieme, Anthony	$6,500 – 75,000
Thomason, Eugene	$3,500 – 45,000
Tucker, Allen	$35,000 – 75,000
Turner, Helen	$7,500 – 135,000
Verner, Elizabeth O'Neill	$45,000 – 95,000
Vonnoh, Robert	$40,000 – 70,000
Walker, W.A.	$10,000 – 350,000
Walter, Martha	$35,000 – 350,000
Weeden, Maria Howard	$6,500 – 24,000
Weir, J. Alden	$6,500 – 80,000
Wharton, James P.	$2,500 – 8,500
Wheeler, Clifton	$4,500 – 25,000
White, Edwin	$5,500 – 25,000
Whiteman, S.E.	$2,500 – 17,500
Whiteman, Thomas	$3,500 – 5,500
Whittaker, George W.	$3,500 – 17,500
Wilcox, J.A.	$2,500 – 4,500
Wilcox, John R.	$1,000 – 4,500
Wiley, Catherine	$3,500 – 75,000
Wiley, Eleanor McAdoo	$1,500 – 6,500
Williams, Edward K.	$2,750 – 16,500
Willis, Iola	$1,500 – 6,500
Wrenn, Harold	$500 – 2,500
Wright, Charles	$10,000 – 35,000
Yates, Cullen	$1,500 – 7,500
Zogbaum, Rufus	$2,500 – 12,500

The price guidelines are taken from value reference texts, auction records, art newsletters, dealer requests, opinions of other collectors, and interpretations by the author. They are meant only as general guidelines for a range of values an artist might be expected to achieve. The particular value for any individual work is subject to the variables discussed in this text and these sums should be considered in the broadest general context.

COLLECTOR BOOKS
informing today's collector

www.collectorbooks.com

For over two decades we have been keeping collectors informed on trends and values in all fields of antiques and collectibles.

DOLLS, FIGURES & TEDDY BEARS

6315	**American Character Dolls**, Izen	$24.95
6317	**Arranbee Dolls**, The Dolls that Sell on Sight, DeMillar/Brevik	$24.95
2079	**Barbie Doll** Fashion, Volume I, Eames	$24.95
4846	**Barbie Doll** Fashion, Volume II, Eames	$24.95
6546	Coll. Ency. of **Barbie** Doll Exclusives & More, 3rd Ed., Augustyniak	$29.95
6451	Collector's Encyclopedia of **Composition Dolls**, Volume II, Mertz	$29.95
5904	Collector's Guide to **Celebrity Dolls**, Spurgeon	$24.95
5599	Collector's Guide to **Dolls of the 1960s and 1970s**, Sabulis	$24.95
6030	Collector's Guide to **Horsman Dolls**, Jensen	$29.95
6455	**Doll Values**, Antique to Modern, 8th Edition, DeFeo/Stover	$14.95
5689	**Nippon Dolls** & Playthings, Van Patten/Lau	$29.95
5365	**Peanuts Collectibles**, Podley/Bang	$24.95
6336	Official **Precious Moments** Coll. Gde. to Company **Dolls**, Bomm	$19.95
6026	**Small Dolls of the 40s & 50s**, Stover	$29.95
5253	Story of **Barbie**, 2nd Ed., Westenhouser	$24.95
5277	**Talking Toys** of the 20th Century, Lewis	$15.95
2084	**Teddy Bears, Annalee's & Steiff** Animals, 3rd Series, Mandel	$19.95
4880	World of **Raggedy Ann** Collectibles, Avery	$24.95

TOYS & MARBLES

2333	Antique & Collectible **Marbles**, 3rd Edition, Grist	$9.95
6649	Big Book of **Toy Airplanes**, Miller	$24.95
5150	**Cartoon Toys** & Collectibles, Longest	$19.95
5900	Collector's Guide to **Battery Toys**, 2nd Edition, Hultzman	$24.95
6471	Collector's Guide to **Tootsietoys**, 3rd Edition, Richter	$24.95
5169	Collector's Guide to **TV Toys** & Memorabilia, 2nd Ed., Davis/Morgan	$24.95
3970	Grist's Machine-Made & Contemporary **Marbles**, 2nd Edition	$9.95
6633	**Hot Wheels**, The Ultimate Redline Guide, 2nd Ed., Clark/Wicker	$29.95
6466	**Matchbox Toys**, 1947 to 2003, 4th Edition, Johnson	$24.95
5830	**McDonald's** Collectibles, 2nd Edition, Henriques/DuVall	$24.95
6840	**Schroeder's Collectible Toys**, Antique to Modern, 10th Ed.	$17.95
6638	The Other **Matchbox Toys**, 1947 to 2004, Johnson	$19.95
6650	**Toy Car** Collector's Guide, 2nd Edition, Johnson	$24.95

FURNITURE

3716	American **Oak** Furniture, Book II, McNerney	$12.95
1118	Antique **Oak** Furniture, Hill	$7.95
6474	Collector's Guide to **Wallace Nutting** Furniture, Ivankovich	$19.95
5359	Early **American** Furniture, Obbard	$12.95
3906	**Heywood-Wakefield** Modern Furniture, Rouland	$18.95
6338	**Roycroft** Furniture & Collectibles, Koon	$24.95
6343	**Stickley Brothers** Furniture, Koon	$24.95
1885	**Victorian** Furniture, Our American Heritage, McNerney	$9.95

JEWELRY, HATPINS, WATCHES & PURSES

4704	Antique & Collectible **Buttons**, Wisniewski	$19.95
6323	**Christmas Pins**, Past & Present, 2nd Edition, Gallina	$19.95
4850	Collectible **Costume Jewelry**, Simonds	$24.95
5675	Collectible **Silver Jewelry**, Rezazadeh	$24.95
6468	Collector's Ency. of Pocket & Pendant **Watches**, 1500 – 1950, Bell	$24.95
6453	**Costume Jewelry** 101, Carroll	$24.95
4940	**Costume Jewelry**, A Practical Handbook & Value Guide, Rezazadeh	$24.95
5812	Fifty Years of Collectible **Fashion Jewelry**, 1925 – 1975, Baker	$24.95
6330	**Handkerchiefs**: A Collector's Guide, Guarnaccia/Guggenheim	$24.95
6833	**Handkerchiefs**: Volume 2, Guarnaccia/Guggenheim	$24.95

5695	**Ladies' Vintage Accessories**, Johnson	$24.95
1181	100 Years of Collectible **Jewelry**, 1850 – 1950, Baker	$9.95
6645	100 Years of **Purses**, 1880s to 1980s, Aikins	$24.95
6337	**Purse Masterpieces**, Schwartz	$29.95
4729	**Sewing Tools** & Trinkets, Thompson	$24.95
6038	**Sewing Tools** & Trinkets, Volume 2, Thompson	$24.95
6039	Signed Beauties of **Costume Jewelry**, Brown	$24.95
6341	Signed Beauties of **Costume Jewelry**, Volume II, Brown	$24.95
6555	20th Century **Costume Jewelry**, Aikins	$24.95
5620	Unsigned Beauties of **Costume Jewelry**, Brown	$24.95
4878	Vintage & Contemporary **Purse Accessories**, Gerson	$24.95
5923	**Vintage Jewelry** for Investment & Casual Wear, Edeen	$24.95

ARTIFACTS, GUNS, KNIVES, TOOLS, PRIMITIVES

6021	**Arrowheads** of the Central Great Plains, Fox	$19.95
1868	Antique **Tools**, Our American Heritage, McNerney	$9.95
6469	Big Book of **Pocket Knives**, 2nd Edition, Stewart/Ritchie	$19.95
4943	Field Gde. to Flint **Arrowheads & Knives** of the N. Am. Indian, Tully	$9.95
3885	**Indian Artifacts** of the Midwest, Book II, Hothem	$16.95
4870	**Indian Artifacts** of the Midwest, Book III, Hothem	$18.95
5685	**Indian Artifacts** of the Midwest, Book IV, Hothem	$19.95
6565	**Modern Guns**, Identification & Values, 15th Ed., Quertermous	$16.95
2164	**Primitives**, Our American Heritage, McNerney	$9.95
6031	Standard **Knife** Collector's Guide, 4th Ed., Ritchie & Stewart	$14.95

PAPER COLLECTIBLES & BOOKS

5902	**Boys' & Girls' Book** Series, Jones	$19.95
5153	Collector's Guide to **Children's Books**, 1850 to 1950, Vol. II, Jones	$19.95
6553	Collector's Guide to **Cookbooks**, Daniels	$24.95
1441	Collector's Guide to **Post Cards**, Wood	$9.95
6627	Early 20th Century **Hand-Painted Photography**, Ivankovich	$24.95
3973	**Sheet Music** Reference & Price Guide, 2nd Ed., Pafik/Guiheen	$19.95

GLASSWARE

5602	Anchor Hocking's **Fire-King** & More, 2nd Ed., Florence	$24.95
6321	**Carnival Glass**, The Best of the Best, Edwards/Carwile	$29.95
5823	Collectible **Glass Shoes**, 2nd Edition, Wheatley	$24.95
6821	Coll. **Glassware from the 40s, 50s & 60s**, 8th Edition, Florence	$19.95
6626	Collector's Companion to **Carnival Glass**, 2nd Ed., Edwards/Carwile	$14.95
1810	Collector's Encyclopedia of **American Art Glass**, Shuman	$29.95
6830	Collector's Encyclopedia of **Depression Glass**, 17th Ed., Florence	$19.95
1664	Collector's Encyclopedia of **Heisey Glass**, 1925 – 1938, Bredehoft	$24.95
3905	Collector's Encyclopedia of **Milk Glass**, Newbound	$24.95
5820	Collector's Guide to **Glass Banks**, Reynolds	$24.95
6454	**Crackle Glass** From Around the World, Weitman	$24.95
6559	**Elegant Glassware** of the Depression Era, 11th Edition, Florence	$24.95
6334	Encyclopedia of **Paden City Glass**, Domitz	$24.95
3981	Evers' Standard **Cut Glass** Value Guide	$12.95
6126	**Fenton Art Glass**, 1907 – 1939, 2nd Edition, Whitmyer	$29.95
6628	**Fenton Glass** Made for Other Companies, Domitz	$29.95
6462	Florences' **Glass Kitchen Shakers**, 1930 – 1950s	$19.95
5042	Florences' **Glassware Pattern Identification** Guide, Vol. I	$18.95
5615	Florences' **Glassware Pattern Identification** Guide, Vol. II	$19.95
6142	Florences' **Glassware Pattern Identification** Guide, Vol. III	$19.95
6643	Florences' **Glassware Pattern Identification** Guide, Vol. IV	$19.95
6641	Florences' **Ovenware** from the 1920s to the Present	$24.95

6226 **Fostoria** Value Guide, Long/Seate $19.95
5899 **Glass & Ceramic Baskets**, White $19.95
6460 **Glass Animals**, 2nd Edition, Spencer $24.95
6127 The **Glass Candlestick** Book, Vol. 1, Akro Agate to Fenton, Felt/Stoer .$24.95
6228 The **Glass Candlestick** Book, Vol. 2, Fostoria to Jefferson, Felt/Stoer .$24.95
6461 The **Glass Candlestick** Book, Vol. 3, Kanawha to Wright, Felt/Stoer ...$29.95
6648 **Glass Toothpick Holders**, 2nd Edition, Bredehoft/Sanford...........$29.95
6329 **Glass Tumblers**, 1860s to 1920s, Bredehoft $29.95
5827 **Kitchen Glassware** of the Depression Years, 6th Edition, Florence $24.95
6133 **Mt. Washington Art Glass**, Sisk $49.95
6556 Pocket Guide to **Depression Glass** & More, 14th Edition, Florence $12.95
6448 Standard Encyclopedia of **Carnival Glass**, 9th Ed., Edwards/Carwile ..$29.95
6449 Standard **Carnival Glass** Price Guide, 14th Ed., Edwards/Carwile $9.95
6035 Standard Encyclopedia of **Opalescent Glass**, 4th Ed., Edwards/Carwile .$24.95
6644 Standard Encyclopedia of **Pressed Glass**, 4th Ed., Edwards/Carwile $29.95
6241 Treasures of **Very Rare Depression Glass**, Florence $39.95
6476 **Westmoreland Glass**, The Popular Years, 1940 – 1985, Kovar.........$29.95

POTTERY

4929 **American Art Pottery**, Sigafoose $24.95
1425 An Illustrated Value Guide to **Cookie Jars**, Westfall $9.95
6549 **California Pottery** Scrapbook, Chipman $29.95
4851 Collectible **Cups & Saucers**, Harran $18.95
6326 Collectible **Cups & Saucers**, Book III, Harran $24.95
6344 Collectible **Vernon Kilns**, 2nd Edition, Nelson $29.95
6331 Collecting **Head Vases**, Barron $24.95
6621 Collector's Ency. of **American Dinnerware**, 2nd Ed., Cunningham $29.95
6034 Collector's Encyclopedia of **California Pottery**, 2nd Ed., Chipman $24.95
6629 Collector's Encyclopedia of **Fiesta**, 10th Ed., Huxford....................$24.95
3431 Collector's Encyclopedia of **Homer Laughlin China**, Jasper $24.95
1276 Collector's Encyclopedia of **Hull Pottery**, Roberts $19.95
5609 Collector's Encyclopedia of **Limoges Porcelain**, 3rd Ed., Gaston $29.95
6637 Collector's Encyclopedia of **Made in Japan Ceramics**, 1st Ed., White .$24.95
2334 Collector's Encyclopedia of **Majolica Pottery**, Katz-Marks $19.95
5677 Collector's Encyclopedia of **Niloak**, 2nd Edition, Gifford $29.95
5679 Collector's Encyclopedia of **Red Wing Art Pottery**, Dollen $24.95
5618 Collector's Encyclopedia of **Rosemeade Pottery**, Dommel $24.95
5841 Collector's Encyclopedia of **Roseville Pottery**, Vol. 1, Huxford/Nickel $24.95
5842 Collector's Encyclopedia of **Roseville Pottery**, Vol. 2, Huxford/Nickel. $24.95
5917 Collector's Encyclopedia of **Russel Wright**, 3rd Edition, Kerr $29.95
6646 Collector's Ency. of **Stangl Artware**, Lamps, and Birds, 2nd Ed., Runge .$29.95
3314 Collector's Encyclopedia of **Van Briggle Art Pottery**, Sasicki $24.95
5680 Collector's Guide to **Feather Edge Ware**, McAllister $19.95
6124 Collector's Guide to **Made in Japan Ceramics**, Book IV, White $24.95
6634 Collector's Ultimate Ency. of **Hull Pottery**, Volume 1, Roberts $29.95
6829 The Complete Guide to **Corning Ware & Visions Cookware**, Coroneos $19.95
6316 Decorative **American Pottery & Whiteware**, Wilby $29.95
5909 **Dresden Porcelain** Studios, Harran $29.95
5918 Florences' Big Book of **Salt & Pepper Shakers** $24.95
6320 Gaston's **Blue Willow**, 3rd Edition $19.95
6630 Gaston's **Flow Blue China**, The Comprehensive Guide...................$29.95
2379 Lehner's Ency. of **U.S. Marks** on Pottery, Porcelain & China $24.95

4722 **McCoy Pottery**, Collector's Reference & Value Guide, Hanson/Nissen ..$19.95
5913 **McCoy Pottery**, Volume III, Hanson & Nissen $24.95
6333 **McCoy Pottery Wall Pockets** & Decorations, Nissen $24.95
6135 **North Carolina Art Pottery**, 1900 – 1960, James/Leftwich $24.95
6335 Pictorial Guide to **Pottery & Porcelain Marks**, Lage $29.95
5691 **Post86 Fiesta**, Identification & Value Guide, Racheter $19.95
1440 **Red Wing Stoneware**, DePasquale/Peck/Peterson $9.95
6037 **Rookwood Pottery**, Nicholson/Thomas $24.95
3443 **Salt & Pepper Shakers** IV, Guarnaccia $18.95
3738 **Shawnee Pottery**, Mangus $24.95
6828 The Ultimate Collector's Encyclopedia of **Cookie Jars**, Roerig $29.95
6640 Van Patten's ABC's of Collecting **Nippon Porcelain** $29.95
5924 **Zanesville Stoneware** Company, Rans/Ralston/Russell $24.95

OTHER COLLECTIBLES

5838 Advertising **Thermometers**, Merritt $16.95
5898 Antique & Contemporary **Advertising Memorabilia**, Summers ...$24.95
5814 Antique **Brass & Copper**, Gaston $24.95
1880 Antique **Iron**, McNerney $9.95
6622 The Art of American **Game Calls**, Lewis $24.95
6472 The A – Z Guide to Collecting **Trivets**, Rosack $24.95
6552 B.J. Summers' Guide to **Coca-Cola**, 5th Edition $24.95
6827 B.J. Summers' Pocket Guide to **Coca-Cola**, 5th Edition $12.95
1128 **Bottle** Pricing Guide, 3rd Ed., Cleveland $7.95
6345 **Business & Tax Guide** for Antiques & Collectibles, Kelly $14.95
3718 Collectible **Aluminum**, Grist $16.95
6342 Collectible **Soda Pop** Memorabilia, Summers $24.95
5060 Collectible **Souvenir Spoons**, Bednersh $19.95
5676 Collectible **Souvenir Spoons**, Book II, Bednersh $29.95
5666 Collector's Encyclopedia of **Granite Ware**, Book 2, Greguire $29.95
5836 Collector's Guide to **Antique Radios**, 5th Edition, Bunis $19.95
4947 Collector's Guide to **Inkwells**, Book II, Badders $19.95
5558 The Ency. of Early American **Sewing Machines**, 2nd Ed., Bays $29.95
6561 Field Guide to **Fishing Lures**, Lewis $16.95
5683 **Fishing Lure** Collectibles, Volume 1, Murphy/Edmisten $29.95
6328 **Flea Market Trader**, 14th Edition, Huxford $12.95
6458 **Fountain Pens**, Past & Present, 2nd Edition, Erano $24.95
6631 **Garage Sale** & Flea Market Annual, 13th Edition, Huxford $19.95
4945 **G-Men and FBI Toys** and Collectibles, Whitworth $18.95
2216 **Kitchen Antiques**, 1790 – 1940, McNerney $14.95
6639 **McDonald's Drinkware**, Kelly $24.95
6028 Modern **Fishing Lure** Collectibles, Volume 1, Lewis $24.95
6131 Modern **Fishing Lure** Collectibles, Volume 2, Lewis $24.95
6322 Pictorial Guide to **Christmas Ornaments** & Collectibles, Johnson $29.95
6839 **Schroeder's Antiques** Price Guide, 24th Edition $14.95
5007 **Silverplated Flatware**, Revised 4th Edition, Hagan $18.95
6647 **Star Wars** Super Collector's Wish Book, 3rd Edition, Carlton $29.95
4935 The W.F. Cody **Buffalo Bill** Collector's Guide, Wojtowicz $24.95
6632 Value Gde. to **Gas Station Memorabilia**, 2nd Ed., Summers/Priddy ...$29.95
6841 Vintage **Fabrics**, Gridley/Kiplinger/McClure $19.95
6036 Vintage **Quilts**, Aug/Newman/Roy $24.95

This is only a partial listing of the books on antiques that are available from Collector Books. All books are well illustrated and contain current values. Most of these books are available from your local bookseller, antique dealer, or public library. If you are unable to locate certain titles in your area, you may order by mail from **COLLECTOR BOOKS**, P.O. Box 3009, Paducah, KY 42002-3009. Customers with Visa, Master Card, or Discover may phone in orders from 7:00 a.m. to 5:00 p.m. CT, Monday – Friday, toll free **1-800-626-5420**, or online at **www.collectorbooks.com**. Add $4.00 for postage for the first book ordered and 50¢ for each additional book. Include item number, title, and price when ordering. Allow 14 to 21 days for delivery.

1-800-626-5420 Fax: 1-270-898-8890

www.collectorbooks.com

Schroeder's ANTIQUES Price Guide

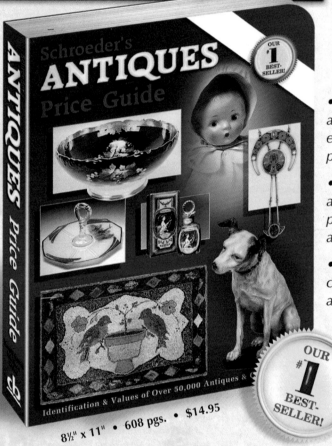

Schroeder's
ANTIQUES
Price Guide

OUR #1 BEST-SELLER!

Identification & Values of Over 50,000 Antiques &

8½" x 11" • 608 pgs. • $14.95

...is the #1 bestselling antiques & collectibles value guide on the market today, and here's why...

• *More than 400 advisors, well-known dealers, and top-notch collectors work together with our editors to bring you accurate information regarding pricing and identification.*

• *More than 50,000 items in over 500 categories are listed along with hundreds of sharp original photos that illustrate not only the rare and unusual, but the common, popular collectibles as well.*

• *Each large close-up shot shows important details clearly. Every subject is represented with histories and background information, a feature not found in any of our competitors' publications.*

• *Our editors keep abreast of newly developing trends, often adding several new categories a year as the need arises.*

OUR #1 BEST-SELLER!

Without doubt, you'll find

Schroeder's Antiques Price Guide

the only one to buy for reliable information and values.

If it merits the interest of today's collector, you'll find it in *Schroeder's*. And you can feel confident that the information we publish is up-to-date and accurate. Our advisors thoroughly check each category to spot inconsistencies, listings that may not be entirely reflective of market dealings, and lines too vague to be of merit. Only the best of the lot remains for publication.

COLLECTOR BOOKS
P.O. Box 3009, Paducah, KY 42002–3009
www.collectorbooks.com

W9-BQW-372

Art by AARON MCBRIDE

Art by WARREN FU

STAR WARS®
VISIONARIES

DARK HORSE BOOKS™

publisher
MIKE RICHARDSON

collection designer
JOSHUA ELLIOTT

art director
LIA RIBACCHI

editor
JEREMY BARLOW

special thanks to
**Fay David and Rick McCallum at
Lucasfilm, and Jonathan Rinzler,
Leland Chee, Sue Rostoni, and
Amy Gary at Lucas Licensing.**

published by
**Dark Horse Books
A division of Dark Horse Comics, Inc.
10956 SE Main Street
Milwaukie, OR 97222**

**darkhorse.com
starwars.com**

To find a comics shop in your area,
call the Comic Shop Locator Service
toll-free at 1-888-266-4226

**First edition: April 2005
ISBN: 1-59307- 311-9**

1 2 3 4 5 6 7 8 9 10

Printed in Canada

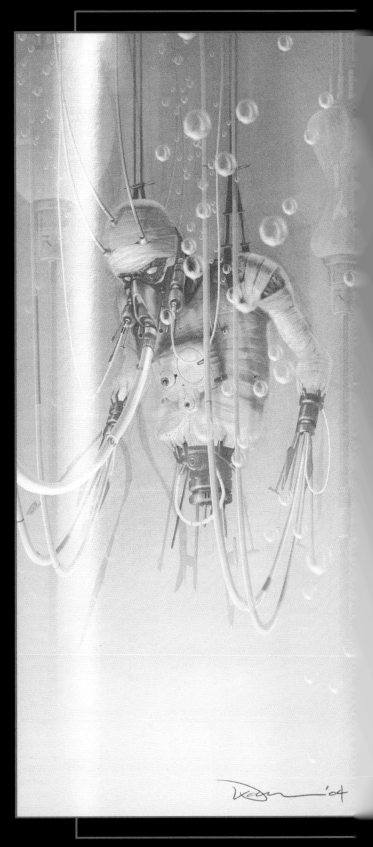

Star Wars Visionaries
Star Wars © 2005 Lucasfilm Ltd. & TM. All rights
reserved. Used under authorization. Text and
illustrations for Star Wars are © 2005 Lucasfilm
Ltd. Dark Horse BooksTM is a trademark of Dark
Horse Comics, Inc. Dark Horse Comics® is
trademark of Dark Horse Comics, Inc., registered
in various categories and countries. All rights
reserved. No portion of this publication may be
reproduced or transmitted, in any form or by any
means, without the express written permission
of Dark Horse Comics, Inc. Names, characters,
places, and incidents featured in this publication
either are the product of the author's imagination
or are used fictitiously. Any resemblance to actual
persons (living or dead), events, institutions, or
locales, without satiric intent, is coincidental.

CONTENTS

During the fourteen months of preproduction on *Star Wars*: Episode III *Revenge of the Sith*, from April 2002 to June 2003, George Lucas would walk up the stairs to the Skywalker Ranch art department every Friday morning. The purpose of these visits was to approve concept art based on the previous week's assignments and to provide material for the following weeks. Lucas might say he needed an asteroid planet, a lizard-like mount, costumes for a love scene, or a new battle cruiser. It would then be up to the concept artists, led by concept design supervisors Ryan Church and Erik Tiemens, to come up with a variety of visions for a variety of subjects. Approved concepts would eventually be made into actual sets, props, clothes, and vehicles, either practical or computer-generated.

Because Lucas was also writing the script during this period, the fascinating aspect of his weekly interactions with the art department was the continuous exchange of ideas. Although he had much of the story already plotted out, the artists — Church, Tiemens, Robert E. Barnes, Warren Fu, Alexander Jaeger, Sang Jun Lee, Michael Murnane, Derek Thompson, Feng Zhu, and others — were often coming up with their own story possibilities: giant windmills on Utapau, a dragonfly-steed for Yoda, or an upside-down world. Not only were they bouncing off Lucas's script ideas, they were brainstorming and inspiring each other.

As I was researching two books on Episode III, I regularly attended these meetings — and each time I was astounded by the group's artistry, imaginings, and productivity. As Erik said, "it was like attending a gallery opening every Friday." Indeed, the artists produced over 4,000 paintings, sketches, and storyboards during preproduction, and each one of these contained dozens of ideas. To create so much so quickly, they completely immersed themselves not only in the design ethos of the saga, but in the character of the players, vehicles, planets, and species. They also worked long hours, often sleeping in the art department; it was almost a form of method-acting — and it resulted in the creation of General Grievous; the planets Felucia, Polis Massa, and Mustafar; the P-38 starfighter, a flying Wookiee catamaran, and on and on.

Yet for each concept that made it into the movie, many did not. Occasionally Lucas would say that an idea was really interesting, but not for his movie. This process is inevitable. Nevertheless, it seemed a shame not to give a voice to those artists who had perhaps more to say — to those who had become initiates in an arcane if popular artform. An obvious solution was to create a medium for this group to tell their own *Star Wars* stories. Fortunately Dark Horse agreed, Jeremy Barlow signed on as editor, and the result is *Star Wars: Visionaries* — intimate views by some of the key creators of a galaxy far, far away....

— J.W. Rinzler
   (Author of *The Art of* and *The Making of Episode III: Revenge of the Sith*)
   Skywalker Ranch, March 2005

OLD WOUNDS

TATOOINE. THE OUTER RIM --
THE THIRD YEAR OF IMPERIAL OCCUPATION.

"VAPORATOR"?

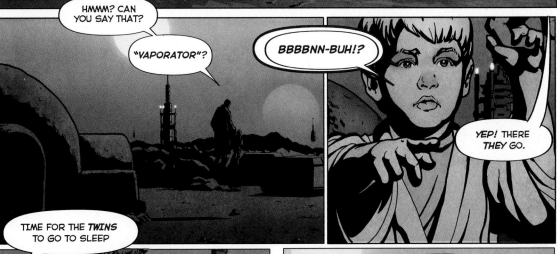

HMMM? CAN YOU SAY THAT?

"VAPORATOR"?

BBBBNN-BUH!?

YEP! THERE *THEY* GO.

TIME FOR THE *TWINS* TO GO TO SLEEP

SSSSHHHH?

UH-HUH. WE HAVE TO BE *QUIET* SO THEY CAN *REST.*

THEY HAVE A *BIG DAY* TOMMOROW BAKING THE SANDS.

I KNOW *SOMEONE ELSE* WHO NEEDS SOME *REST.*

RUMBLE RUMBLE RUMBLE RUMBLE RUMBL

CLICK

BERU!

YES, OWEN?

BERU, BRING ME THE *RIFLE*.

CLICK

OWEN, WHAT IS *IT*?

TUSKEN RAIDER?

DON'T THINK SO. IT LOOKS TO BE *ALONE*.

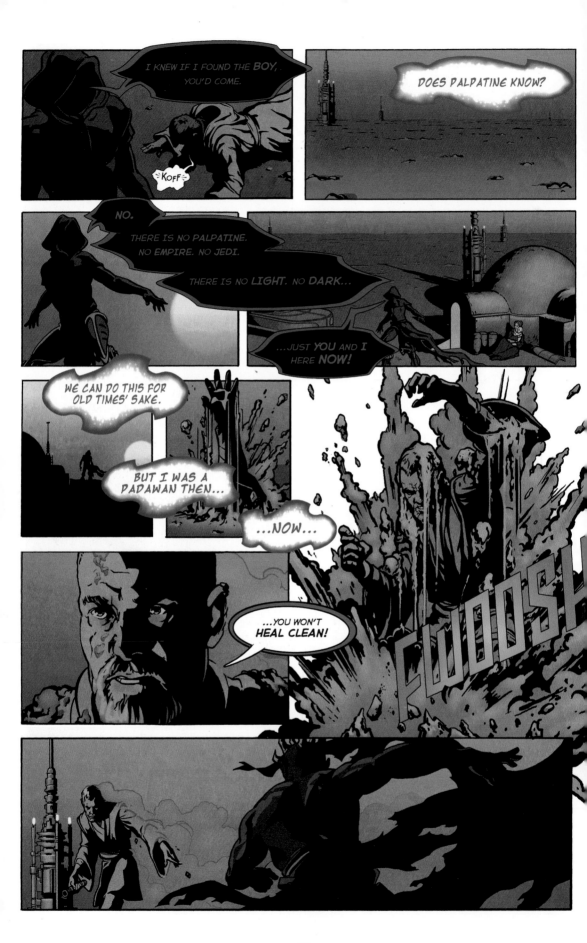

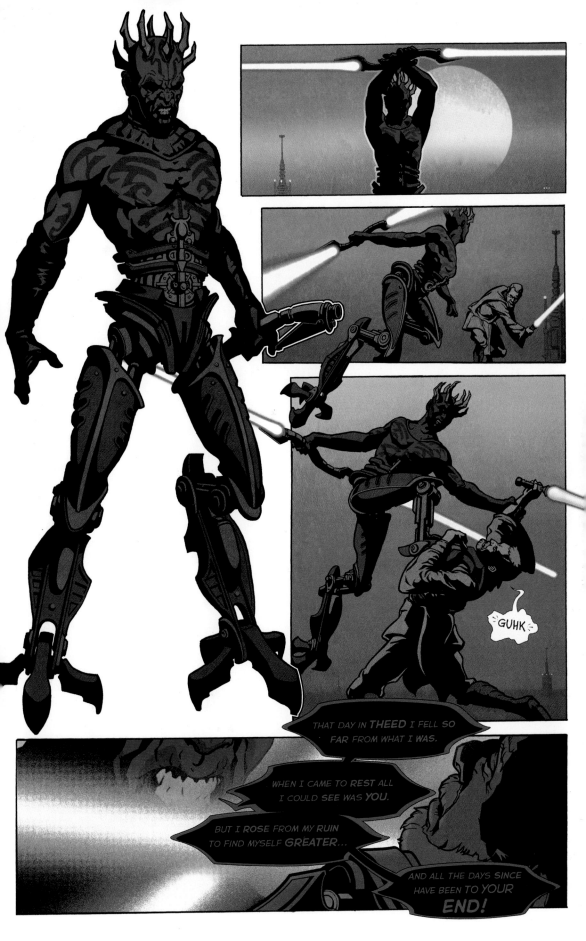

Art by AARON MCBRIDE

Just north of Theed, an artist lived and worked in his studio at the base of an abandoned castle.

THE ARTIST OF NABOO

The artist was a recluse who was consumed with painting suns and moons.

Meanwhile, closer to the capital, Padmé enjoyed the beauty of her gardens.

The days ended in glowing, warm peace.

On the outskirts of Theed, everyone visited the exotic and fragrant bazaar.

A chance encounter, and Padmé's gaze transfixed the artist.

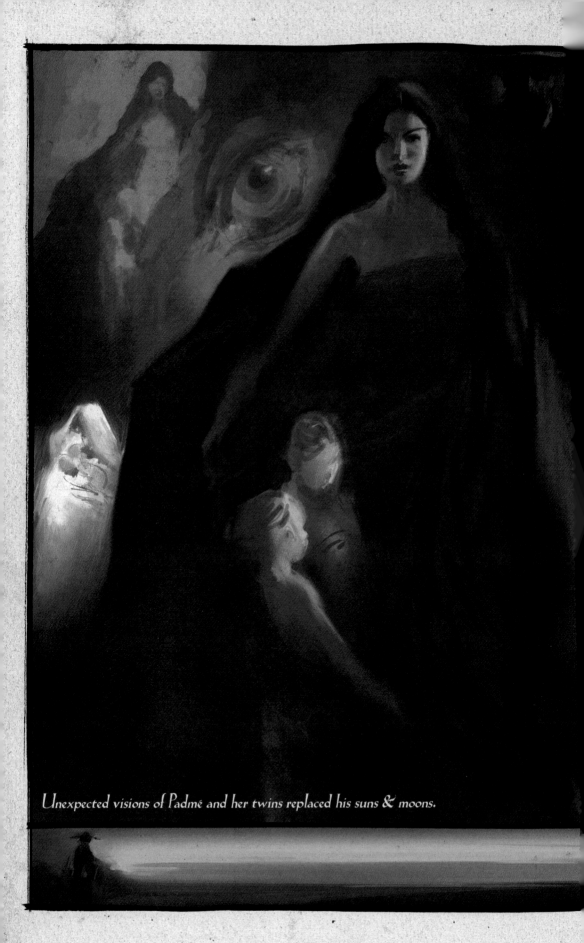

Unexpected visions of Padmé and her twins replaced his suns & moons.

Aware of nothing but what played in his mind, he somehow made his way home.

Perplexed and trying to make sense of it all, he painted for twenty-four weeks straight...

Finally.... an epiphany.

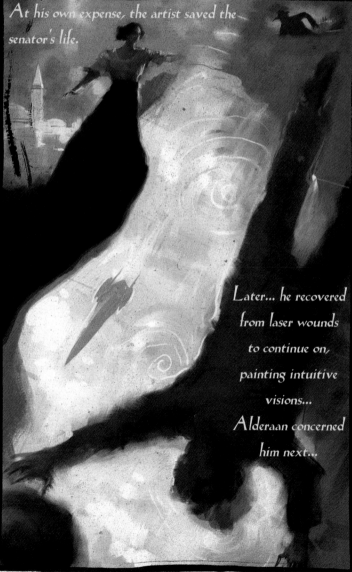

At his own expense, the artist saved the senator's life.

Later... he recovered from laser wounds to continue on, painting intuitive visions... Alderaan concerned him next...

End

Art by MICHAEL MURNANE

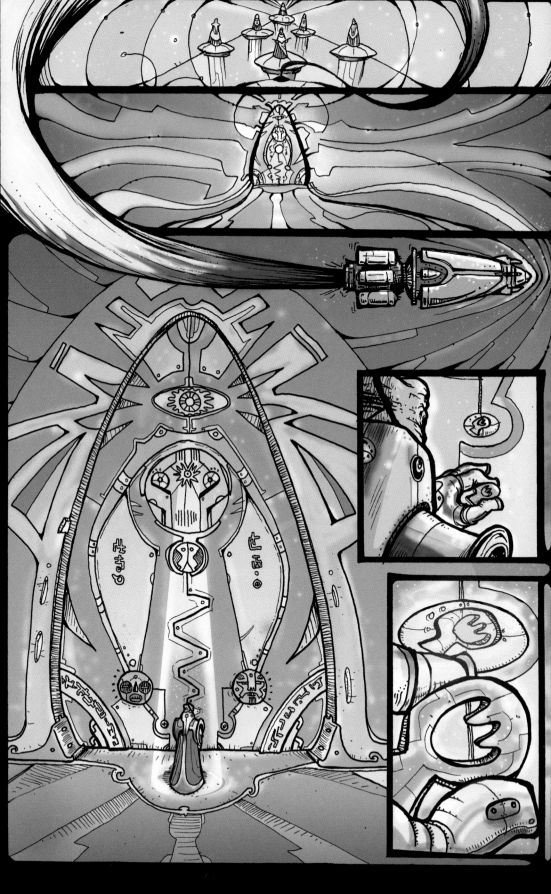

39

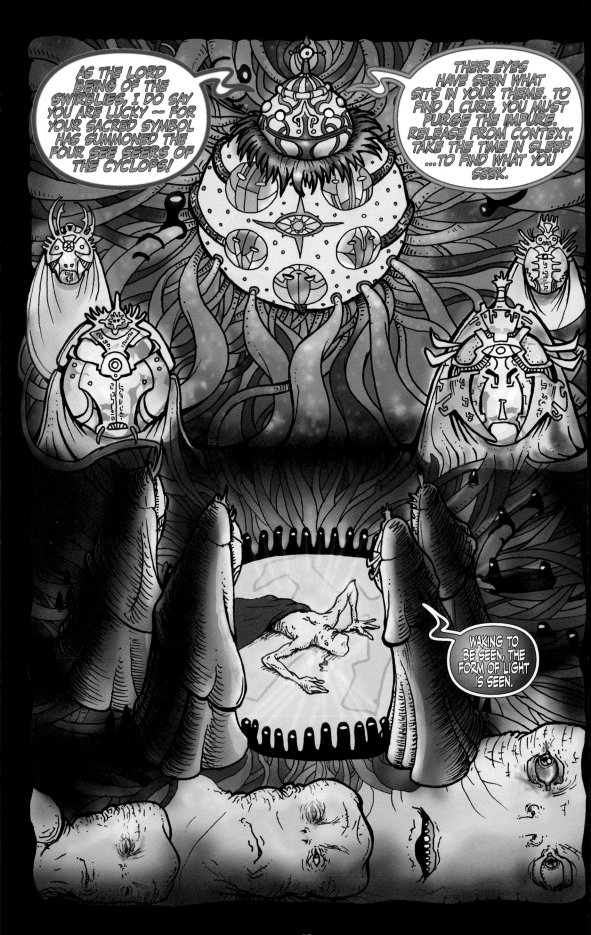

SEE EPISODE III
FOR THE FINAL FATE
OF WAT TAMBOR!

THE END

44

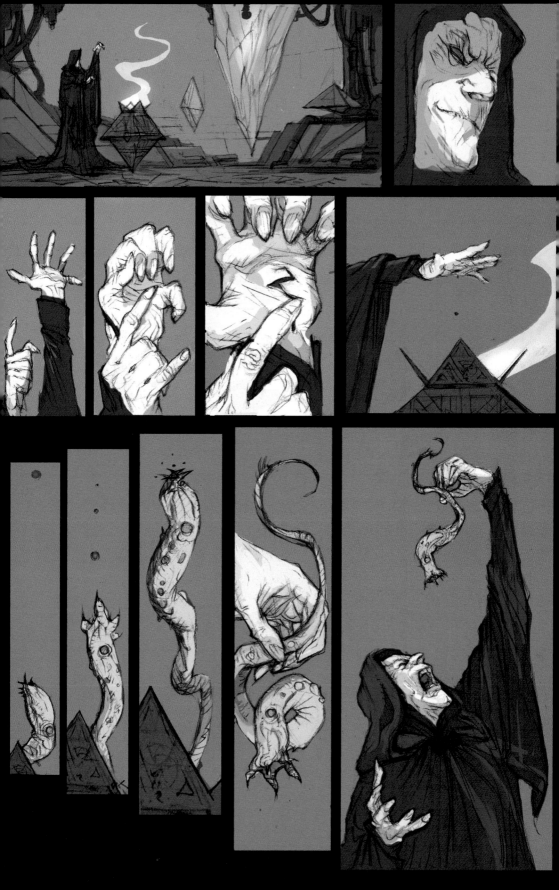

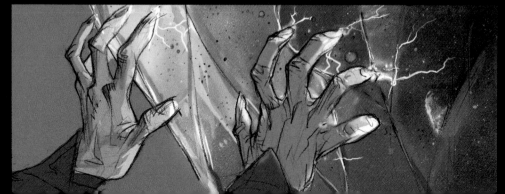

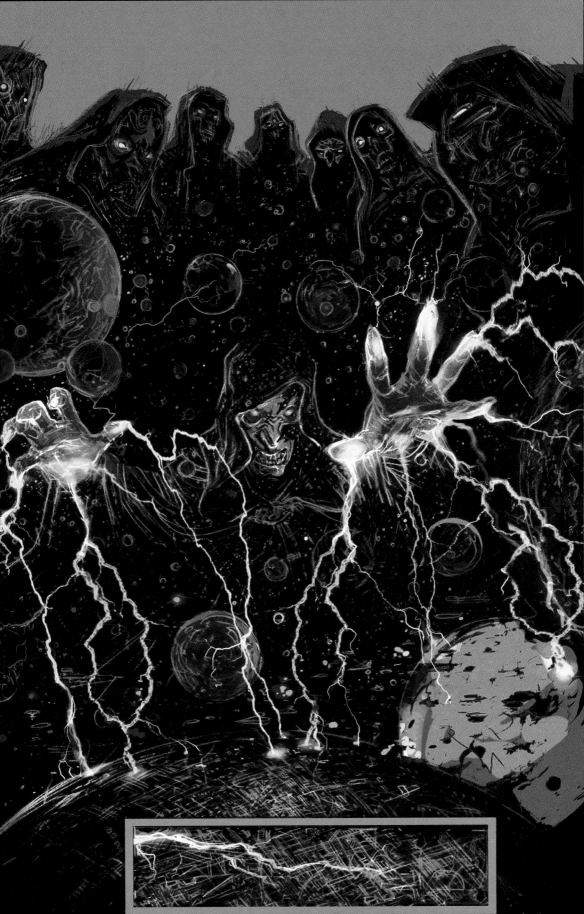

END

ENTRENCHED

DEAR MOTHER,
   FIRST I WANT TO APOLOGIZE FOR NOT BEING ABLE TO WRITE HOME. THE REBELLION, AS YOU KNOW, HAS US ON THE MOVE QUITE A BIT AND WE'VE BEEN WORKING TOO HARD TO HAVE ANY "DOWN TIME" FOR ANYTHING PERSONAL.

ACTUALLY OUR BATTALION COMMANDER ORDERED US *NOT* TO WRITE. HE'S AFRAID REMEMBRANCES OF FAMILY WILL MAKE US HOMESICK, TAKING OUR MINDS OFF THE TASKS AHEAD--

--BUT WITH THE PRESSURES OF WHAT I FEEL, WHAT *I KNOW* IS ABOUT TO COME...

...I DIDN'T THINK I SHOULD WAIT ANY LONGER.

EVEN THOUGH I'M THE YOUNGEST NONCOM IN THE BATTALION, MAJOR DERLIN PERSONALLY ASSIGNED ME TO BE THE LEADER OF 4TH SQUAD.

MOVING INTO A NEW UNIT'S DIFFICULT, BUT THE GUYS DO EVERYTHING THEY CAN TO MAKE ME FEEL LIKE PART OF THE GROUP.

THOUGH MOST OF THEM TALK TOUGH, I CAN TELL THEY'RE ALL STILL AFRAID...

...AFRAID OF THE UNKNOWN...

OUR MEN ARE THE MOST TRAINED FIGHTERS THE REBELLION'S EVER HAD. MOST OF THEM ARE SURVIVORS FROM THE BATTLES OF YAVIN AND DALUUJ.

WHICH DEFINITELY HELPS OUT MORALE WITH THE YOUNGER KIDS.

...AFRAID OF THE FUTURE...

...AFRAID OF *DYING*.

UNFORTUNATELY I CAN'T SAY WHERE WE ARE, BUT I *CAN* TELL YOU THAT IT'S *COLD*.

IT'S SO COLD THAT THE SPEEDERS WON'T FLY HERE WITHOUT MODIFICATIONS--

--SO THEY'VE TRAINED THE LONG-RANGE SCOUTS TO RIDE ONE OF THE LOCAL ANIMALS FOR RECON PATROLS!

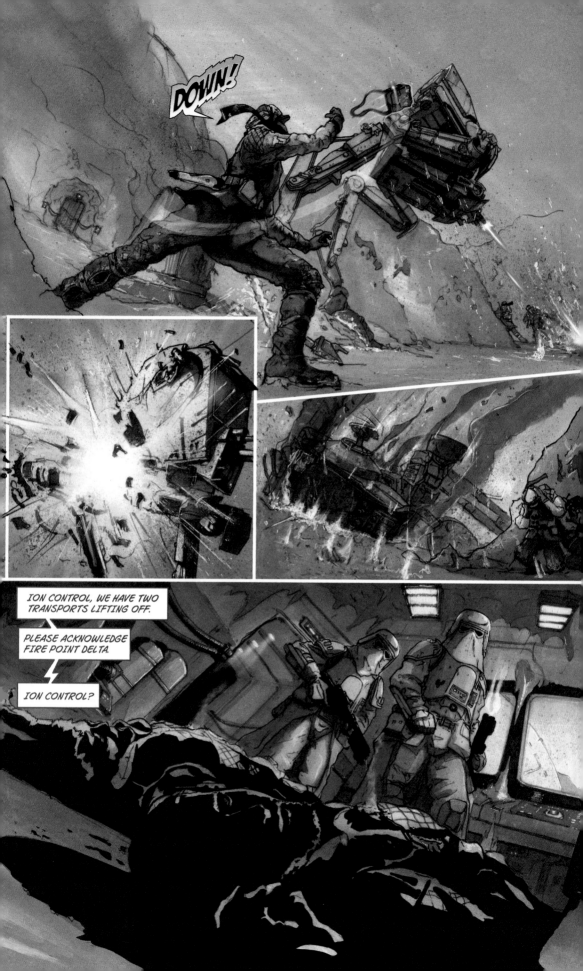

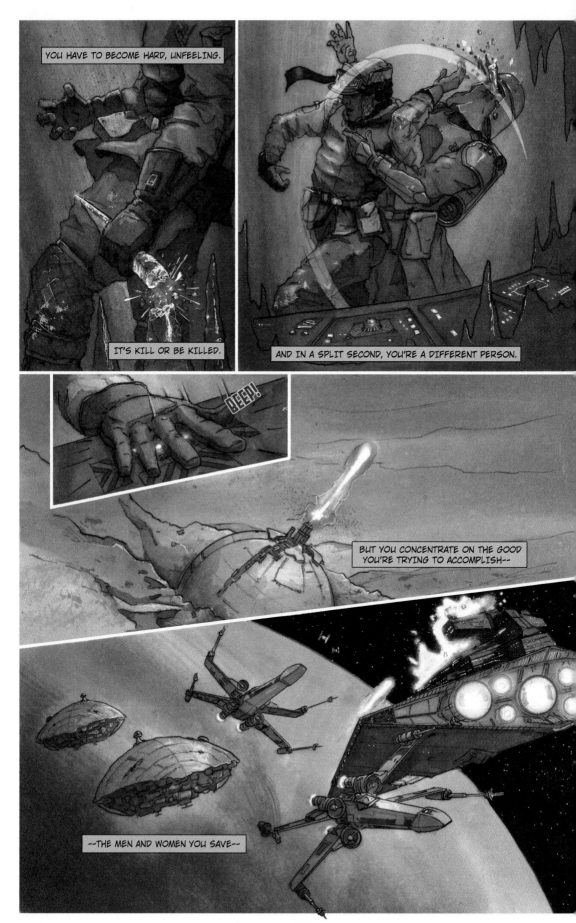

JOBIN, I'VE SET THE SELF-DESTRUCT! WE HAVE TO MOVE!

IF WE CAN MAKE IT TO HANGAR BAY SEVEN--

--WE CAN GRAB A RIDE OUTTA HERE!

--AND NOT DWELL ON THE ONES YOU LEAVE BEHIND.

OH CRAP....

ALL WE HAVE TO--

TAKE THEM.

THE WHOLE PLACE IS COMING APART!

HANGAR TEN!

GET TO HANGAR TEN!

Art by STEPHAN MARTINIÉRE

PROTOTYPES

An industrial wasteland in the outer rim...

KEEP YOUR GUARD UP, *DURGE.* REMEMBER WHAT I TAUGHT YOU...

NNNNGGG!

WITHOUT THE ELEMENT OF SURPRISE, YOU HAVE TO THROW YOUR OPPONENT OFF BALANCE--

-- ATTACK AS YOU DEFEND --

BDEN!

STAY BACK. THE BEAST IS DISABLED, BUT STILL DANGEROUS.

THIS WAS A TEST. WE WERE INVITED HERE, YET THIS GUARD ANIMAL WASN'T LET OUT BY ACCIDENT...

YOUR UNIQUE PHYSIOLOGY PRESENTED SOME CHALLENGES...

...IT KEPT TRYING TO *HEAL OVER* MY WORK.

IT'S QUITE A GIFT YOU HAVE.

DURGE...?

YOU OKAY?

SURE. A LITTLE NAUSEOUS, BUT GETTING USED TO IT.

YOU'RE LOOKING SPIFFY.

SUCH A TOUCHING REUNION. IT'S TIME TO MEET YOUR SPARRING PARTNER.

WE'RE TRAINING WITH YOUR PROTOCOL DROID?!

YOU OF ALL PEOPLE SHOULD KNOW NOT TO TRUST APPEARANCES...

WHAT YOU SEE NOW IS AN *AMALGAMATION* OF MY DROID...AND A REBORN DR. NUBYL --

-- AND *SHE* IS MOST *ANXIOUS* TO BEGIN YOUR *TRAINING.*

LET'S SEE IF YOU CAN *LIVE UP* TO THE DOCTOR'S WORK...

I'VE ENHANCED MOST OF YOUR ARMORS' COMBAT SYSTEMS, UPGRADING YOUR INDEPENDENTLY CONTROLLED CONCUSSION CHARGES...

"...YOUR ARMORS' COMPUTER SYSTEMS NOW WORK IN TANDEM WITH YOUR OWN HEIGHTENED NEURO-NETWORKS...

"...ENABLING YOU TO AUTOMATICALLY TRACK ANY INCOMING HOSTILE FIRE...

"...YOUR HELMETS' VISUAL ARRAYS EMPLOY A TARGETING SYSTEM LINKED TO YOUR OPTIC NERVES. SIMPLY *LOOK* AT YOUR TARGET AND YOUR WEAPON WILL FIND ITS MARK.

"PROVIDED YOUR TARGET ISN'T AS *WELL-EQUIPPED* AS YOU ARE."

"YOUR SUITS ALSO PROVIDE INTERNAL EQUILIBRIUM FEEDBACK, FOR ENHANCED BALANCE, RECOVERY...

"...AND COUNTER-ATTACKS.

"THE ARMOR WILL DELIVER AS MUCH OR AS LITTLE PHYSICAL FORCE AS YOU REQUIRE...

"...ENABLING YOU TO MOVE AS YOU WISH.

"SIMPLY MOVE AS YOU NORMALLY WOULD, AND THE SUIT WILL COMPENSATE...

"...YOU'LL FIND YOUR SPEED AND ACCURACY GREATLY IMPROVED."

THAT'S ENOUGH-- NO NEED TO DESTROY EACH OTHER! YOU'VE DISPLAYED YOUR ABILITIES WELL ENOUGH.

READY FOR THE REAL WORLD, I THINK.

NOW, CONCERNING *YOUR* END OF THE BARGAIN...

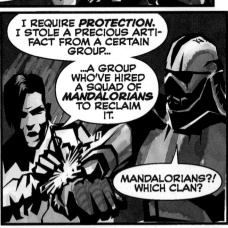

I REQUIRE *PROTECTION.* I STOLE A PRECIOUS ARTIFACT FROM A CERTAIN GROUP...

...A GROUP WHO'VE HIRED A SQUAD OF *MANDALORIANS* TO RECLAIM IT.

MANDALORIANS?! WHICH CLAN?

ONE LOYAL TO *UNG KUSP.*

YOU THREE ARE TO *INTERCEPT* THEM.

WE WERE BOUND TO CROSS PATHS WITH THEM EVENTUALLY.

WHERE ARE THEY NOW?

I BELIEVE THEY'VE JUST BREACHED THE FRONT DOOR.

K KOOM

84

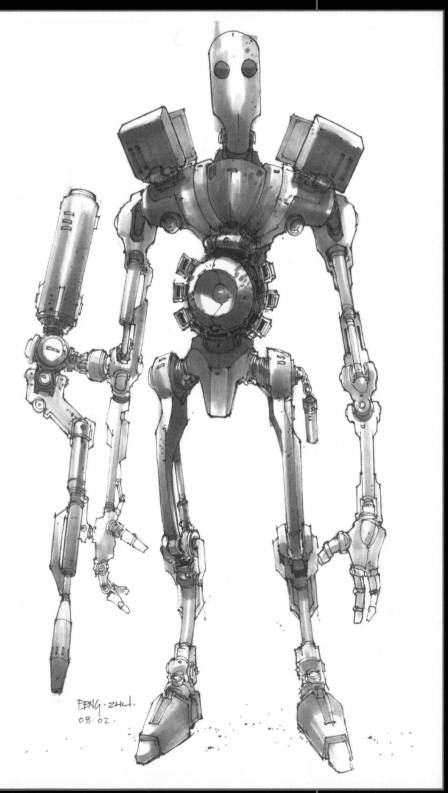

Art by FENG ZHU

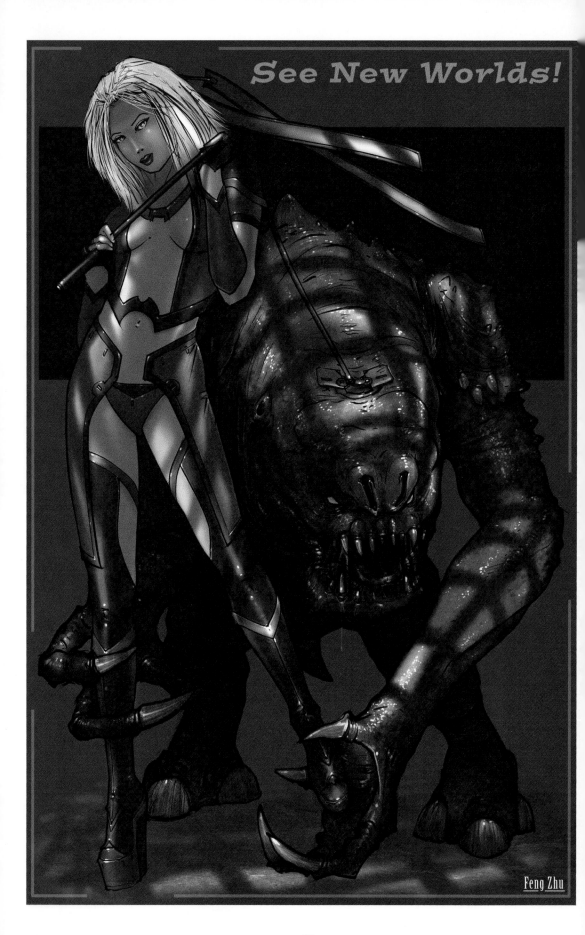

See New Worlds!

Feng Zhu

Art by SANG JUN LEE

DEEP FOREST

THE PLANET KASHYYYK. EIGHTEEN MONTHS AFTER THE BATTLE OF GEONOSIS.

HAVE THE KASHYYYK ROYAL FAMILIES -- ≥KAFF KAFF≤ JOINED THE CONFEDERACY?

WE ARE STILL WAITING FOR THEIR ANSWER.

THOSE FILTHY SIMIANS! WE DON'T HAVE TIME TO WAIT. HELP THEM DECIDE -- SEND THE DROIDS!

DROIDS? BUT THAT WAS NOT PART OF OUR PLAN--

IT IS NOW.

DROIDS DISPATCHED.

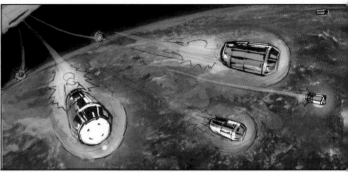

KASHYYYK ROYAL CITY: EARLY MORNING.

"CAREFUL, YOU MUST BE. DECEIVE YOU, THE SEPARATISTS WILL..."

...TRUST THEM, YOU MUST NOT, *KING GRAKCHAWWAA.*

SEND AID, THE REPUBLIC WILL, IF NEED IT YOU DO.

⟨I...KASHYYYK IS NOT YET READY TO COMMIT TO THIS WAR.⟩

⟨THE SEPARATIST DELEGATE ASKS TO SPEAK WITH YOU, YOUR HIGHNESS.⟩

WE TRUST YOU'VE HAD TIME TO CONSIDER OUR OFFER...

98

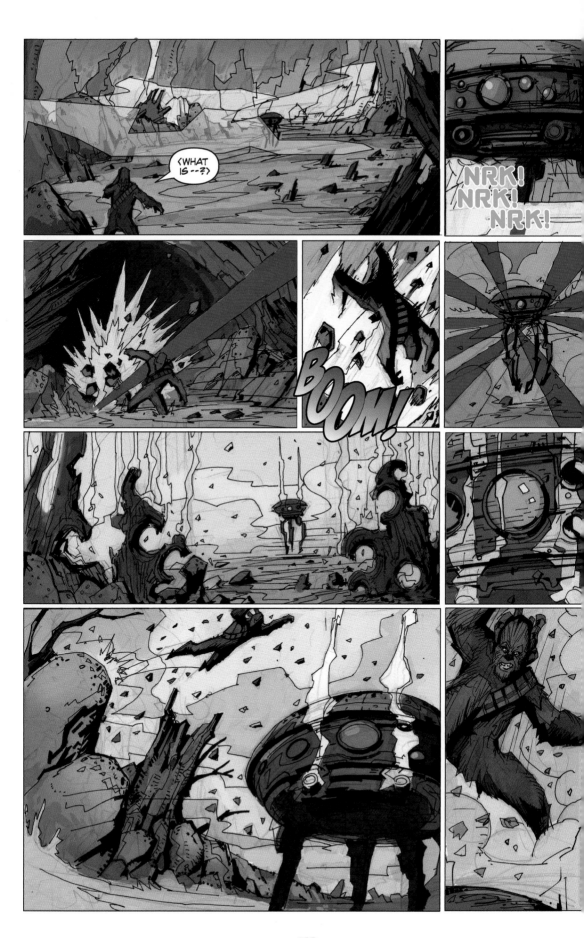

101

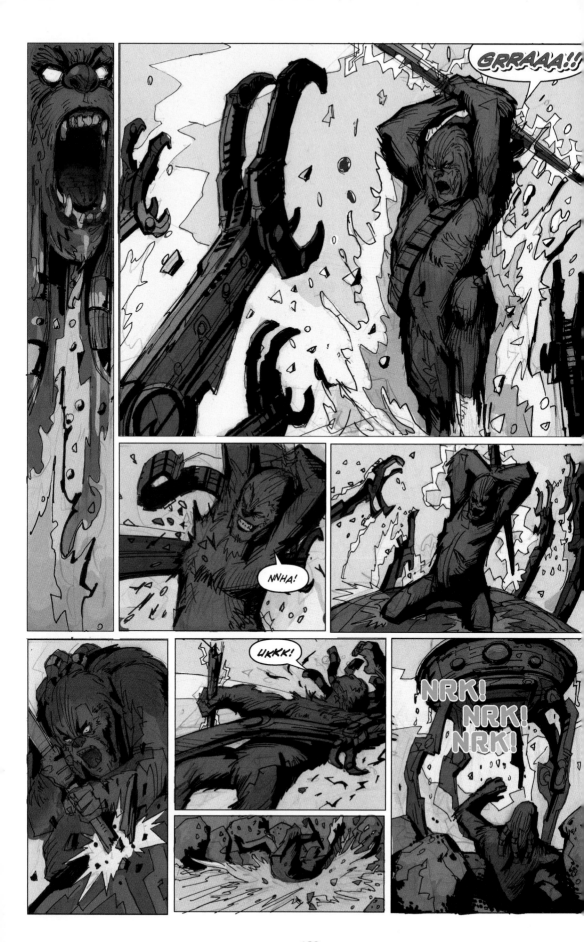

103

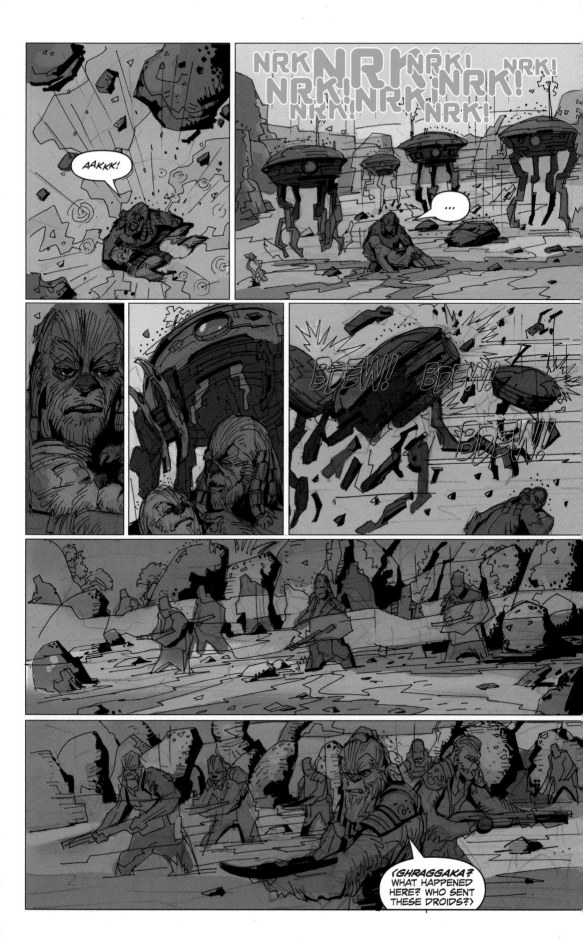

THE REPUBLIC DOES NOT CARE ABOUT YOU. WE WILL PROVIDE PROTECTION.

〈YOUR HIGHNESS, WE CAN'T HAND OVER OUR PLANET TO THE SEPARATISTS. WE MUST FIGHT!〉

〈THAT WOULD BE *SUICIDE!* WE CAN'T WIN A WAR!〉

HE IS CORRECT. YOU MUST THINK ABOUT YOUR *FUTURE!*

〈YOUR HIGHNESS -- YOUR SON...WAS KILLED TODAY IN THE WESTERN FOREST. KILLED BY SEPARATIST DROIDS.〉

〈MY SON...?〉

ER...A REGRETTABLE ACCIDENT...BUT WE MUST HAVE YOUR DECISION!

〈MY DECISION...?〉

〈WAR AGAINST THE INVADERS!〉

END

Art by ERIK TIEMENS

CELESTIA GALACTICA PHOTOGRAFICA

RYAN CHURCH

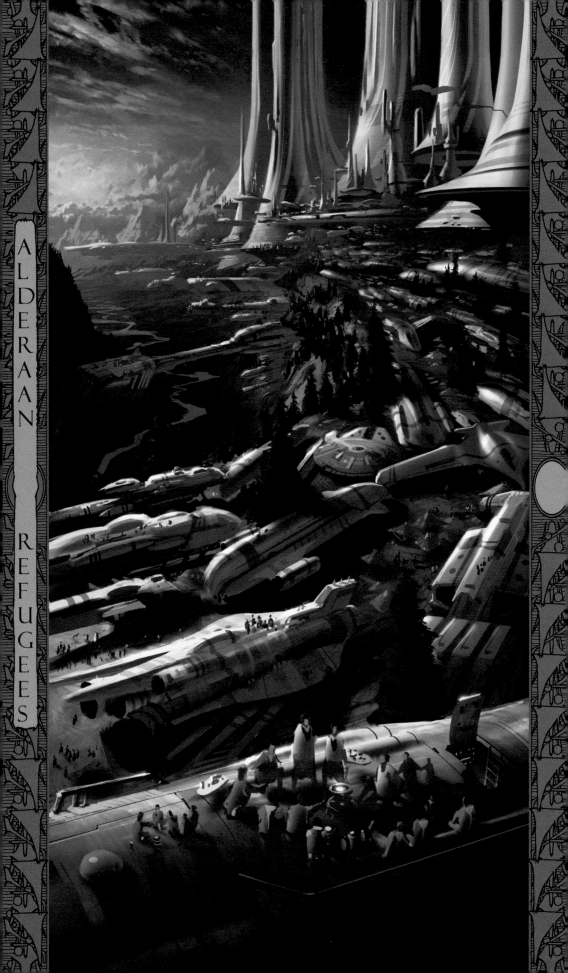

ALDERAAN REFUGEES

DEATH STAR DRYDOCK

AT-AT VILLA

RECLAIMED WRECK

BAD PET

BRIDGEWORLD LOST

UTAPAU SURRENDERS

THE PLANET KALEE...

CAAAW!

"OUR APPEALS HAVE BEEN IGNORED.

FLAP.
FLAP.
FLAP.

"IT IS NOW APPARENT THAT THE REPUBLIC AND THE JEDI FAVOR OUR ENEMY."

GENERAL, YOU ARE OUR LAST HOPE AGAINST THE HUK IN THIS WAR.

MAY THE SPIRITS OF OUR ANCESTORS WATCH OVER YOU AND YOUR TROOPS.

AS LONG AS THIS OLD THING HOLDS TOGETHER, WE'LL BE OKAY.

BLIP... BLIP... BLIP... BLIP...

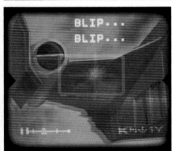

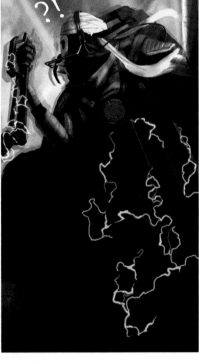

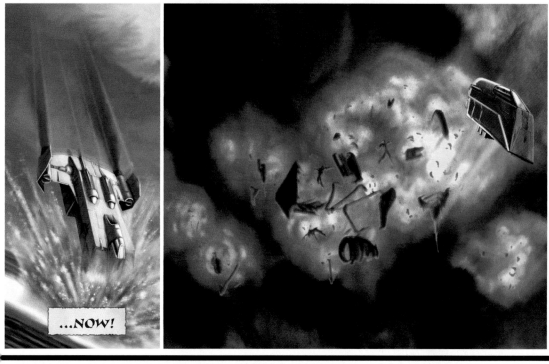

...NOW!

DID HE SURVIVE?

BREATHING, BUT UNCONSCIOUS--

TURN HIM OVER.

CLICK!

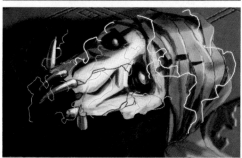

THAT HEART STUN WILL WEAR OFF SHORTLY. WHEN HE AWAKENS, HE WILL BEGIN TO DIE.

TRANSPORT HIM TO GEONOSIS AT ONCE. I MUST TRAVEL TO SERENNO FOR ONE OTHER IMPORTANT PIECE OF CARGO.

I HAVE THE KALEESH GENERAL. HE WAS NOT CONSCIOUS TO WITNESS HIS "JEDI" CAPTOR. IN FACT, HE IS COMPLETELY UNAWARE OF WHAT HAS TRANSPIRED.

YOU MAY BEGIN PREPARATIONS FOR YOUR... EXPERIMENT.

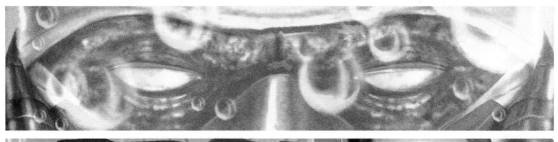

AM...I ...DEAD?

AH, YOU ARE AWAKE MY FRIEND. AND YES, YES, VERY MUCH ALIVE.

BUT YOUR BODY HAS SUSTAINED NEARLY FATAL WOUNDS, DUE TO YOUR ACCIDENT--

WHO... ARE--?

MY APOLOGIES. I AM SAN HILL, CHAIRMAN OF THE INTERGALACTIC BANKING CLAN.

AND JUDGING FROM THE CLOAK WE FOUND, YOU ARE A KALEESH GENERAL, ARE YOU NOT?

A VERY FORTUNATE ONE I MIGHT ADD. A BANKING CLAN FRIGATE ACCIDENTALLY PICKED UP YOUR ESCAPE POD'S EMERGENCY BEACON IN THE JENUWAA SEA.

YOUR CREW WAS NOT SO LUCKY, I'M AFRAID--

BUT YOU, DEAR GENERAL, YOUR MIND AND VITAL ORGANS ARE SAFELY IN OUR CARE, HERE ON GEONOSIS--

GEONOSIS?!...AN HONORABLE LEADER DIES ALONGSIDE HIS SOLDIERS! I ORDER YOU TO BRING ME BACK TO KALEE!

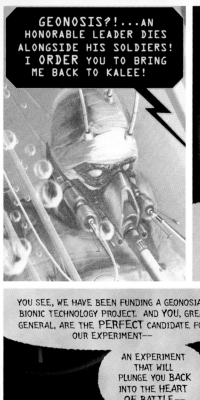

HOW TOUCHING, GENERAL. DO YOU REALLY THINK THE IBC WOULD GO THROUGH ALL THIS TROUBLE ONLY TO LET YOU DIE? YOU WOULD NOT EVEN SURVIVE A JOURNEY BACK TO KALEE...

...LET ALONE ANOTHER FOUR HOURS HERE WITHOUT A BLOOD TRANSFUSION.

HOWEVER, AS FATE WOULD HAVE IT, YOUR ACCIDENT IS ALMOST ...A BLESSING.

YOU SEE, WE HAVE BEEN FUNDING A GEONOSIAN BIONIC TECHNOLOGY PROJECT. AND YOU, GREAT GENERAL, ARE THE PERFECT CANDIDATE FOR OUR EXPERIMENT––

AN EXPERIMENT THAT WILL PLUNGE YOU BACK INTO THE HEART OF BATTLE––

WHAT GOOD IS AN AMPUTEE IN THE HEART OF BATTLE?!

THEREIN LIES THE BEAUTY OF THIS TECHNOLOGY.

WE CAN GUARANTEE YOU A NEW SELF-SUSTAINING BODY WITH APPENDAGES, FREE OF CUMBERSOME LIFE-SUPPORT SYSTEMS.

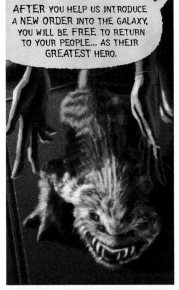

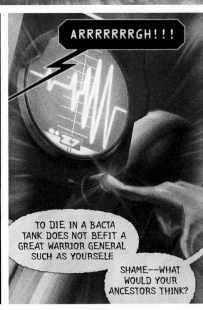

MONTHS LATER, ABOARD A SEPARATIST CRUISER ORBITING GEONOSIS...
THIS ONCE BELONGED TO AN OLD FRIEND OF MINE. AND NOW IT IS YOURS, AS REWARD FOR YOUR IMPRESSIVE TRAINING.
THE JEDI SHALL FALL TO THEIR OWN WEAPON.
NO ONE HAS EVER RECEIVED A LIGHTSABER AS A "GIFT." ESPECIALLY, NOT... ...A DROID.
A SIGN OF GRATITUDE WOULD NOT BE COMPLETELY OUT OF PLACE AT THE MOMENT.

MASTER, THE EXPERIMENT HAS EXCEEDED MY EXPECTATIONS. HIS HONOR AND NOBILITY HAVE BEEN ECLIPSED...

"...BY COLD VENGEANCE...

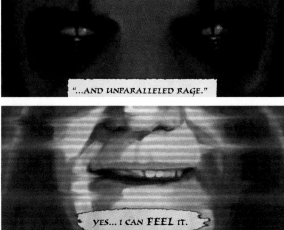

"...AND UNPARALLELED RAGE."

YES... I CAN FEEL IT.

"BENEATH THE NEARLY INDESTRUCTIBLE SHELL..."

"...LIVES THE STRATEGIC MIND OF A GENERAL...

"...WHO HAS EMBRACED THE WAY OF THE SITH."

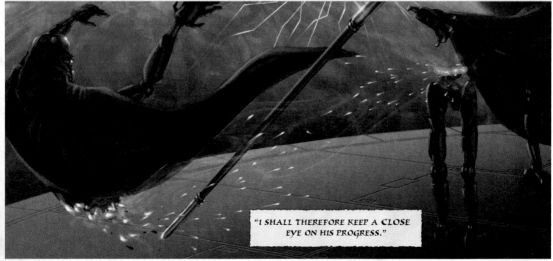

YES... YES. BE MINDFUL OF ANY PROBLEMS THE EXPERIMENT MAY BREED...

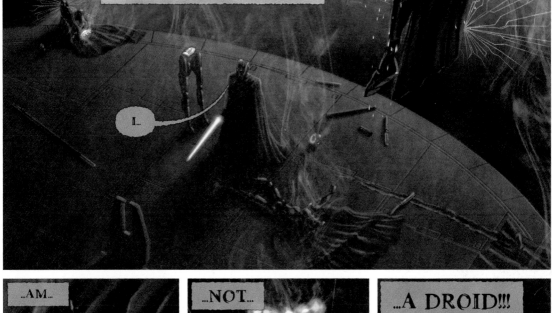

"...THIS BIONIC TECHNOLOGY MAY PROVE TO BE A USEFUL TOOL FOR THE DARK SIDE IN THE YEARS TO COME."

I..

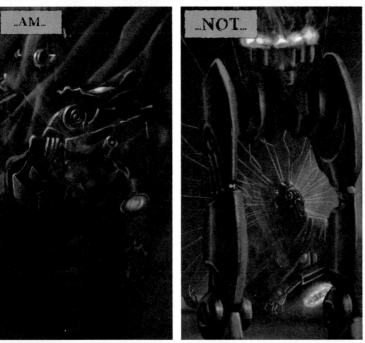

..AM..

...NOT...

...A DROID!!!

WHAAAAAT'S WROOONG?... WHAA..AA....AA

...I AM
GENERAL GRIEVOUS!

ROBERT E. BARNES is a partially nocturnal designer, sculptor and illustrator who valiantly survived working on the concept teams of all three *Star Wars* prequels. He has also contributed illustrations and creatures for the *Star Wars Cross-Section* and *Visual Dictionary* books. Following the inspiring footsteps of previous design graduates of California State University Long Beach, Robert happily landed at Industrial Light & Magic and then Lucasfilm, where he has designed numerous *Star Wars* beings including Durge, mercenary nemesis to Jedi of the Clone Wars. Robert is tolerated by his wife and two daughters, and would like to be a zoologist when he grows up.

RYAN CHURCH likes drawing spaceships and explosions. Luckily for him he was able to design and illustrate a bunch of cool stuff working as concept design supervisor on *Star Wars:* Episode II and III. Clients and employers include Walt Disney Imagineering, Electronic Arts, Paramount and Universal Studios, Industrial Light & Magic, and Lucasfilm. Ryan makes his home in Southern California where he enjoys watching bad movies about spaceships and explosions.

The year 1975 gave us Industrial Light & Magic, Saturday Night Live, and WARREN FU; who would later go on to invent what is known today as *drawing*. Since then, drawing has gone on to become a popular sport amongst many nerds, especially artists. He also invented sarcasm. Following a short-lived attempt at turning his drawing act into a Las Vegas show, he retired penniless. Reviewers called the show "pathetic," "a terrible miscalculation," and that it "lacked the sex-appeal of river-dancing." Warren now spends his days judging pageants, appearing on Hollywood Squares, and writing autobiographies in the third-person that are exactly 100 words long.

ALEX JAEGER has worked at Industrial Light & Magic as a modelmaker, concept designer and art director for the past 10 years. With more than a dozen feature films under his belt, Alex has established a vast portfolio of memorable movie moments. Hardware design is his favorite subject, but more important is making sure the design fits the story. "Making people believe things once impossible are possible is the goal. Both in story and design." Expanding his talents to the graphic novel world is the beginning of his chance to influence both story and design. His website can be found at www.aixart.com.

Having grown up with a deeply curious nature, SANG JUN LEE tries to infuse the wonder of the natural world into his artwork. As a concept artist for the movie industry, he focuses on Character and Costume Design, and has helped define the look for feature film projects such as *Men in Black II, The Hulk, Peter Pan, Pirates of the Caribbean,* and *Star Wars:* Episode III. He continues exploring nature for inspiration and to fuel his imagination, just as he did as a child. You can find his website at www.sangjunart.com.

Over the past 20 years, STEPHAN MARTINIÉRE has become known for his talent, versatility and imagination in every entertainment field. From director to concept illustrator, Stephan has worked on such projects including: *I, Robot, The Time Machine, Virus, Red Planet, Dragon Heart 2,* and *Titan A.E.* Stephan was nominated for an Emmy Award and is the recipient of several Spectrum and Expose Awards. He is currently the visual design director for Midway Games.

AARON MCBRIDE is an art director at Industrial Light & Magic. He has worked on such films as *Star Wars*: Episode III *Revenge of the Sith, Pirates of the Caribbean: The Curse of the Black Pearl, Minority Report, Hulk,* and *A.I.* He currently lives in San Francisco with his wife Nancy and faithfully waits for a Jem and the Holograms reunion tour. His website address is www.sagania.com.

MIKE MURNANE loves Edward Gorey, Dr. Suess, Moebius books, David Lynch films, astral plaining and sentient robots among other things. Top it off with a tasty paint ball injury to Mike's right eye, good family love and support … and you arrive at his contribution to this book. He has sculpted and drawn for *Star Wars* Episode II and Episode III, Industrial Light & Magic, PDI and numerous other projects while he makes movies and tries to teach kids to do the same. Mike is currently reconnecting with the multidimensional time traveling space mystical crew who reside at www.superadvanced.com.

DEREK THOMPSON started working in comics in 1993, illustrating several titles for Dark Horse, including *Predator: Bad Blood, Monster,* and *Abe Sapien.* After moving into game design work for Rhythm & Hues, he landed a job as a concept artist at Industrial Light & Magic. There, he contributed designs and storyboards for numerous features, including *Men In Black, Spawn, The Mummy, The Mummy Returns, Deep Impact,* and *Van Helsing.* Derek recently fulfilled a longtime dream to work at Skywalker Ranch in the *Star Wars*: Episode III art department. Check out his website at www.derekmonster.com.

ERIK TIEMENS has contributed to many films, including *Forrest Gump, Contact,* and *Star Wars*: Episode II and Episode III. Tiemens is also featured in *The Art of Star Wars* books, as well as in *The Art of Star Trek.* Tiemens describes his work on the *Star Wars* films, where he is a concept design supervisor, as extensive shot design and color/lighting direction. Painters Sargent and Turner are among his major influences. He enjoys painting en plein air and currently shows traditional paintings in galleries in California and Connecticut. Samples of his work can be found at www.watersketch.com.

FENG ZHU is a highly recognized and established concept designer in the entertainment industry. His work has expanded across many platforms, ranging from video games, feature films, television commercials, to theme park rides, toy designs, and his own line of training DVDs. Besides working in-house for other studios, Feng has also established himself as a successful freelance designer, under his own studio: Feng Zhu Design. Some of his clients include Electronic Arts, Epic Games, Warner Bros, 3D Realms, Film Roman, Monster Garage, Playboy, Sony Games, Wacom, and Microsoft. He is currently developing his own line of toys, to be launched in 2005.

STAR WARS®

TIMELINE OF TRADE PAPERBACKS AND GRAPHIC NOVELS!

OLD REPUBLIC ERA:
25,000-1000 YEARS BEFORE
STAR WARS: A NEW HOPE

Tales of the Jedi—
Knights of the Old Republic
ISBN: 1-56971-020-1 $14.95

Dark Lords of the Sith
ISBN: 1-56971-095-3 $17.95

The Sith War
ISBN: 1-56971-173-9 $17.95

The Golden Age of the Sith
ISBN: 1-56971-229-8 $16.95

The Freedon Nadd Uprising
ISBN: 1-56971-307-3 $5.95

The Fall of the Sith Empire
ISBN: 1-56971-320-0 $15.95

Redemption
ISBN: 1-56971-535-1 $14.95

Jedi vs. Sith
ISBN: 1-56971-649-8 $17.95

RISE OF THE EMPIRE ERA:
1000-0 YEARS BEFORE
STAR WARS: A NEW HOPE

The Stark Hyperspace War
ISBN: 1-56971-985-3 $12.95

Prelude to Rebellion
ISBN: 1-56971-448-7 $14.95

Jedi Council—Acts of War
ISBN: 1-56971-539-4 $12.95

Darth Maul
ISBN: 1-56971-542-4 $12.95

Jedi Council—
Emissaries to Malastare
ISBN: 1-56971-545-9 $15.95

Episode I—
The Phantom Menace
ISBN: 1-56971-359-6 $12.95

Episode I—
The Phantom Menace Adventures
ISBN: 1-56971-443-6 $12.95

Outlander
ISBN: 1-56971-514-9 $14.95

Star Wars: Jango Fett—
Open Seasons
ISBN: 1-56971-671-4 $12.95

The Bounty Hunters
ISBN: 1-56971-467-3 $12.95

Twilight
ISBN: 1-56971-558-0 $12.95

The Hunt for Aurra Sing
ISBN: 1-56971-651-X $12.95

Darkness
ISBN: 1-56971-659-5 $12.95

The Rite of Passage
ISBN: 1-59307-042-X $12.95

Episode II—Attack of the Clones
ISBN: 1-56971-609-9 $17.95

Clone Wars Volume 1:
The Defense of Kamino
ISBN: 1-56971-962-4 $14.95

Clone Wars Volume 2:
Victories and Sacrifices
ISBN: 1-56971-969-1 $14.95

Clone Wars Adventures Volume 1
ISBN: 1-59307-243-0 $6.95

Clone Wars Volume 3:
Last Stand on Jabiim
ISBN: 1-59307-006-3 $14.95

Clone Wars Volume 4: Light and Dark
ISBN: 1-59307-195-7 $16.95

Droids—The Kalarba Adventures
ISBN: 1-56971-064-3 $17.95

Droids—Rebellion
ISBN: 1-56971-224-7 $14.95

Classic Star Wars—
Han Solo At Stars' End
ISBN: 1-56971-254-9 $6.95

Boba Fett—Enemy of The Empire
ISBN: 1-56971-407-X $12.95

Dark Forces—
Soldier for the Empire GSA
ISBN: 1-56971-348-0 $14.95

Mara Jade—By the Emperor's Hand
ISBN: 1-56971-401-0 $15.95

Underworld
ISBN: 1-56971-618-8 $15.95

Empire Volume 1: Betrayal
ISBN: 1-56971-964-0 $12.95

Empire Volume 2: Darklighter
ISBN: 1-56971-975-6 $17.95

REBELLION ERA:
0-5 YEARS AFTER
STAR WARS: A NEW HOPE

Classic Star Wars, Volume 1:
In Deadly Pursuit
ISBN: 1-56971-109-7 $16.95

Classic Star Wars, Volume 2:
The Rebel Storm
ISBN: 1-56971-106-2 $16.95

Classic Star Wars, Volume 3:
Escape to Hoth
ISBN: 1-56971-093-7 $16.95

Classic Star Wars—
The Early Adventures
ISBN: 1-56971-178-X $19.95

Jabba the Hutt—The Art of the Deal
ISBN: 1-56971-310-3 $9.95

Vader's Quest
ISBN: 1-56971-415-0 $11.95

Splinter of the Mind's Eye
ISBN: 1-56971-223-9 $14.95

A Long Time Ago... Volume 1:
Doomworld
ISBN: 1-56971-754-0 $29.95

A Long Time Ago... Volume 2:
Dark Encounters
ISBN: 1-56971-785-0 $29.95

A Long Time Ago... Volume 3:
Resurrection of Evil
ISBN: 1-56971-786-9 $29.95

A Long Time Ago... Volume 4:
Screams in the Void
ISBN: 1-56971-787-7 $29.95

A Long Time Ago... Volume 5:
Fool's Bounty
ISBN: 1-56971-906-3 $29.95

A Long Time Ago... Volume 6:
Wookiee World
ISBN: 1-56971-907-1 $29.95

A Long Time Ago... Volume 7:
Far, Far Away
ISBN: 1-56971-908-X $29.95

Battle of the Bounty Hunters
Pop-Up Book
ISBN: 1-56971-129-1 $17.95

Shadows of the Empire
ISBN: 1-56971-183-6 $17.95

The Empire Strikes Back—
The Special Edition
ISBN: 1-56971-234-4 $9.95

Return of the Jedi—The Special Edition
ISBN: 1-56971-235-2 $9.95

NEW REPUBLIC ERA:
5-25 YEARS AFTER
STAR WARS: A NEW HOPE

X-Wing Rouge Squadron
The Phantom Affair
ISBN: 1-56971-251-4 $12.95

Battleground Tatooine
ISBN: 1-56971-276-X $12.95

The Warrior Princess
ISBN: 1-56971-330-8 $12.95

Requiem for a Rogue
ISBN: 1-56971-331-6 $12.95

In the Empire's Service
ISBN: 1-56971-383-9 $12.95

Blood and Honor
ISBN: 1-56971-387-1 $12.95

Masquerade
ISBN: 1-56971-487-8 $12.95

Mandatory Retirement
ISBN: 1-56971-492-4 $12.95

Shadows of the Empire
Evolution
ISBN: 1-56971-441-X $14.95

Heir to the Empire
ISBN: 1-56971-202-6 $19.95

Dark Force Rising
ISBN: 1-56971-269-7 $17.95

The Last Command
ISBN: 1-56971-378-2 $17.95

Dark Empire
ISBN: 1-59307-039-X $16.95

Dark Empire II
ISBN: 1-56971-119-4 $17.95

Empire's End
ISBN: 1-56971-306-5 $5.95

Boba Fett—Death, Lies, & Treachery
ISBN: 1-56971-311-1 $12.95

Crimson Empire
ISBN: 1-56971-355-3 $17.95

Crimson Empire II—Council of Blood
ISBN: 1-56971-410-X $17.95

Jedi Academy—Leviathan
ISBN: 1-56971-456-8 $11.95

Union
ISBN: 1-56971-464-9 $12.95

NEW JEDI ORDER ERA:
25+ YEARS AFTER
STAR WARS: A NEW HOPE

Chewbacca
ISBN: 1-56971-515-7 $12.95

INFINITIES:
DOES NOT APPLY TO TIMELINE

Infinities — A New Hope
ISBN: 1-56971-648-X $12.95

Infinities—The Empire Strikes Back
ISBN: 1-56971-904-7 $12.95

Infinities—Return of the Jedi
ISBN: 1-59307-206-6 $12.95

Star Wars Tales Volume 1
ISBN: 1-56971-619-6 $19.95

Star Wars Tales Volume 2
ISBN: 1-56971-757-5 $19.95

Star Wars Tales Volume 3
ISBN: 1-56971-836-9 $19.95

Star Wars Tales Volume 4
ISBN: 1-56971-989-6 $19.95

AVAILABLE AT YOUR LOCAL COMICS SHOP OR BOOKSTORE
To find a comics shop in your area, call 1-888-266-4226
For more information or to order direct: • On the web: www.darkhorse.com • E-mail: mailorder@darkhorse.com
• Phone: 1-800-862-0052 or (503) 652-9701 Mon.-Sat. 9 A.M. to 5 P.M. Pacific Time